# LIVING LANGUAGE®
# ADVANCED FRENCH

## REVISED AND UPDATED

# THE LIVING LANGUAGE SERIES

**Living Language Basic Courses, Revised & Updated**

Spanish*                  Italian*
Japanese*                 French*
German*                   Russian
Portuguese (Continental)
Portuguese (Brazilian)

**Living Language Intermediate Courses— Skill Builder: Verbs**

Spanish                   Italian
French                    German

**Living Language Advanced Courses**

Spanish                   French

**Living Language Ultimate Series: Beginner—Intermediate**

Spanish*                  Italian*
Japanese*                 Russian
French*                   German*
Inglés/English for Spanish Readers
Portuguese                Mandarin Chinese

**Living Language Ultimate Series: Advanced**

Spanish*                  Italian
Japanese                  Russian
French                    German
Inglés/English for Spanish Readers

**Fodor's/Living Language Travelers Series**

Spanish for Travelers
Italian for Travelers
French for Travelers
German for Travelers

**Living Language Business Companion**

Chinese        German        Spanish

**Living Language/Terra Cognita In the Know**

China                         Germany
Mexico & Central America

**Living Language English for the Real World**

for Chinese Speakers
for Korean Speakers
for Japanese Speakers
for Spanish Speakers
for Russian Speakers

**Living Language American English Pronunciation Program**

**Living Language English for New Americans**

Everyday Life          Health & Safety
Work & School

**Living Language Easy English**

**Living Language Sign Language Courses**

Getting Started in Signing
Say It by Signing

**Living Language Non-Connoisseur's Menu Guide to French, Italian, and Spanish/Latin American Cuisine**

**Living Language Instant Scholar Series**

A Shortcut to Art & Literature
A Shortcut to Good Grammar
A Shortcut to a Sophisticated Vocabulary

*Available on Cassette and Compact Disc

If you're traveling, we recommend

**Fodor's guides**

Available in bookstores everywhere, or call 1-800-726-0600 for additional information.

Visit our website at www.livinglanguage.com

Living Language® publications are available at special discounts for bulk purchases for sales promotions or premiums, as well as for fund-raising or educational use. Special editions can be created in large quantities for special needs. For more information, write to Special Sales Manager, Living Language, 280 Park Avenue, New York, NY 10017.

# LIVING LANGUAGE®
# ADVANCED FRENCH

## REVISED AND UPDATED

Revised by
THE EDITORIAL STAFF OF LIVING LANGUAGE
AND
SUSAN HUSSERL-KAPIT, PH.D.

Based on the original by
MARY FINOCCHIARO AND REMUNDA CADOUX,
HUNTER COLLEGE

Previously published as *French 3*

Living Language, A Random House Company
New York

This work was previously published under the titles *Living Language Conversation Manual, French Advanced Course* and *Living Language Advanced Conversational Spanish* by Mary Finocchiaro and Remunda Cadoux, Hunter College. This work was also previously published as *Living Language French 3*, revised by the Editorial Staff of Living Language and Susan Husserl-Kapit, Ph.D.

Published by Living Language, A Random House Company, New York, New York. Living Language is a member of the Random House Information Group.

Originally published by Living Language in 1968, 1969, and 1996.

Random House, Inc. New York, Toronto, London, Sydney, Auckland

www.livinglanguage.com

Living Language and colophon are registered trademarks of Random House, Inc

Manufactured in the United States of America

Design by Peter A. Davis

Library of Congress Cataloging-in-Publication Data is available upon request

ISBN 0-609-80449-9

10   9   8   7   6   5   4   3

1999 Updated Edition

Living Language® publications are available at special discounts for bulk purchases for sales promotions or premiums, as well as for fund-raising or educational use. Special editions can be created in large quantities for special needs. For more information, write to Special Sales Manager, Living Language, 280 Park Avenue, New York, NY 10017.

# CONTENTS

# INTRODUCTION

*Living Language® Advanced French* is a continuation of the beginner to intermediate level *French Complete Course*. This program has been thoroughly revised and updated to reflect currect and idiomatic usage of French. If you have already mastered the basics of French in school, while traveling abroad, or with other Living Language courses, then *Advanced French* is right for you.

The complete program includes this manual, along with four hours of recordings. However, if you are confident of your pronunciation, you can also use this manual on its own.

With *Advanced French* you'll continue to learn how to speak and understand idiomatic French. The program follows an American couple visiting friends in France. While participating in their adventures you'll improve your proficiency to a level that allows you to take part in engaging conversations easily and comfortably.

## COURSE MATERIALS

### THE MANUAL

*Living Language Advanced French* consists of 20 lessons. Every lesson includes a dialogue, notes, a grammar and usage section, and exercises.

DIALOGUE: Each lesson begins with a dialogue in standard, idiomatic French presenting a realistic situation frequently encountered when traveling abroad. The dialogues follow the adventures of Charles and Jane, an American couple in France. All dialogues are translated into colloquial English.

NOTES: The notes refer to specific expressions and phrases in the dialogue. They'll allow you to see the grammar rules and vocabulary "in action," and they comment on the cultural and historical background of the particular expression. The notes are numbered according to the corresponding exchange in the dialogue, and the specific phrases covered are marked by the ° symbol.

GRAMMAR AND USAGE: This section reviews and expands upon basic French grammar. You'll learn how to express yourself more accurately using advanced grammatical structures idiomatically.

EXERCISES: This section allows you to review the grammar and vocabulary covered in the lessons. With the ANSWER KEY in the back of the book you can check your progress. Note that the answers to the first exercise in each lesson do not appear in the Answer Key, as this is primarily an oral and written drill.

The clear and concise SUMMARY OF FRENCH GRAMMAR and the easy-to-use VERB CHARTS make this manual a valuable reference for future use.

## THE RECORDINGS

The recordings include the complete dialogues of all 20 lessons in the manual, plus a number of example sentences from the Grammar and Usage section. The recorded material appears in **boldface** in your manual. Each dialogue is first read at normal conversational speed without interruption, and then a second time, phrase by phrase with pauses for you to repeat after the native speakers. By listening to and imitating the native speakers you'll improve your pronunciation and comprehension while learning to use new phrases and structures.

# INSTRUCTIONS

1. Look at page 1. The material in **boldface** type will appear on the recordings. Read each lesson through first, and pay careful attention to the vocabulary and grammar points emphasized in the NOTES and GRAMMAR AND USAGE sections. Examples of grammatical structures that appear on the recordings are in ***boldface italic type***.

2. Then listen to the recordings as the dialogues are read at normal conversational speed. When the dialogues are read more slowly a second time, repeat after the native speakers in the pauses provided. Don't worry if your pronunciation is not perfect the first time around. Practice makes perfect. Study with the manual and listen to the recordings as often as you wish.

3. The EXERCISES at the end of the lessons will help you review the material covered in each lesson and help you check your progress toward proficiency.

4. If you take breaks between lessons, it is always a good idea to review the previous lessons before you begin your studies again.

5. For future reference use the SUMMARY OF FRENCH GRAMMAR and also the VERB CHARTS at the end of the manual.

LIVING LANGUAGE®

# ADVANCED
# FRENCH

## REVISED AND UPDATED

# LESSON 1

### RENDEZ-VOUS AU CAFÉ
### APPOINTMENT AT A CAFÉ

## A. DIALOGUE

*On fixe le rendez-vous.*° Making the appointment.

1. Michel: **Allô?**°
   Hello?

2. Charles: **Allô, Michel? C'est Charles Lewis, de New York.**
   Hello, Michel? It's Charles Lewis from New York.

3. Michel: **Quel *plaisir*° de vous entendre! Où vous trouvez-vous° en ce moment?**
   What a pleasure to hear from you! Where are you right now?

4. Charles: **À l'Hôtel Merceau. *Nous venons d'arriver,* ma femme et moi.**
   At the Hotel Merceau. My wife and I have just arrived.

5. Michel: **Je *tiens à vous voir* le plus tôt possible! Vous êtes libre cet après-midi? À deux heures?**
   I'm eager to see you as soon as possible. Are you free this afternoon? At two o'clock?

6. Charles: **C'est parfait. Où nous retrouverons-nous?**
   Perfect. Where should we meet?

7. Michel: **Au Café des Deux Magots,° Place Saint-Germain. Prenez un taxi.**

At the *Café des Deux Magots,* Place Saint-Germain.
Take a taxi.

8. Charles: **D'accord.°  Est-ce qu'on trouvera une
   table libre à cette heure-là?**
   Okay. Will we get a table at that time?

9. Michel: **Sans doute. À tout à l'heure.°**
   Probably. See you in a little while.

10. Charles: **Entendu. À plus tard. Au revoir.**
    Right. See you later. So long.

*On se retrouve au café.*    Meeting at the café.

11. Michel: **Charles, je suis content de vous revoir.
    Soyez° le bienvenu à Paris!°**
    Charles, it's good to see you again. Welcome to Paris!

12. Charles: **Merci, Michel. Nous sommes tellement°
    *contents,* Jane et moi, *d'être* à Paris.**
    Thank you, Michel. Jane and I are so happy to be in
    Paris.

13. Michel: **Mais, où est Jane?**
    But, where's Jane?

14. Charles: **Elle est restée° à l'hôtel pour défaire les
    bagages. Vous savez, le voyage a été long et fati-
    gant.**
    She stayed at the hotel to unpack. You know the trip
    was long and tiring.

15. Michel: **Voulez-vous vous asseoir à l'intérieur ou
    à la terrasse?**
    Do you want to sit indoors or out on the terrace?

16. Charles: **À la terrasse, bien entendu!**
    Outdoors, of course.

17. Michel: **Ah! *Voilà une table libre* près de la fenêtre.**
    Ah! There's an empty table near the window.

18. Serveur: **Qu'est-ce que vous prenez,° messieurs?°**
    What will you have, gentlemen?

19. Michel: **Un citron pressé,° s'il vous plaît. Il fait si chaud!°**
    A lemonade, please. It's so warm!

20. Charles: **Et pour moi° un demi.°**
    And for me a draft beer.

21. Serveur: **Tout de suite,° messieurs.**
    Right away, gentlemen.

22. Charles: **Quelle° agréable initiation à la vie° française! Tiens!° *Voici déjà°* le serveur qui nous apporte° les boissons!° À votre santé!**
    What a pleasant introduction to French life! Look! Here's the waiter bringing our drinks already! Cheers!

23. Michel: **À la vôtre!° Et bon séjour° à Paris!**
    Cheers! Here's to an enjoyable stay in Paris!

24. Charles: **On est° vraiment bien ici. *J'ai envie* d'y rester° toute la journée.°**
    It's really nice here. I feel like staying here the whole day.

25. Michel: **Vous avez le *droit de passer°* toute l'après-midi au café.**
    You have the right to spend all afternoon at the café.

26. Charles: ***On ne demande* jamais° *aux clients de partir?***
    They never ask the customers to leave?

27. Michel: **Pas du tout! Et, si vous voulez, vous pouvez lire le journal, écrire des lettres, bavarder avec des amis, ou, tout simplement, regarder passer les gens.**
Not at all! And, if you want, you can read a newspaper, write letters, chat with friends, or simply watch the people passing by.

28. Charles: **Quand on habite à New York on oublie bien vite° *l'art de se détendre.***
When you live in New York, you quickly forget the art of relaxing.

29. Michel: **J'espère° que vous avez fait bon voyage.° Vous avez pris un vol d'Air France, n'est-ce pas?**
I hope you've had a good trip. You took an Air France flight, didn't you?

30. Charles: **Oui, et c'était très agréable. Nous étions assis à côté de deux touristes hollandais qui étaient très sympathiques.**
Yes, and it was very pleasant. We sat next to two Dutch tourists who were very nice.

31. Michel: **Si vous n'avez pas de projets° pour demain, on pourra peut-être faire un petit tour° à pied.°**
If you don't have any plans for tomorrow, maybe we can take a little walk.

32. Charles: **Quelle bonne idée!° Je suis sûr que Jane *aura envie de nous accompagner.***
What a good idea! I'm sure Jane will want to come with us.

33. Michel: **Monsieur, l'addition,° s'il vous plaît. Je vais régler l'addition, donner un pourboire,° et nous partons ... Mais non, Charles. C'est moi**

**qui vous invite pour fêter votre arrivée à Paris.**
Waiter! The check, please. I'm going to pay the bill,
leave a tip, and we'll go ... No, no, Charles, I'm
treating you to celebrate your arrival in Paris.

## B. NOTES

*On fixe le rendez-vous: On* is a catch-all pronoun meaning
"we," "they," indefinite "you," "people," etc.
See Lesson 4 for a full explanation. See also Note 24
below.

1. *Allô!:* What to say when answering the telephone.
   *J'écoute* is also used.

3. *Quel plaisir:* Note the use of *quel* to express "What
   a ... !" This is discussed fully in Lesson 5.
   *vous trouvez-vous:* Forms of *se trouver* (lit.: to find
   oneself) are often used in place of *être* (to be). *Se
   trouver* is a reflexive verb. Other reflexive verbs in
   this lesson are *se rencontrer, s'asseoir, se détendre.*
   Reflexive verbs are discussed in detail in Lesson 5.

7. *(le) Café des Deux Magots:* A famous café on the
   Left Bank in Paris.

8. *D'accord:* Agreed, okay. *Entendu,* in sentence 10 of
   the text, means the same thing.

9. *À tout à l'heure:* See you in a little while. A frequently used expression.

11. *Soyez:* imperative form of the verb *être.*
    *Soyez le bienvenu:* lit.: Welcome. A common cour-
    tesy formula.
    *à Paris:* See Lesson 2.

12. *tellement = si* (so).

14. *Elle est restée:* Note the use of *être* as a helping verb instead of *avoir*. See Lesson 8 for full discussion.

18. *Prendre* is used when offering or asking for food. *messieurs:* plural of *monsieur* (similarly: *mesdames, mesdemoiselles*).

19. *un citron pressé:* lemonade (lit.: a squeezed lemon). There is another drink called *limonade,* which is carbonated.
    *il fait si chaud:* The verb *faire* is often used in weather expressions. Examples: *il fait froid* (''it's cold''); *il fait beau* (''the weather is fine''); *Qu'il faisait doux!* (''How nice it was!'').

20. *pour moi:* Note the use of the disjunctive pronoun after preposition *pour*. See Lesson 5 for explanation of disjunctive pronoun forms and uses.
    *un demi:* short for *un demi-litre* (a half-liter). A liter is approximately equal to a quart.

21. *Tout de suite:* immediately, right away.

22. *Quelle agréable initiation:* See Note 3 above. Notice that *quelle* is feminine, to agree with the feminine noun *initiation*.
    *la vie française:* The definite article is used with nouns to express a general concept or idea. Examples: *La vie est belle.* Life is beautiful. *La santé est importante.* Health is important.
    *Tiens!:* Look! What do you know! A familiar exclamation.
    *déjà:* Notice its position in the sentence immediately after *voici*.
    *le serveur qui nous apporte:* lit.: ''the waiter who is bringing us . . .''
    *boissons:* from the verb *boire,* to drink.

23. *À la vôtre = à votre santé:* a familiar toast.
   *bon séjour:* lit." good sojourn, stay."

24. *on est:* equivalent to *nous sommes.*
   *j'ai envie de:* equivalent to *je voudrais, j'ai-merais* (I'd like to, I feel like). For fuller explana-tion, see Grammatical Item 4 in this lesson. *y rester:* y is an adverbial pronoun that precedes the verb and replaces phrases introduced by *à* or other preposi-tions that refer to location. *Je vais à Paris = J'y vais.*
   *la journée:* This feminine form of "day" is used to indicate duration or extension of time. Note also *toute la matinée* ("all morning," "the entire morn-ing"), *toute la soirée* ("all evening," "the entire evening"). Contrast with the masculine *tous les jours* ("every day"), *tous les matins* ("every morn-ing"), *tous les soirs* ("every evening").

25. *passer:* to spend (time); *dépenser,* to spend (money).

26. *ne . . . jamais:* never.

28. *bien vite = très vite* (very quickly). *Bien* is used to intensify the word it precedes. Examples: *Il est bien gentil.* ("He's quite nice."); *Elle danse ici bien sou-vent.* ("She dances here quite often.")

29. *j'espère:* from verb *espérer.* In verbs which have *é* as the last vowel of the stem, the *é* changes to *è* before the silent endings *-e, -es,* and *-ent.* However, the *é* remains throughout the future and conditional tenses. Other verbs similarly conjugated: *préférer* (to prefer), *répéter* (to repeat), *céder* (to yield), *s'in-quiéter* (to worry), *posséder* (to possess), *protéger* (to protect).

31. *pas de projets: de* and not *des* because of the neg-ative partitive construction. See Lesson 8 for de-tailed explanation of the partitive.

*projets:* plans, projects.
*faire un petit tour: faire une petite promenade* (take a walk).
*à pied:* on foot.

32. *Quelle bonne idée!:* What a good idea!

33. *l'addition:* a bill in a restaurant or café.
*un pourboire:* Although service is, by law, included in the bill at cafés, bars, and restaurants, it is customary to leave a small tip for the waiter. Notice *pour boire* (lit.: "for drinking") but used to indicate a tip for any service.

## C. GRAMMAR AND USAGE

1. *Venir de:* to have just (lit.: "to come from")

| Subject | *venir* | *de* | Pronoun | Infinitive | Object |
|---------|---------|------|---------|------------|--------|
| a. *Je* | *viens* | *de* | *lui* | *parler.* | |
| b. *Il* | *venait* | *de* | *l'* | *acheter.* | |
| c. *Il* | *venait* | *de* | | *lire* | *le journal.* |

a. I have just spoken to him.
b. He had just bought it.
c. He had just read the newspaper.

Note:
• See Summary of French Grammar for review of object pronouns and the Irregular Verb Charts for forms of *venir.*

2. *Tenir à:* to be eager to, to want to very much

| Subject | *tenir* | *à* | Pronoun | Infinitive | Objective |
|---------|---------|-----|---------|------------|-----------|
| a. *Il* | *tient* | *à* | *vous* | *parler.* | |
| b. *Nous* | *tenions* | *à* | | *voir* | *Michel.* |

a. He wants very much to talk to you.
b. We were eager to see Michel.

Note:
- See the Irregular Verb Charts for forms of *tenir*.

3. *Voici/voilà*

| Direct object pronoun | *voici* or *voilà* |
|---|---|
| a. *Me* | *voici.* |
| b. *Les* | *voilà.* |

a. Here I am.
b. There they are.

Note:
- In modern usage, *voilà* is often used instead of *voici*.

| | |
|---|---|
| a. *Me voici.* | Here I am. |
| b. *Te voici.* | Here you are. |
| c. *Le voici.* | Here he/it is. |
| d. *La voici.* | Here she/it is. |
| e. *Nous voici.* | Here we are. |
| f. *Vous voici.* | Here you are. |
| g. *Les voici.* | Here they are. |

4. *Avoir envie de:* to feel like, to want to (used primarily in the present, imperfect past, and future)

| Subject | *avoir* | *envie* | *de* | Object Pron. | Infin. | Object |
|---|---|---|---|---|---|---|
| a. *J'* | *ai* | *envie* | *de* | | *dormir.* | |
| b. *Il* | *avait* | *envie* | *de* | *le* | *voir.* | |
| c. *Elle* | *aura* | *envie* | *d'* | | *acheter* | *le livre.* |

    a. I feel like sleeping.
    b. He wanted to see him.
    c. She will want to buy the book.

Note:
    • Review forms of *avoir* in the Irregular Verb Charts.

5. Prepositions before infinitives

*de*

After certain nouns that describe emotion, doubt or feeling:

|        | Noun     | Prep. | Infinitive | Object  |
|--------|----------|-------|------------|---------|
| a. *J'ai* | *envie*  | *de*  | *partir.*  |         |
| b. *Quel* | *plaisir* | *de* | *voir*     | *Paris!* |
| c. *Il a* | *le droit* | *de* | *rester.* |         |

    a. I feel like leaving.
    b. What a pleasure to see Paris!
    c. He has the right to stay.

After certain adjectives that describe emotion, doubt, or feeling:

|        | Adjective | Prep. | Infinitive | Object |
|--------|-----------|-------|------------|--------|
| a. *Nous sommes* | *contents* | *de* | *partir.* | |
| b. *Je suis* | *enchanté* | *de* | *faire* | *votre connaissance.* |

    a. We are happy to leave.
    b. I am pleased to make your acquaintance.

After certain verbs:

|  | Verb | Prep. | Infinitive |
|---|---|---|---|
| a. *Il* | *refuse* | *de* | *venir.* |
| b. *Il* | *essaie* | *de* | *parler.* |
| c. *Il* | *demande aux clients* | *de* | *partir.* |

a. He refuses to come.
b. He tries to speak.
c. He asks the clients to leave.

*à*

After nouns when the infinitive expresses the purpose or outcome of that noun:

|  | Noun | Prep. | Infinitive |
|---|---|---|---|
| a. *Avez-vous* | *une chambre* | *à* | *louer?* |
| b. *C'est* | *une machine* | *à* | *écrire.* |
| c. *J'ai entendu* | *un bruit* | *à* | *rendre sourd.* |

a. Do you have a room to rent?
b. It's a typewriter.
c. I heard a deafening noise.

After certain adjectives when the infinitive qualifies the adjective:

|  | Adjective | Prep. | Infinitive |
|---|---|---|---|
| a. *Nous sommes* | *prêts* | *à* | *partir.* |
| b. *C'est* | *facile* | *à* | *faire.* |

a. We are ready to go.
b. It's easy to do.

After certain verbs:

| Verb | Prep. | Infinitive | Object |
|---|---|---|---|
| a. *Je commence* | *à* | *parler* | *français.* |
| b. *Il tient* | *à* | *régler* | *l'addition.* |

a. I am beginning to speak French.
b. He insists on settling the bill.

No preposition after certain verbs (following are the most common):

| | Verb | Infinitive | Object |
|---|---|---|---|
| a. *aller:* | *Je vais* | *téléphoner.* | |
| b. *vouloir:* | *Je voudrais* | *laisser* | *un pourboire.* |
| c. *falloir:* | *Il faut* | *faire* | *une réservation.* |
| d. *pouvoir:* | *Vous pouvez* | *lire* | *le journal.* |
| e. *savoir:* | *Nous savons* | *nager.* | |

a. I'm going to phone.
b. I'd like to leave a tip.
c. One must make a reservation.
d. You can read the paper.
e. We know how to swim.

Note:

- Forms of the above irregular verbs are given in the Irregular Verb Charts.


EXERCISES

A. Substitute each of the words or expressions in parentheses for the underlined word or expression in the pattern sentence. Write each new sentence and say it aloud.

1. Example: *Il fait beau./Il fait chaud.* (*chaud, froid, frais, doux, bon, mauvais, du soleil, du vent*)

2. *C'est moi qui l'invite.* (*son ami, lui, elle, son père, Michel, sa soeur*)
3. *Quel plaisir de vous voir!* (*connaître, entendre, parler, revoir, écouter*)

B. Replace the subject pronoun *je* by the other subject pronouns (*tu, il, elle, nous, vous, ils, elles*). Make the appropriate changes in the verb. (Study verb forms in the Irregular Verb Charts.)

1. *Je viens de l'acheter.*
2. *Je tiens à le voir.*
3. *J'ai envie de lui parler.*

C. Replace the underlined object pronoun by the other appropriate pronouns (*me, te, le, la, nous, vous, les*), and translate.

1. *Me voici.*
2. *Te voilà.*

D. Translate the following sentences into French. Then say them aloud.

1. I'm going to meet Charles.
2. He's not going to see Jane.
3. Are we going to find a free table at that time?
4. I want to call my friend.
5. Do you want to speak French?
6. She wants to make an appointment.
7. It's necessary to sit indoors (*à l'intérieur*).
8. It is necessary to pay the bill.
9. She can take a little walk.
10. We can celebrate your arrival.
11. I know how to read a French newspaper.
12. Do you know how to write a letter in French?

13. I'm beginning to unpack.
14. Are you beginning to understand?
15. She wants very much to see him.
16. I refuse to stay here.
17. He has asked Robert to stay.
18. I'm happy to be in Paris.
19. It's time to meet Michel.
20. I have the right to accompany Michel.
21. Do we have the right to enter?

E. From among the three choices given, choose the best translation for the word or phrase given at the beginning of each sentence. Write the complete sentence, and translate.

1. (have just) *Je* _____ *arriver.*
   (a) *tiens à*
   (b) *ai envie d'*
   (c) *viens d'*
2. (right away) _____, *messieurs.*
   (a) *À la vôtre*
   (b) *Heureusement*
   (c) *Tout de suite*
3. (drinks) *Tiens, voici déjà le serveur qui nous apporte les* _____.
   (a) *verres*
   (b) *boissons*
   (c) *pourboires*
4. (never) *Et on ne demande* _____ *aux clients de partir?*
   (a) *jamais*
   (b) *plus*
   (c) *rien*
5. (of course) *À la terrasse,* _____.
   (a) *pas du tout*
   (b) *bien entendu*
   (c) *tout à fait*

6. (It's) _____ *chaud.*
   - (a) *Il est*
   - (b) *C'est*
   - (c) *Il fait*
7. (I feel like) _____ *marcher.*
   - (a) *Je me sens*
   - (b) *Je demande*
   - (c) *J'ai envie de*
8. (pay) *Je vais* _____ *l'addition et laisser un pourboire.*
   - (a) *rejoindre*
   - (b) *retrouver*
   - (c) *régler*

# LESSON 2

## AU KIOSQUE°
## AT THE NEWSSTAND

### A. DIALOGUE

1. Charles: (*Au marchand de journaux*) **Nous venons d'arriver à Paris, monsieur, et je ne connais° pas les journaux français. Pourriez°-vous nous aider?**
   (To the news vendor) We've just arrived in Paris, sir, and I'm not familiar with French newspapers. Could you help us?

2. Marchand: **Volontiers, monsieur. Pour la politique et l'information générale, nous avons bon nombre de quotidiens° parisiens. Puis, nous avons aussi des journaux littéraires...**
   Certainly, sir. For politics and general information, we have many dailies in Paris. Then, we also have literary journals

3. Jane: **"Quotidiens," vous avez dit? Je ne connais pas** *ce mot-là.*
   *"Quotidiens,"* did you say? I don't know that word.

4. Marchand: **Cela veut dire qu'il y a un numéro tous les jours,° madame. Il y a aussi des hebdomadaires,° qui ne° paraissent qu'une fois par semaine.**
   That means that there's an edition every day, ma'am. There are also weeklies, which come out only once a week.

5. Charles: **Si je ne me trompe pas, je vois là une quinzaine° de quotidiens!**
   If I'm not mistaken, I see about fifteen dailies there!

6. Jane: **Mais quel journal a un très grand tirage, monsieur? Si on veut connaître un pays . . .**
   But which paper has a very large circulation, sir? If one wants to get to know a country . . .

7. Marchand: *Ouest-France,* **par exemple.** *En choisissant celui-ci* **vous ne vous tromperez pas. Tenez, vous voulez regarder?°**
   *Ouest-France,* for example. You can't go wrong choosing this one. Here, would you like to look at it?°

8. Charles: **Mais je ne vois que des histoires régionales. Regardez, voici un article sur une école en Bretagne, en voilà un autre sur le tourisme au Mont-Saint-Michel. N'auriez-vous pas quelque chose de° national? C'est la France en général qui nous intéresse.**
   But I see only regional stories. Look, here's an article on a school in Brittany, there's another on tourism at Mont-Saint-Michel. Don't you have anything national? It's France in general that interests us.

9. Marchand: **Si, si°, *Ouest-France* donne aussi des informations nationales et internationales. Ce ne sont pas seulement des gens de l'ouest de la France qui le lisent. Mais si ce sont les actualités° nationales qui vous intéressent surtout, vous pouvez acheter *Le Monde* ou *Libération*.**
Yes, yes, *Ouest-France* also gives national and international news. It's not only people from the west of France who read it. But if you're especially interested in national and international news, you can buy *Le Monde* or *Libération*.

10. Charles: **Est-ce que les spectacles et les sports figurent dans ces journaux?**
Are there sports and entertainment in these newspapers?

11. Marchand: **Bien sûr! Vous avez tout ce qu'il vous faut.°**
Of course! You have everything you need.

12. Charles: **Eh bien, je commence par *Le Monde*.**
All right, I'll begin with *Le Monde*.

13. Jane: **Je vois que vous avez là des revues de tous les pays—revues *françaises, italiennes, allemandes, anglaises, américaines,* et *russes*.**
I see you have magazines from every country—French, Italian, German, English, American, and Russian.

14. Marchand: **Oui, madame, et de tous les genres. Il y a des revues hebdomadaires et mensuelles, et d'autres qui paraissent tous les quinze jours.**
Yes, ma'am, and all kinds. There are weekly and monthly magazines, and others that come out every other week.

15. Jane: **Celles-là sont d'intérêt général, n'est-ce pas—*Paris-Match* et *Jours de France?***
Those over there are of general interest, aren't they—*Paris-Match* and *Jours de France?*

16. Marchand: **C'est ça, madame, et de ce *côté-ci* nous avons des revues de mode, *Marie-France* et *Elle* . . .**
That's right, ma'am, and on this side we have some fashion magazines, *Marie France* and *Elle* . . .

17. Jane: **Que c'est ennuyeux! En° avez-vous une sur l'informatique?**
What a bore! Do you have any on computer science?

18. Marchand: **Oui, madame. Voilà *Informatique Magazine* et *l'Ordinateur*.**
Yes ma'am. Here is *Informatique Magazine* and *l'Ordinateur*.

19. Marchand: **Est-ce que je peux vous suggérer aussi *cette petite revue, l'officiel des spectacles*?° Elle vous donne le programme de tous les spectacles à Paris.**
May I also suggest to you this little magazine, *l'officiel des spectacles?* It gives you the programs of all the entertainment in Paris.

20. Charles: **C'est exactement *ce qu*'il nous faut.**
That's exactly what we need.

21. Charles: **Auriez-vous aussi un plan de la ville avec tous les monuments importants?**
Would you also have a map of the city with all the important monuments?

22. Marchand: **Bien sûr. En voilà un qui se vend° bien.**
Certainly. Here's one [of them] that is very popular.

23. Jane: **Nous avons naturellement notre _Michelin_,°**
    **mais il nous faut un guide illustré format de**
    **poche.**
    We have our _Michelin_, of course, but we need an
    illustrated pocket guide.

24. Marchand: **Voici quelque chose qui fera votre af-**
    **faire.**
    Here is something that will do the trick.

25. Charles: **Jane, regarde ces cartes routières. Elles**
    **montrent° toutes les nouvelles routes et se ven-**
    **dent dix francs cinquante chacune.**
    Jane, look at these road maps. They show all the
    new roads and are sold for ten francs fifty each.

26. Charles: **Vous avez été si aimable, monsieur.**
    **Pourriez-vous nous indiquer un magasin tout**
    **près d'ici où l'on vend des cassettes° et des**
    **disques compacts?**
    You have been so helpful, sir. Could us direct us to
    a store near here where they sell cassettes and com-
    pact discs?

27. Marchand: **Il y en a un à deux pas d'ici, au coin de**
    **la rue. Au revoir, monsieur, madame.**
    There is one very close by, on the corner. Good-bye,
    sir, madam.

## B. NOTES

Title. _kiosque:_ a newsstand. There are kiosks on many street
    corners in Paris, where one can buy newspapers, maga-
    zines, postcards, street maps, guides, and sometimes road
    maps. Kiosks are very colorful because they display
    posters announcing theater programs, concerts, art ex-
    hibits, and other attractions.

1. *connais:* present tense of *connaître*, "to know," in the sense of "to be acquainted with," "to be familiar with." See also 3 and 6 of text.
*Pourriez-vous:* Note that the conditional is used in many expressions of courtesy. See Irregular Verb Charts for conditional forms of *pouvoir* and *avoir*, and Lesson 6 for discussion of the conditional of courtesy.

2. *quotidien:* daily.

4. *tous les jours:* every day. See Lesson 1, note 24 for a discussion of this use of *tout*.
*hebdomadaire:* weekly. (Other words in this family are *mensuel:* monthly, and *annuel:* yearly.)
*ne . . .* [verb] *. . . que:* only.

5. *quinzaine:* *"aine"* at the end of a number indicates an approximate amount. Note, however, *douzaine,* which means "a dozen."

7. Notice the omission of "it" in the French.

8. *quelque chose de* + adjective: something + adjective. As in *quelque chose d'intéressant* (something interesting); *quelque chose de nécessaire* (something necessary). Note that the adjective is always masculine. Also notice *Donnez-moi quelque chose.* (Give me something.)

11. *il vous faut:* you need (lit.: It is necessary to you). This is the present tense of the verb *falloir*, "to be necessary to." It is used only in the third person singular. Note also, in 20 and 23 of the text: *il nous faut:* we need. See Lesson 3 for full discussion.
*Si:* The affirmative answer to a negative question cannot be *oui*. Think of *si* as meaning "on the contrary—yes."

*actualités:* from *actuel* (contemporary, at the present time, at this moment). Do not confuse it with the English "actual," which is equivalent to the French *réel* or *véritable.*

17. *en:* a catchall pronoun meaning "some of it," "some of them," "any of it," "any of them," "about it," etc. This pronoun is always expressed in French, though it may be merely implied in English. *En* is discussed in Lesson 11.

19. *L'officiel des spectacles:* a pocket-sized weekly guide to events of cultural and general interest; names of restaurants, hotels, movies, plays, etc.

22. *se vend:* Notice that the reflexive form of the verb *vendre* is used to express the passive "is sold." Contrast with the active use of *vend* in 26 of the text.

23. *Michelin:* comprehensive detailed guides to the various regions of France and other countries.

25. *Elles montrent:* An alternative way to express the same idea would be: *Elles indiquent toutes les nouvelles routes . . .*

26. Some related terms are:
    *un walkman/un baladeur:* Walkman
    *une radio cassette:* cassette player/radio
    *une chaîne (stéréo):* stereo set
    *une vidéo-cassette:* videocassette
    *un magnétoscope:* VCR
    *un caméscope:* camcorder
    *un lecteur de disques compacts:* CD player

## C. GRAMMAR AND USAGE

1. *Ce qui:* that which, what (used as subject of a dependent clause)

| Verb | *ce qui* | Verb | |
|---|---|---|---|
| a. | *Ce qui* | *n'est pas* | *clair n'est pas raisonnable.* |
| b. *Je vois* | *ce qui* | *est* | *sur la table.* |

   a. That which is not clear is not reasonable.
   b. I see what is on the table.

2. *Ce que:* that, which, what (used as *object* of a dependent clause)

| Verb | *ce que* | Subject | Verb | |
|---|---|---|---|---|
| a. | *Ce que* | *vous* | *dites* | *est intéressant.* |
| b. *Je comprends* | *ce que* | *Michel* | *a dit.* | |

   a. What you're saying is interesting.
   b. I understand what Michel said.

3. Demonstrative adjectives
   *ce, cet, cette:* this/that; *ces:* these/those

| MASCULINE | | FEMININE | |
|---|---|---|---|
| Sing. | Plu. | Sing. | Plu. |
| a. *ce garçon* | *ces garçons* | d. *cette femme* | *ces femmes* |
| b. *cet ami* | *ces amis* | e. *cette amie* | *ces amies* |
| c. *cet hôtel* | *ces hôtels* | f. *cette histoire* | *ces histoires* |

   a. this boy, these boys      d. this woman, these women

   b. this friend, these friends e. this friend, these friends

   c. this hotel, these hotels    f. this story, these stories

*-ci* (derived from *ici:* here) designates something close to the speaker, and *-là* (there) indicates something at a distance.

| a. *Je n'aime pas* | *cette revue-ci.* |
|---|---|
| b. *Je préfère* | *ce journal-là.* |
| c. *Je ne veux pas* | *ces compacts-là.* |
| d. *Je veux* | *ces cassettes-ci.* |

a. I don't like this magazine.
b. I prefer that newspaper.
c. I don't want those CDs.
d. I want these tapes.

4. Adjectives of nationality (always written in lower case)

| FEMININE | MASCULINE | |
|---|---|---|
| *belge* | *belge* | Belgian |
| *suisse* | *suisse* | Swiss |
| *espagnole* | *espagnol* | Spanish |
| *française* | *français* | French |
| *anglaise* | *anglais* | English |
| *chinoise* | *chinois* | Chinese |
| *danoise* | *danois* | Danish |
| *américaine* | *américain* | American |
| *sénégalaise* | *sénégalais* | Senegalese |
| *algérienne* | *algérien* | Algerian |
| *marocaine* | *marocain* | Moroccan |
| *italienne* | *italien* | Italian |
| *canadienne* | *canadien* | Canadian |
| *allemande* | *allemand* | German |

Note:

- The above adjectives, like all adjectives, agree in gender and number with the nouns they modify or describe.
- When adjectives of nationality are used as nouns, they are capitalized. Contrast:

| | |
|---|---|
| *C'est un livre français.* | It's a French book. |
| *C'est un Français.* | He is a Frenchman. |

5. *En* + present participle

| | |
|---|---|
| a. *En parlant, il a fait des erreurs.* | a. While speaking, he made some mistakes. |
| b. *En choisissant ceci, vous ne vous trompez pas.* | b. You can't go wrong in choosing this one. |
| c. *Elle a pleuré en apprenant la vérité.* | c. She cried upon learning the truth. |
| d. *En lisant, on apprend beaucoup.* | d. One learns a great deal through reading. |

Note:

- *En* may be translated by "while," "by," "upon," "through," "in."
- *En* + present participle may come at the beginning, in the middle, or at the end of a sentence.
- See the Irregular Verb Charts for present participles of irregular verbs.
- Note that this is not the same use of *en* mentioned in Note 17 of this lesson.

## EXERCISES

A. Substitute the word(s) or expressions in parentheses for the underlined word(s) or expressions in the pattern sentence. Write the complete sentence and say it aloud.

1. *Je ne comprends pas ce que vous <u>dites</u>.* (*voulez, écrivez, faites, expliquez, voulez dire*)
2. *Je vois ce <u>qui est sur la table</u>.* (*arrive, se passe, ne va pas, vous inquiète*)
3. *J'aime ce <u>manteau</u>-ci.* (*livre, compact, complet, journal, garçon*)

B. Make each of the following masculine. Write complete sentences.
   Example: *C'est une Française: C'est un Français.*

   *Anglaise*
   *Chinoise*
   *Américaine*
   *Marocaine*
   *Espagnole*

C. Expand the following sentences by placing *En choisissant ce compact* in front of each; then say aloud and translate.

   1. _____, *il s'est trompé.*
   2. _____, *elle a bien fait.*
   3. _____, *elle ne s'est pas trompée.*
   4. _____, *elle avait raison.*
   5. _____, *nous avons payé trop cher.*

D. Translate the following sentences into French; then say them aloud.

   1. Could you tell us . . . ?
   2. Could you show us a magazine on computer science?
   3. Could you direct us to (*nous indiquer*) a store?
   4. Would you have a good literary journal?
   5. If I'm not mistaken, here's a Canadian daily.
   6. Here is something interesting on the newsstand.
   7. Here is something boring.
   8. There is something important in that weekly.

9. We need some cassettes and some CDs.
10. May I see Jane?
11. May I speak to Charles?
12. Let's choose between this edition (*numéro*) and that edition.
13. Look at this monument. Don't look at that article.
14. I don't like these newspapers. I prefer those newspapers.
15. I don't like this city map. I prefer that city map.
16. Show me that stereo.
17. Take those cassettes.
18. Buy these guides.
19. Here's what you're looking for.
20. Here's what I mean.
21. What I want? A road map!
22. What he's looking for? A Walkman!
23. What she's reading? Our *Michelin!*
24. They sell everything you're looking for.
25. I understand everything she's saying.
26. He knows what's important.
27. We read what's necessary.
28. Do you see what's happening?
29. By reading one learns to read.
30. By writing one learns to write.


E. From among the three choices given, choose the best translation for the word or phrase at the beginning of each sentence. Write the complete sentence, and translate.


1. (I don't know) _____ *les journaux.*
   (a) *Je ne sais pas*
   (b) *Je ne vois pas*
   (c) *Je ne connais pas*
2. (Could you) _____ *nous aider?*
   (a) *Pourriez-vous*
   (b) *Auriez-vous*
   (c) *Seriez-vous*

3. (a week) *Ces journaux paraissent une fois* _____.
   - (a) *la semaine*
   - (b) *par semaine*
   - (c) *une semaine*

4. (So many) _____ *images!*
   - (a) *Trop d'*
   - (b) *Beaucoup d'*
   - (c) *Tant d'*

5. (with) *Je commence* _____ *Le Monde.*
   - (a) *par*
   - (b) *sans*
   - (c) *comme*

6. (all) *Nous avons des revues de* _____ *les genres.*
   - (a) *toutes*
   - (b) *tous*
   - (c) *tout*

7. (That's right) _____, *madame.*
   - (a) *C'est raison*
   - (b) *C'est droite*
   - (c) *C'est ça*

8. (a map) *Avez-vous* _____ *de la ville?*
   - (a) *un plan*
   - (b) *une route*
   - (c) *une mappe*

# LESSON 3

## AU TÉLÉPHONE°
## ON THE TELEPHONE

## A. DIALOGUE

*Un appel Paris-Bordeaux.*  A call from Paris to Bordeaux.

*Charles parle à l'employée près des cabines téléphoniques à la poste.* Charles is speaking to the employee near the phone booths at the post office.

1. Charles: **Je ne comprends pas tout à fait votre système téléphonique. Est-ce que vous *pourriez m'aider* à passer un coup de fil?**
   I don't quite understand your phone system. Could you please help me make a phone call?

2. Employée: **Bien sûr, monsieur. C'est pour quelle ville?**
   Certainly, sir. What city are you calling?

3. Charles: **C'est pour Bordeaux, mais je ne connais pas le numéro de téléphone de mon correspondant.**
   Bordeaux, but I don't know the phone number of my party.

4. Employée: **Cela *ne* fait *rien,* monsieur. Vous avez un Minitel° à votre disposition à côté des cabines.**
   That doesn't matter, sir. There's a Minitel available next to the phone booths.

5. Charles: **Je ne sais pas comment *m'en servir.***
   I don't know how to use it.

6. Employée: **C'est très simple. Il suffit de composer le 11 pour avoir accès à l'annuaire électronique. Ensuite, vous taperez le nom de votre correspondant et le nom de ville, et vous *verrez* le numéro sur votre écran.**
   It's very simple. All you have to do is dial 11 for access to the electronic directory. Then, you type the name of your party and the city, and the number will appear on the screen.

*Charles revient à l'employée.* Charles returns to the employee.

7. Charles: **Ça y est. J'ai trouvé mon numéro.**
   That's it. I've found the number.

8. Employée: **Très bien, monsieur. Vous pouvez composer le numéro vous-même.°Allez dans la cabine cinq, et vous *viendrez régler* la communication quand vous *aurez terminé.***
   Very well. You can dial the number yourself. Go to booth five and come pay for the call when you have finished.

*Charles va dans la cabine.* Charles goes into the booth.

9. Charles: **Allô. Je voudrais parler à M. Duclos, s'il vous plaît.**
   Hello, I'd like to speak to Mr. Duclos, please.

10. Assistante: **C'est de la part de qui?**
    Who shall I say is calling?

11. Charles: **C'est Charles Lewis à l'appareil.**
    This is Charles Lewis speaking.

12. Assistante: **Je vais voir s'il est là. Ne quittez pas. . . . Non, il vient de sortir. Voudriez-vous laisser un message?**
    I'll see if he's there. Hold on. . . . No, he just left. Would you like to leave a message?

13. Charles: ***Quel* dommage! Pourriez-vous lui dire que *je le rappelerai* ce soir? Il faut qu'on se parle.**
    What a pity! Would you please tell him that I will call him back tonight? We have to talk to each other.

14. Assistante: **Très bien, monsieur. *Je lui ferai* la communication.**
    Very well, sir. I'll give him the message.

15. Charles: **Merci beaucoup, madame. Au revoir.**
Thank you very much, ma'am. Good-bye.

*Charles revient à l'employée.*   Charles returns to the employee.

16. Charles: **Voilà, madame. Combien je vous dois?**
There you go, ma'am. How much do I owe you?

17. Employée: **Ce *sera* huit francs pour trois minutes, monsieur.**
That'll be eight francs for three minutes, sir.

*Un appel local.*   A local call.

18. Charles: **Je regrette de vous déranger encore, madame, mais . . .**
I'm sorry to bother you again, ma'am, but . . .

19. Employée: **Je vous en prie, monsieur. Je suis là pour ça.**
That's quite all right, sir. That's what I'm here for.

20. Charles: **Cette fois-ci je dois passer un coup de fil dans Paris-même, et je connais le numéro.**
This time I have to make a phone call within Paris, and I know the number.

21. Employée: **Avez-vous une télécarte?°**
Do you have a phone card?

22. Charles: **Non, je n'ai pas de télécarte.**
No, I don't have a phone card.

23. Employée: **Alors, *il vous faut* des pièces d'argent. Décrochez le combiné, mettez cinquante centimes dans la fente, et vous pouvez composer votre numéro.**

Then, you need French coins. Take the receiver off the hook, put fifty centimes in the slot, and you can dial your number.

24. Charles: **Vous êtes bien aimable, madame. Merci beaucoup.**
You're very kind, ma'am. Thank you very much.

## B. NOTES

Title. *Téléphone:* Calls can be made from a café, a post office, and many other public places. Most public telephones, especially in the larger cities, take the *télécarte* (see Note 21) rather than coins.

4. *Minitel:* a small computer terminal connected to the telephone that allows the user access to many services such as the *annuaire électronique,* transportation and theater reservations, e-mail, stock quotes, and computer games, to name a few.

8. *vous-même:* yourself. Study the following:

| | |
|---|---|
| *moi-même* | myself |
| *toi-même* | yourself |
| *lui-même* | himself |
| *elle-même* | herself |
| *nous-mêmes* | ourselves |
| *vous-mêmes* | yourself or yourselves |
| *eux-mêmes* | themselves (masc. or gen.) |
| *elles-mêmes* | themselves (fem.) |
| *soi-même* | oneself |

21. *télécarte:* These telephone credit cards can be bought in varying numbers of *unités* (units of value) in post offices, tobacco shops, train stations, subway stations, and newspaper stands.

## C. GRAMMAR AND USAGE

1. *Quel*—what

   *quel* (as an interrogative)

| | |
|---|---|
| a. **Quel numéro voulez-vous?** | What number do you want? |
| b. **Quelle ville voulez-vous?** | What city to do you want? |
| c. **Quels livres désirez-vous?** | What books do you want? |
| d. **Quelles robes désirez-vous?** | What dresses do you want? |

*quel* (in exclamations). Notice the English equivalents, particularly. The forms are like those of the interrogative.

| | |
|---|---|
| a. **Quel système compliqué!** | What a complicated system! |
| b. **Quelle belle robe!** | What a beautiful dress! |
| c. **Quels beaux yeux!** | What beautiful eyes! |
| d. **Quelles belles maisons!** | What beautiful homes! |

2. *ne . . . rien*—nothing/not . . . anything

| Subject | *ne* | Ind. Obj. | Main Verb | *rien* |
|---|---|---|---|---|
| a. *Je* | *ne* | | *vois* | *rien.* |
| b. *Il* | *ne* | *me* | *disait* | *rien.* |

   a. I see nothing. (I don't see anything.)
   b. He said nothing to me. (He wasn't saying anything to me.)

Past tense:

| Subject | *ne* | Object | Auxiliary | *rien* | Past Participle |
|---|---|---|---|---|---|
| a. *Je* | *n'* | | *ai* | *rien* | *vu.* |
| b. *Nous* | *n'* | | *avons* | *rien* | *trouvé.* |
| c. *Il* | *ne* | *s'* | *est* | *rien* | *acheté.* |
| d. *Je* | *ne* | *lui* | *ai* | *rien* | *donné.* |

a. I saw nothing. (I didn't see anything.)
b. We found nothing. (We didn't find anything.)
c. He bought nothing for himself. (He didn't buy anything for himself.)
d. I gave him nothing. (I didn't give him anything.)

As a subject:

| Rien | ne | Verb |
|------|-----|------|
| 1. **Rien** | **n'** | **est si beau.** |
| 2. **Rien** | **ne** | **s'est passé.** |

a. Nothing is so beautiful.
b. Nothing happened.

*rien*—used alone:

a. *Qu'est-ce qui se*     What is happening?
   *passe? Rien.*          Nothing.
b. *Que vois-tu? Rien.*     What do you see?
                     Nothing.

Note:

• When *rien* is used as a one-word utterance, *ne* is omitted.

3. Object pronouns before complementary infinitives. Note that they immediately precede the infinitive.

| Subject | Main Verb | Object pronouns | Infinitive |
|---------|-----------|-----------------|------------|
| a. *Je* | *dois* | *lui* | *téléphoner* |
| b. *Je* | *peux* | *le* | *chercher.* |
| c. *Je* | *sais* | *m'en* | *servir.* |
| d. *Je* | *vais* | *l'* | *acheter.* |

a. I have to call him.
b. I can look for it.
c. I know how to use it. (*savoir* before an infinitive means "to know how.")
d. I'm going to buy it.

4. The future tense

| 1st Conjugation | 2nd Conjugation | 3rd Conjugation |
|---|---|---|
| *arriver,* to arrive | *choisir,* to choose | *attendre,* to wait |
| infin. + endings | infin. + endings | Drop final -e of infinitive + endings |
| *j'arriverai* (I'll arrive, etc.) | *choisirai* (I'll choose, etc.) | *attendrai* (I'll wait, etc.) |
| *tu arriveras* | *choisiras* | *attendras* |
| *il arrivera* | *choisira* | *attendra* |
| *elle arrivera* | *choisira* | *attendra* |
| *nous arriverons* | *choisirons* | *attendrons* |
| *vous arriverez* | *choisirez* | *attendrez* |
| *ils arriveront* | *choisiront* | *attendront* |
| *elles arriveront* | *choisiront* | *attendront* |

Note:
- The future tense is formed by adding the endings *-ai, -as, -a, -ons, -ez, -ont* either (1) to the infinitive, or (2) to an irregular stem. The irregular stem is a modification of the infinitive and always ends in *r*.

Future tense of the three most common irregular verbs.

| avoir, to have | être, to be | aller, to go |
|---|---|---|
| stem + endings | stem + endings | stem + endings |
| *j'aurai* (I'll have, etc.) | *serai* (I'll be, etc.) | *irai* (I'll go, etc.) |
| tu auras | seras | iras |
| il aura | sera | ira |
| elle aura | sera | ira |
| nous aurons | serons | irons |
| vous aurez | serez | irez |
| ils auront | seront | iront |
| elles auront | seront | iront |

Note:
- For additional examples of the formation of the future tense of regular verbs, see the Regular Verb Charts.
- For the formation of the future tense of verbs with irregular future stems, see the Irregular Verb Charts.
- The future tense in French is generally used in the same way as the future tense in English. However, important exceptions are noted in Section 5 below.

5. Future after *quand, lorsque, dès que, aussitôt que* when futurity is implied.

| Word | Subject | Object Pronoun | Future Verb | Future or Imperative Verb Phrase |
|---|---|---|---|---|
| a. **Quand** | il | | viendra, | je lui parlerai. |
| b. **Lorsque** | tu | | rentreras, | téléphone-moi. |
| c. **Dès qu'** | il | me | verra, | il dira, "Bonjour." |
| d. **Aussitôt que** | vous | | arriverez, | venez me voir. |

a. When he comes, I shall speak to him.
b. When you get home, call me.
c. As soon as he sees me, he will say, "Good day."
d. As soon as you arrive, come to see me.

6. Indirect objects used with *il faut* (third person singular of *falloir*).

| *Il* | Indirect Obj. | *faut* | Direct obj. | Meanings |
|------|------|------|------|------|
| a. *Il* | *me* | *faut* | *dix francs.* | I need ten francs. |
| b. *Il* | *te* | *faut* | *un jeton.* | You [fam.] need a token. |
| c. *Il* | *lui* | *faut* | *le numéro.* | He [She] needs the number. |
| d. *Il* | *nous* | *faut* | *l'annuaire.* | We need the directory. |
| e. *Il* | *vous* | *faut* | *une cabine.* | You need a booth. |
| f. *Il* | *leur* | *faut* | *de l'espoir.* | They need (some) hope. |

(See also Lesson 2, Note 11.)

## EXERCISES

A. Substitute each of the words or expressions in parentheses for the underlined word in the model sentence. Write the complete sentence and say it aloud.

1. *Je peux le demander.* (*choisir, comprendre, voir, lire, faire, acheter*)
2. *Je peux le demander.* (*dois, vais, veux, sais*)
3. *Je ne sais rien.* (*vois, comprends, lis, dis, mange, veux*)
4. *Il n'a rien vu.* (*compris, acheté, choisi, lu, fini, appris*)

B. Transform the following sentences into exclamations by using the proper form of *quel*. Say and translate them.

Example: *C'est une belle maison./Quelle belle maison!*

1. *C'est un livre intéressant.*
2. *C'est un bon garçon.*
3. *C'est une robe exquise.*
4. *Ce sont de jolies images.*
5. *Ce sont de beaux arbres.*

C. Replace *dès que, lorsque,* and *aussitôt que* by *quand* in each of the following sentences. Say, write, and translate each sentence.

1. *Dès que je le verrai, je le saluerai.*
2. *Aussitôt qu'il viendra, dites-lui de manger.*
3. *Lorsqu'il sortira, fermez la porte.*
4. *Dès que vous quitterez la salle, on commencera la discussion.*
5. *Aussitôt qu'il achètera la voiture, il fera un voyage.*

D. Translate the following sentences into French. Then say them aloud.

1. I'd like to look up a number.
2. Would you like to speak to Charles?
3. What an interesting system!
4. I see nothing.
5. He finds nothing.
6. You don't want anything?
7. She saw nothing.
8. We didn't find anything.
9. They didn't want anything.
10. What did you find? Nothing.
11. What do you want? Nothing.
12. He needs the directory. (with *il faut*)
13. Please speak more loudly.

E. Match the English phrases in the first column with their correct French equivalents in the second column. Say and write the French sentences.

| | |
|---|---|
| 1. Buy a telephone credit card. | *Décrochez le récepteur.* |
| | *Raccrochez si vous avez fait un faux numéro.* |
| 2. Look up the number in the directory. | *Achetez une télécarte.* |
| 3. Pick up the receiver. | *Composez votre numéro.* |
| 4. Insert the telephone credit card. | *Attendez le signal.* |
| | *Introduire la télécarte.* |
| 5. Wait for the dial tone. | *Recommencez de nouveau.* |
| 6. Ask Information for the number. | *Demandez le numéro au service des renseignements.* |
| 7. Dial your number. | |
| 8. Speak with your party. | *Cherchez le numéro dans l'annuaire.* |
| 9. Hang up if you have a wrong number. | *Parlez avec votre correspondant.* |
| 10. Begin again. | |

F. Translate the dialogue into French.

Mme: Hello! Is this 42-81-58-17?

M.: Yes, ma'am.

Mme: I'd like to speak to Mr. Dupont, please.

M.: Who's calling?

Mme: This is Mrs. Lenclos.

M.: Hold on, please . . . I'm sorry, ma'am, but his line is busy. Do you want to wait?

Mme: No, thank you. I prefer to leave a message. Please tell him that I'll call back tomorrow.

M.: I'll give him the message.

Mme: Thank you very much. Good-bye, sir.

M.: Good-bye, ma'am.

G. From among the three choices given, choose the best translation for the word or phrase given at the beginning of each sentence, write the complete sentence, and translate.

1. (which) *C'est pour _____ ville?*
   - (a) *quelle*
   - (b) *cette*
   - (c) *quoi*

2. (It doesn't matter) _____, *monsieur.*
   - (a) *Cela ne dit pas*
   - (b) *Cela n'est pas*
   - (c) *Cela ne fait rien*

3. (on the right) *La cabine est à _____.*
   - (a) *gauche*
   - (b) *droite*
   - (c) *bas*

4. (I have) *Dès que _____ la communication, je vous ferai signe.*
   - (a) *j'ai*
   - (b) *j'avais*
   - (c) *j'aurai*

5. (Please) _____ *entrer.*
   - (a) *Voulez*
   - (b) *Veuillez*
   - (c) *Voudriez*

6. (once again) *Je vous dérange _____.*
   - (a) *encore une fois*
   - (b) *toujours*
   - (c) *autrefois*

7. (itself) *C'est dans Paris _____.*
   - (a) *soi-même*
   - (b) *même*
   - (c) *lui-même*

8. (You will need) _____ *une télécarte.*
   - (a) *Vous faudrez*
   - (b) *Vous faudra*
   - (c) *Il vous faudra*

9. (I understand) _____, *jusqui'ici.*
   - (a) *J'y sais*
   - (b) *J'y suis*
   - (c) *J'y comprends*
10. (I'll know how) _____ *me débrouiller.*
    - (a) *Je sais*
    - (b) *Je saurai*
    - (c) *Je savais*

# LESSON 4

## LES TRANSPORTS EN VILLE
## CITY TRANSPORTATION

### A. DIALOGUE

*Le Métro.*    The Metro.

1. Jane: **Le Marais° est même** *plus beau* **que je ne croyais.°**
   The Marais is even more beautiful than I thought.

2. Charles: **C'est vrai. J'aurais pu passer plus de temps dans le quartier.**
   That's right. I could have spent more time in the quarter.

3. Jane: **Oui, moi aussi, mais regarde l'heure.** *Il faut qu'on rentre* **à l'hôtel si** *on* **va rejoindre° Nicole ce soir. Heureusement le métro est rapide!**
   Yes, me too, but look at the time. We'd better get back to the hotel if we're going to meet Nicole this evening. Luckily, the metro is fast!

4. Charles: **Un carnet, s'il vous plaît.**
   A book of tickets, please.

5. Employee: **Oui, monsieur.**
   Yes, sir.

6. Charles: **Comment fait-on** *pour aller*° **à Saint-Jacques?**
   How do we get to Saint-Jacques?

7. Employee: **Eh bien,** *passez* **votre ticket dans la machine et puis,** *prenez* **la direction° Place d'Italie.** *Descendez* **sur le quai par l'escalier qui se trouve au bout du couloir. D'ici à la Place d'Italie, il n'y a que cinq arrêts. Là, vous ferez une correspondence° pour aller à Saint-Jacques. Vous prendrez la ligne 6,° direction Étoile. Saint-Jacques est la troisième station.**
   Well, put your ticket through the machine and then take the Place d'Italie train. Take the stairs at the end of the corridor to get down to the platform. From here to the Place d'Italie, there are only five stops. There you'll change trains to go to Saint-Jacques. You'll take the number six train to Etoile. Saint-Jacques is the third station.

8. Charles: **Merci, madame.**
   Thank you.

*Le Bus.*   The Bus.

9. Jane: *Écoute,* **chéri, j'ai une merveilleuse idée. Puisque nous avons déjà pris le métro aujourd'hui, prenons un bus pour aller nous rejoindre avec Nicole. Ça sera plus sympa comme on pourra voir un peu plus de la ville.**
   Listen, dear, I've got a great idea. Since we've already taken the metro today, let's take a bus to go meet Nicole. That will be nicer since we'll be able to see a little more of the city.

10. Charles: **Tu° as raison. Et en plus, l'arrêt de bus est juste là.**
You're right. Plus, the bus stop is right there.

11. Jane: **Quel monde!**
What a crowd!

12. Charles: **Oui, malheureusement c'est l'heure d'affluence. Voyons, je crois que c'est cette ligne-ci qu'il nous faut.**
Yes, unfortunately it's rush hour. Let's see, I think that this is the line that we need.

13. Jane: *Pourvu qu'on puisse monter!* **Il est bien bondé!**
I only hope we can get on! It's pretty packed.

14. Charles: **Mais il y a encore de la place, heureusement.** (*au conducteur*) **Nous allons à la Place des Ternes, monsieur.**
But there is still some space, luckily. (to the driver) We're going to the Place des Ternes, sir.

15. Conducteur: **Il faut composter votre ticket avant d'aller à l'arrière. Appuyez sur la bande magnétique pour signaler que vous voulez descendre et sur le bouton pour faire ouvrir les portes d'arrière.**
You've got to punch your ticket before going to the back. Press on the strip to signal that you want to get off and on the button to open the rear door.

16. Jane: **Tiens, deux places à côté de la fenêtre. C'est moins rapide que le métro, mais c'est aussi beaucoup plus intéressant.**
Look, two spaces next to the window. It's not as fast as the subway, but it's also more interesting.

*Le Taxi.* The Taxi

17. Charles: **Merci beaucoup, Nicole, pour une soirée très agréable.**
Thank you very much, Nicole, for a very pleasant evening.

18. Nicole: **Ah, pas de quoi.**
Don't mention it.

19. Jane: **Vous avez bien choisi le restaurant et le spectacle.**
You did a good job choosing the restaurant and the show.

20. Charles: **Mais il est tard! Vous voulez nous accompagner jusqu'à la station de métro?**
But it's late. Do you want to walk with us to the metro station?

21. Nicole: **J'aimerais bien, mais à cette heure-ci, il n'y a plus de métro. Il y a un bus de nuit, mais un taxi serait beaucoup plus facile. Il y a une station de taxis juste là.**
I would love to, but at this hour, the metro isn't running anymore. There is a night bus, but a taxi would be much easier. There is a taxi stand right over there.

22. Charles: **Merci, Nicole.** (*au chauffeur*) **C'est combien pour aller au Boulevard Saint-Jacques?**
Thank you, Nicole. (to the driver) How much is it to go to the Boulevard Saint-Jacques?

23. Chauffeur: **Vous payerez le prix inscrit au compteur, monsieur.**
You pay the price shown on the meter.

24. Jane: **Je dois avouer que je voyagerais toujours en taxi si c'était possible. C'est de loin le moyen de transport *le plus confortable*.**
I have to admit that I would always travel by taxi if it were possible. It's by far the most comfortable means of transportation.

25. Charles: **Et le plus cher aussi, malheureusement.**
And the most expensive as well, unfortunately.

26. Jane: **Mais à cette heure-ci, comme il n'y a pas beaucoup de circulation, on arrivera bientôt à l'hôtel.**
But at this hour, since there isn't much traffic, we'll get to our hotel soon.

27. Charles: **Tu as raison. Et moi, j'ai sommeil. Tu veux me réveiller dès qu'on y sera arrivé?**
You're right. And I'm tired. Do you want to wake me up as soon as we get there?

## B  NOTES

Title: *le Métro* is short for *le Métropolitain*, the subway system of Paris.

1. *Le Marais* is a scenic quarter of Paris full of mansions restored as museums. It is especially known for the *Centre Pompidou* and the *Place des Vosges.*
*plus que je ne croyais:* After the comparative of an adjective, *ne* generally precedes the verbs *croire* and *penser*. For example: *Elle est plus pressée que je ne pensais.* She is more rushed than I thought.

3. *on va se rejoindre:* Note the use of *aller* plus an infinitive to denote the future tense, as in the English "We are going to get together."

6. *pour aller: pour* plus an infinitive means "in order to . . ."

7. *direction Place d'Italie:* Parisian subway lines are generally identified by the names of the stops at either end of the line. The lines can also be identified by number. Therefore, a person traveling on line 4 may be headed *direction Porte de Clignancourt* or *direction Porte d'Orléans.*
   *correspondence:* a transfer to another subway line. Outside of each subway station and on each platform there is a large map of the entire subway system and the possible transfers from one line to another. In the larger stations, a passenger can press a button indicating his station destination and the most convenient route will immediately light up on the map.

10. *tu:* The use of the *tu* form is traditionally limited to members of one's family, intimate friends, and children. Young people generally use this form among themselves, as do adults involved in the same activity, such as a sports team, office personnel, etc. Although the *tu* form has become more commonly used, it is always best to use *vous* whenever uncertain.

## C. GRAMMAR AND USAGE

1. Comparison of adjectives

|  | aussi/ plus/ moins | Adjective | que | Object |
|---|---|---|---|---|
| a. *Cette idée est* | *plus* | *originale* | *que* | *l'autre.* |
| b. *Ce projet-ci est* | *plus* | *intéressant* | *que* | *celui-là.* |
| c. *Mon complet est* | *moins* | *beau* | *que* | *le vôtre.* |
| d. *Ces hommes-ci sont* | *moins* | *riches* | *que* | *ceux-là.* |
| e. *Cet hôtel est* | *aussi* | *bon* | *que* | *l'autre.* |
| f. *Ses repas sont* | *aussi* | *délicieux* | *que* | *ceux de sa soeur.* |

a. This idea is more original than the other one.
b. This project is more interesting than that one.
c. My suit is less beautiful than yours.
d. These men are less rich than those.
e. This hotel is as good as the other one.
f. Her meals are as delicious as her sister's.

2. Imperative

| Infinitive | Fam. Sing. | Fam. Pl. and Polite Form | Suggestion (Let's) |
|---|---|---|---|
| a. *parler* | *Parle!* | *Parlez!* | *Parlons!* |
| b. *finir* | *Finis!* | *Finissez!* | *Finissons!* |
| c. *apprendre* | *Apprends!* | *Apprenez!* | *Apprenons!* |

a. (to) speak Speak! Speak! Let's speak!
b. (to) finish Finish! Finish! Let's finish!
c. (to) learn Learn! Learn! Let's learn!

Note:

- To form the imperative, take the *tu, vous,* and *nous* forms of the present indicative, and omit the subject pronoun.
- In general, drop the final "s" of the familiar singular form for *-er* verbs.

Examples:

|   |   |   |
|---|---|---|
| a. | *Parle français.* | Speak French. |
| b. | *Va à l'école.* | Go to school. |
| c. | *Ouvre la porte.* | Open the door. |

Note:

- For easier pronunciation, the "s" *is* included before the pronouns *en* and *y.*

Example:

|   |   |   |
|---|---|---|
| a. | *Parles-en.* | Speak of it. |
| b. | *Vas-y.* | Go there. |

Note:

- The imperative forms of *avoir, être,* and *savoir* are irregular and can be found in the Irregular Verb Charts.

3. *On*

Study the function of *on* in the following sentences:

a. *On perd toujours la tête dans ces cas-là.*
One always loses one's head in these cases.
b. *On parle français ici.*
French is spoken here./We speak French here.
c. *On dit que c'est un voleur.*
People say he's a thief./They say he's a thief.
d. *On va sortir ce soir.*
We're going to go out tonight.

Note:

- *On* is another catchall pronoun (like *en.*) Its literal meaning is "one," as in the first example above, but it is frequently used as well for "you, they, we," or for "people" in the vague, generalized sense. *On* can also express the passive voice, as in:

  *On vend les billets ici.*   Tickets are sold here.

## 4. *Devoir*

Study the forms of *devoir* in the Irregular Verb Charts. Notice some of the functions and equivalents of *devoir* in the following sentences:

| Subject | Auxiliary Verb | *devoir* | Infinitive |
|---------|----------------|----------|------------|
| a. *Je* |                | *dois*   | *partir.*  |
| b. *Je* |                | *devais* | *partir.*  |
| c. *Je* |                | *devrai* | *partir.*  |
| d. *Je* |                | *devrais*| *partir.*  |
| e. *J'* | *ai*           | *dû*     | *partir.*  |
| f. *J'* | *aurais*       | *dû*     | *partir.*  |

a. I must leave.
b. I was supposed to leave.
c. I'll have to leave.
d. I should leave.
e. I had to leave.
f. I should have left.

Note:

- With nouns, *devoir* means "to owe."

Examples:

*Il me doit six francs.*        He owes me six francs.
*Je lui dois la vie.*           I owe my life to him.

5. The subjunctive: This mood expresses doubt, emotion, volition, possibility, necessity. It is generally used in subordinate clauses after verbs that require mood, after *il faut que*, and after certain conjunctions.

Study the regular forms of the subjunctive in the Regular Verb Charts. You will also find the subjunctives of the most common irregular verbs in the Irregular Verb Charts.

Notice the following examples:

|              | Main clause     | Subordinate clause        |
|--------------|-----------------|---------------------------|
| a. Volition  | *Il veut*       | *que j'aille.*            |
| b. Doubt     | *Nous doutons*  | *qu'elles viennent ici.*  |
| c. Emotion   | *Je regrette*   | *qu'il soit bondé.*       |

- a. He wants me to go (that I go).
- b. We doubt that they are coming here
- c. I am sorry (that) it is packed.

Study the following examples of the subjunctive with certain conjunctions:

| Present/Future/ Imperative | Conjunction  | Present Subjunctive        |
|----------------------------|--------------|----------------------------|
| a. *Je viendrai*           | *pourvu que* | *vous m'invitiez.*         |
| b. *Il n'est pas heureux*  | *quoiqu'*    | *il soit riche.*           |
| c. *Je sortirai*           | *à moins qu'*| *il ne pleuve.*            |
| d. *Je le répète*          | *afin que*   | *vous puissiez l'apprendre.* |
| e. *Venez*                 | *pour que*   | *je puisse vous parler.*   |

a. I'll come <u>provided</u> you invite me.
b. He is not happy <u>although</u> he is rich.
c. I shall go out <u>unless</u> it rains.
d. I repeat it <u>in order that</u> you may learn it.
e. Come <u>so that</u> I can speak to you.

Note:

- In example c., notice that with the conjunction *à moins que, ne* is placed before the subjunctive. This is also done with a few other expressions, such as *de peur que* (for fear that) and has no negative connotation.

## EXERCISES

A. Substitute each of the words or expressions in parentheses for the underlined word or expression in the model sentence. Write each new sentence and say it aloud.

1. *Le taxi est plus <u>rapide</u> que le <u>métro</u>. (cher, intéressant, efficace, beau, propre)*
2. *On parle <u>français</u> ici. (anglais, italien, chinois, espagnol, turc)*
3. *Je dois <u>partir</u>. (sortir, étudier, manger, lire, travailler)*
4. *Il me doit <u>dix francs</u>. (vingt francs, cent cinquante francs, deux livres, du respect)*

B. Transform these familiar singular forms of the imperative to (1) the *vous* form, and (2) to the *nous* (Let's . . .) form.

Example: *Parle!/Parlez!/Parlons!*

1. *Finis!*
2. *Sois!*

3. *Apprends!*
4. *Mange!*
5. *Choisis!*
6. *Mets!*

C. Translate the following sentences into French. Then say them aloud.

1. What's your address?
2. We have to take a bus.
3. She must take the subway.
4. That must be the bus stop.
5. I had to take a taxi.
6. They had to take a book of tickets.
7. She'll have to stand in line.
8. They'll have to pay.
9. He should pay, but he doesn't want to pay.
10. He should have left.
11. They (fem.) should have come.
12. Let's go look at the Eiffel Tower.
13. Let's go spend the afternoon with Marie.
14. How does one get to the Place des Vosges?
15. How does one find a taxi?
16. There is only one station before Concorde.
17. There are only two changes to make.
18. He said that she would take a taxi.
19. He said that they would have the money.
20. They are richer than the others.
21. The taxis are more expensive than the bus.
22. English is spoken here.
23. The Eiffel Tower can be seen from here.
24. People travel far to see the Eiffel Tower.
25. She wants you to go.
26. I am glad that she is happy.
27. We doubt that he can do that.
28. I will go unless it rains.

D. From among the three choices given, choose the best translation for the English word or phrase given. Write the complete sentence, and translate.

1. (To get back) _____, *prenons un taxi.*
   (a) *A rentrer*
   (b) *A la rentrée*
   (c) *Pour rentrer*

2. (Let's go) _____ *prendre nos billets.*
   (a) *Va*
   (b) *Allons*
   (c) *Allez*

3. (at the end) *L'escalier se trouve* _____ *du couloir.*
   (a) *à la fin*
   (b) *enfin*
   (c) *au bout*

4. (room) *Il y a encore de la* _____.
   (a) *chambre*
   (b) *place*
   (c) *pièce*

5. (There's a crowd!) _____ *monde.*
   (a) *Il y a un*
   (b) *Quel du*
   (c) *Il y a du*

6. (get off) *On doit* _____ *ici.*
   (a) *partir*
   (b) *descendre*
   (c) *reprendre*

7. (better) *Oui, ça vaudrait* _____
   (a) *bon*
   (b) *bien*
   (c) *mieux*

8. (That one) _____ *doit être occupé.*
   (a) *Cela*
   (b) *Ceci*
   (c) *Celui-là*

9. (what) *C'est* _____ *adresse, s'il vous plaît?*
   (a) *quelle*
   (b) *quel*
   (c) *quoi*
10. (a train change) *Y a-t-il* _____ *avant Molitor?*
    (a) *un changement de train*
    (b) *une correspondance*
    (c) *une connection*

# LESSON 5

## FAISONS UNE PROMENADE À PIED
## LET'S TAKE A WALK

A. DIALOGUE

*Avant la promenade.*   Before the walk.

1. Jane: **Si on faisait° une promenade à pied, tous les deux? Si on allait voir un quartier intéressant, le Quartier Latin,° par exemple?**
   How about taking a walk, the two of us? How about going to visit an interesting neighborhood—the Latin Quarter, for instance?

2. Charles: ***Toi et moi? Seuls? Je me suis baladé à Paris il y a longtemps, mais je ne saurais pas te guider à présent.***
   You and I? Alone? I wandered around Paris a long time ago, but I wouldn't know how to show you around now.

3. Jane: **C'est facile! Il faudra tout simplement demander le chemin au concierge.°**
   It's easy! We only have to ask the concierge the way.

*À la réception.*    At the reception desk.

4. Charles: **Monsieur, pourriez-vous nous dire comment aller au Quartier Latin?**
   Sir, could you tell us how to get to the Latin Quarter?

5. Concierge: **De quel côté voulez-vous aller?**
   Toward what area do you want to go?

6. Charles: **Du côté de la Sorbonne°...**
   Toward the Sorbonne...

7. Concierge: **Eh bien, le Quartier Latin est à deux pas° d'ici, puisque nous sommes sur la Rive Gauche.° Regardez ce plan de Paris.... Nous sommes ici.**
   Well, the Latin Quarter is close by here, since we are on the Left Bank. Look at this map of Paris.... We are here.

8. Charles: **Ah! Je vois bien. Nous ne sommes pas très loin du Quartier Latin.**
   Ah! I see. We're not very far from the Latin Quarter.

9. Concierge: **Vous devez aller vers le boulevard Saint-Michel° et la rue des Écoles.**
   You have to head toward the boulevard Saint-Michel and the rue des Écoles.

10. Charles: **Je comprends. On doit aller dans cette direction-ci...**
    I understand. We have to go in *this* direction...

11. Concierge: **C'est ça! Il faut prendre la rue de Seine et vous continuez tout droit. Une fois arrivé au Boulevard Saint-Germain, vous devez tourner à gauche devant l'église qui fait le coin du boulevard et de la rue Napoléon.**

Right! You have to continue straight ahead on the rue de Seine. Once you arrive at the boulevard Saint-Germain, turn left in front of the church on the corner of the boulevard and the rue Napoléon.

12. Charles: **Puis, on traverse le boulevard, on marche encore deux rues,° et on tourne à droite!**
Then, you cross the boulevard, you walk two more blocks, and you turn to the right!

13. Concierge: **C'est ça. Et *si vous vous égarez,* vous n'avez qu'à demander le chemin à un passant. À propos, ne traversez pas avant que le signal l'indique. Et quand on traverse la rue, il faut marcher sur les bandes blanches dans le passage clouté!**
That's it. And if you get lost, all you have to do is ask a passerby the way. By the way, don't cross before you see the signal turn green. And when you do, you have to stay within the crosswalk.

14. Charles: *Ne vous inquiétez pas!*
Don't worry!

15. Charles: **Voilà, Jane, nous devrons tout simplement faire dix minutes de marche.**
There, Jane, we'll just have to walk for ten minutes.

16. Jane: **C'est parfait. Je n'ai pas envie de° marcher longtemps. Allons-y!**
Perfect! I don't feel like walking a long time. Let's go!

*Quinze minutes plus tard.*　　Fifteen minutes later.

17. Jane: **Charles, voilà la Seine! Mais je vois Notre-Dame.° *Nous nous sommes égarés!***
Charles, there's the Seine. But I see Notre Dame. We've lost our way!

18. Charles: **Un instant. Je vais demander le chemin à
cette dame.°**
**Madame, s'il vous plaît ... pour aller au Quar-
tier Latin ... à la Sorbonne ... quelle rue faut-il
prendre? Je n'ai aucune idée ...**
Just a minute. I'm going to ask this woman the way.
Please, ma'am, to go to the Latin Quarter ... to the
Sorbonne ... which street must you take? I have no
idea ...

19. Madame: **Mais vous marchez° dans le mauvais
sens, monsieur.**
But you're walking in the wrong direction, sir.

20. Charles: **Comment? Je ne marche° pas dans le
bon sens?**
What? I'm not walking in the right direction?

21. Madame: **Je le regrette, monsieur, mais vous devez rebrousser chemin et remonter cette rue.**
I'm sorry, sir, but you must retrace your steps and go
back up this street.

22. Charles: **Tu entends, Jane? Nous devons faire
demi-tour.**
Did you hear, Jane? We have to start all over again.

23. Jane: **Je te parie qu'en quittant l'hôtel nous aurions dû tourner à gauche quand nous avons
tourné à droite!**
I'll bet that on leaving the hotel we should have
turned left when we turned right!

*De retour à l'hôtel.*    Back at the hotel.

24. Concierge: **Bonsoir, messieurs 'dames.° Avez-
vous fait une bonne promenade cet après-midi?**

Good evening, sir, madam. Did you have a nice
walk this afternoon?

25. Charles: **Ah oui. Une fois que nous avons trouvé le
bon chemin.**
Oh, yes, Once we found the right way.

26. Concierge: **Mais comment? Mes indications
n'étaient pas justes?**
What? My directions weren't correct?

27. Jane: **Si, mais c'est _nous_ qui _nous sommes trompés._
Nous avons tourné à droite au lieu de tourner à
gauche.**
Yes, but we're the ones who made a mistake. We
turned right instead of turning left.

28. Concierge: **Quel dommage! Mais vous avez dû
voir des endroits intéressants.**
What a pity! But you must have seen some interesting places.

29. Charles: **Ah, vous avez raison. Nous avons revu
Notre-Dame, les bouquinistes de la Seine, et la
Sainte-Chapelle.°**
Oh, you are right. We saw Notre Dame again, the
secondhand book vendors along the Seine, and the
Sainte Chapelle.

30. Jane: **N'oublie pas que nous avons vu aussi le
musée de Cluny° et le Panthéon.°**
Don't forget that we also saw the Cluny Museum
and the Panthéon.

## B. NOTES

1. _Si on faisait:_ The imperfect is used after _si_ to mean
"How about?" Example: _Si on parlait au concierge?_ (How about speaking to the concierge?)

*le Quartier Latin:* the section of Paris on the Left Bank (of the Seine River) where the University of Paris is located. It is called the Latin Quarter because, during the Middle Ages, all students spoke Latin.

3. *concierge:* Both in hotels and in apartment houses, the concierge acts like a superintendent who also is the recipient and dispenser of all information about tenants, directions, prices, and such things.

6. *Sorbonne:* the seat of the faculties of arts and letters of the University of Paris. The university consists of thirteen public universities designated by a number—Paris I, Paris II, etc.

7. *à deux pas:* lit.: "two steps away," but this is often merely wishful thinking.
   *Rive Gauche:* the Seine River divides Paris into the *Rive Gauche* (Left Bank) and the *Rive Droite* (Right Bank). In general, the student/bohemian/artistic/intellectual quarters of the city are on the Rive Gauche, and the commercial and fashionable quarters on the Rive Droite.

9. *boulevard Saint-Michel:* Often referred to as the "Boul' Mich'," it is the main thoroughfare of the Latin Quarter. It is lined with cafés and bookstores.

12. *deux rues:* Note that the French say *rues* instead of "blocks" when giving directions.

16. *avoir envie de faire:* to feel like doing something.

17. The Cathedral of Notre-Dame is usually referred to simply as "*Notre-Dame.*"

18. *cette dame:* Note the use of *cette dame* for "that woman." In this sort of social context, it is good form to refer to a woman as a "lady," e.g., *une dame.* Similarly, refer to a man as *ce monsieur*, a young woman as *cette demoiselle.*

19/20. *marchez . . . marche:* It would be equally correct to use forms of *aller.* That is, *"Vous allez dans le mauvais sens . . ." "Comment? Je ne vais pas . . ."*

24. *messieurs 'dames:* This abbreviation of *messieurs et mesdames* is frequently used by service people in France.

29. *la Sainte-Chapelle:* a church that is a jewel of Gothic architecture on the Île de la Cité (a small island in the middle of the Seine). Notre Dame is also on the Île de la Cité.

30. *le musée de Cluny:* a small museum in the Latin Quarter.
*le Panthéon:* a building containing the tombs of many famous people of France.

## C. GRAMMAR AND USAGE

1. "Disjunctive" or emphatic pronouns
(See the Summary of French Grammar for all the forms and no. 6 below.)

Study the forms and functions of this class of pronouns:

After prepositions:

|   | | Preposition | Pronoun |
|---|---|---|---|
| a. | *Je travaille* | *pour* | *lui.* |
| b. | *Viens* | *avec* | *moi.* |
| c. | *Partons* | *sans* | *eux.* |

a. I work for him.
b. Come with me.
c. Let's leave without them.

After *que* in comparisons:

|  | plus/moins/ aussi | Adjective | que | Pronoun |
|---|---|---|---|---|
| a. *Il est* | *plus* | *riche* | *que* | *toi.* |
| b. *Nous sommes* | *moins* | *pressés* | *que* | *vous.* |
| c. *Vous êtes* | *aussi* | *intelligent* | *qu'* | *elle.* |

a. He is richer than you (fam.).
b. We are less hurried than you (polite sing. or pl.).
c. You are as intelligent as she.

After imperatives:

a. *Donne-moi ce livre.*    Give me this book.
b. *Couche-toi maintenant.*    Go to bed now.

In compound subjects and objects:

a. *Charles et moi nous*    Charles and I go to the
   *allons au cinéma.*    movies.
b. *Lui et elle viendront*    He and she will come
   *demain.*    tomorrow.
c. *Je vous aime*[1] *beau-*    I like you and Jane very
   *coup, toi et Jane.*    much.

Note:

• In a compound subject, when the two pronouns are of the third person, the subject pronoun is omitted and the verb follows directly (see above).

[1] The verb *aimer*, used alone, means "to love." Ex.: *Je t'aime.* I love you. Note that *Je vous aime beaucoup* means "I like you very much and *Je vous aime bien* simply means "I like you."

- In all other cases, the normal subject or object pronoun is included along with the disjunctive pronouns (see a. and c. above).

In emphatic statements:

a. *Moi, je ne le veux pas.* — I don't want it.

b. *Je ne sais pas, moi.* — I don't know.

After *c'est:*

a. *C'est moi.* — It's I.
b. *C'est toi.* — It's you.
c. *C'est lui.* — It's he.
d. *C'est elle.* — It's she.
e. *C'est nous.* — It's we.
f. *C'est vous.* — It's you.
g. *C'est/Ce sont eux.* — It's they.
h. *C'est/Ce sont elles.* — It's they.

Alone, as a complete utterance:

a. *Qui a fait cela? Moi.* — Who did that? I (did).
b. *Qui est entré? Lui.* — Who entered? He (did).

2. Reflexive verbs—Verbs whose action is performed by the subject on itself: *elle se lave, il se lève.*

Study the forms and equivalents (see also the Regular Verb Charts):

Present tense

a. *Je me lave.* — I wash myself.
b. *Tu te laves.* — You wash yourself.
c. *Il se lave.* — He washes himself.

d. *Elle se lave.*                      She washes herself.

e. *Nous nous lavons.*                  We wash ourselves.

f. *Vous vous lavez.*                   You wash yourself (your-
                                        selves).

g. *Ils se lavent*                      They wash themselves.

h. *Elles se lavent.*                   They wash themselves.

Examples:

| Infinitive | Subject | Reflexive pronoun | Verb | Complement |
|---|---|---|---|---|
| a. *se lever* | *Je* | *me* | *lève* | *à huit heures.* |
| b. *se tromper* | *Vous* | *vous* | *trompez.* | |
| c. *se dépêcher* | *Nous* | *nous* | *dépêchons* | *quand nous sommes en retard.* |

    a. I get up at eight o'clock.

    b. You're making a mistake.

    c. We hurry (ourselves) when we are late.

| Infinitive | | Subj. | Reflexive Pronoun | Verb | Dir. Obj. | Complement |
|---|---|---|---|---|---|---|
| a. *se brosser* | *Est-ce que* | *tu* | *te* | *brosses* | *les dents* | *tous les matins?* |
| b. *se laver* | | *Elle* | *se* | *lave* | *les mains.* | |

    a. Do you brush your teeth every morning?

    b. She is washing her hands.

Note:

- Many verbs that are not reflexive in English are reflexive in French. As you come across reflexive verbs,
  memorize them.

Present Perfect

|   |   |   |
|---|---|---|
| a. | *Je me suis égaré(e).* | I lost my way. (lit.: I lost myself.) |
| b. | *Tu t'es égaré(e).* | You lost your way. |
| c. | *Il s'est égaré.* | He lost his way. |
| d. | *Elle s'est égarée.* | She lost her way. |
| e. | *Nous nous sommes égaré(e)s.* | We lost our way. |
| f. | *Vous vous êtes égaré(e)(s).* | You lost your way. |
| g. | *Ils se sont égarés.* | They lost their way. |
| h. | *Elles se sont égarées.* | They lost their way. |

Note:

- Compound tenses of reflexive verbs, such as the present perfect above, are always formed with the auxiliary *être*.
- The past participle of reflexive verbs agrees with the subject, unless <u>the verb is followed by a direct object,</u> in which case there is no agreement.

Contrast:

|   |   |   |
|---|---|---|
| a. | *Nous nous sommes lavé(e)s.* | We washed ourselves [got washed]. |
| b. | *Nous nous sommes lavé les mains.* | We washed our hands. |
| c. | *Elle s'est coupée.* | She cut herself. |
| d. | *Elle s'est coupé le doigt.* | She cut her finger. |

## EXERCISES

A. Substitute each of the words in parentheses for the underlined word in the pattern sentence. Write the complete sentence and say it aloud.

1. *Il travaille pour* <u>*moi*</u>. (*toi, lui, elle, nous, vous, eux, elles*)
2. *Il est plus riche que* <u>*moi*</u>. (*toi, lui, elle, nous, vous, eux, elles*)
3. *Qui est à la porte? C'est* <u>*moi*</u>. (toi, lui, elle, nous, vous, eux, elles)
4. *Elle s'est* <u>*lavée*</u>. (*couchée, arrêtée, dépêchée, levée, égarée, trompée*)

B. Replace *Je* by the other subject pronouns. Make all necessary verb changes. Write the sentences, say aloud, and translate.

1. *Je me couche à neuf heures.*
2. *Je me suis trompé(e).*

C. Change the present to the present perfect. Say, and translate each.

Example: *Nous nous couchons./Nous nous sommes couché(e)s.*

1. *Nous nous lavons.*
2. *Nous nous levons.*
3. *Nous nous trompons.*
4. *Nous nous dépêchons.*
5. *Nous nous arrêtons.*

D. Translate the following into French. Then say them aloud.

1. Ask the concierge the way.
2. Don't ask this gentleman the way.
3. I wouldn't know how to go on foot.
4. Toward what area do you wish to go? Toward Paris.
5. They (*elles*) looked at each other.
6. How about going to see Sainte Chapelle?
7. How about taking a walk?

8. We've lost our way.
9. We went to the Latin Quarter.
10. Turn to the right.
11. I must turn to the left.
12. You should have continued straight ahead.
13. She must retrace her steps.
14. Is the Sorbonne right near (*à deux pas d'*) here?
    Yes, it's very near (*tout près d'*) here.

E. From among the three choices, select the best translation for the English word or phrase given. Write the complete sentence, and translate.

1. (How about taking) _____ *une promenade à pied?*
   (a) *Comment faire*
   (b) *Si on faisait*
   (c) *Si on prendrait*

2. (easy) *C'est* _____.
   (a) *aisé*
   (b) *facile*
   (c) *agréable*

3. (Look at) _____ *ce plan de Paris.*
   (a) *Cherchez*
   (b) *Voyez*
   (c) *Regardez*

4. (straight ahead) *Il faut continuer* _____.
   (a) *droit devant*
   (b) *à droite*
   (c) *tout droit*

5. (direction) *Vous allez dans le mauvais* _____.
   (a) *sens*
   (b) *côté*
   (c) *coin*

6. (left) *Nous avons tourné* _____.
   (a) *laissé*
   (b) *à gauche*
   (c) *à droite*

7. (once) *Ah, oui,* _____ *nous avons trouvé le bon chemin.*
   (a) *premier*
   (b) *une fois que*
   (c) *maintenant que*

8. (mistaken) *C'est nous qui nous sommes* _____.
   (a) *égaré*
   (b) *trompé*
   (c) *trompés*

9. (What a pity) _____!
   (a) *Quelle pitié!*
   (b) *Quelle sympathie!*
   (c) *Quel dommage!*

10. (Don't forget) _____ *que nous avons vu Notre-Dame.*
    (a) *N'oublie pas*
    (b) *Ne revois pas*
    (c) *Ne dis pas*

# LESSON 6

## DANS UN GRAND MAGASIN°
## IN A DEPARTMENT STORE

### A. DIALOGUE

*Au rayon des gants.* In the glove department.

1. Vendeuse: **Je peux vous aider, madame?**
   Can I help you, madam?

2. Jane: **Je *voudrais* une paire de gants pour tous les jours, s'il vous plaît; comme *les miens,* mais en cuir.°**
   I'd like a pair of gloves for every day, please; like mine, but in leather.

3. Vendeuse: **Nous en avons de tous les styles et de toutes les couleurs. En voici une paire en chevreau ...**
   We have all kinds and colors. Here is a pair in kidskin ...

4. Jane: **Oui, *ceux-là* sont assez jolis. *Pourriez-vous me les montrer* en beige, s'il vous plaît?**
   Yes, those are quite pretty. Could you show them to me in beige, please?

5. Vendeuse: **Quelle est votre pointure,° madame? Les pointures sont les mêmes qu'aux États-Unis.**
   What size do you take, madam? The sizes are the same as in the United States.

6. Jane: **Ah oui? Alors six et demi.**
   Ah, yes? Six and a half, then.

7. Vendeuse: **Un instant, je vais vous les chercher. Les voici. Voulez-vous les essayer, madame?**
   One moment, I'll get them for you. Here they are. Would you like to try them on, madam?

8. Jane: **Ils me vont° parfaitement. Quel en est le prix, s'il vous plaît?**
   They fit me perfectly. What's the price, please?

9. Vendeuse: **Deux cents cinquante francs.**
   Two hundred fifty francs.

10. Jane: **C'est très bien. Voulez-vous *me les emballer,* s'il vous plaît?**
    That's fine. Will you wrap them for me, please?

11. Vendeuse: **Voilà, madame. Merci beaucoup.**
    There you are, madam. Thank you very much.

12. Jane: **Au fait,** *pourriez-vous* **m'indiquer où se trou-
    vent les toilettes?°**
    By the way, could you tell me where the ladies' room
    is?

13. Vendeuse: **Avec plaisir, madame. Tournez à
    gauche et continuez tout droit.**
    Gladly, madam. Turn to the left, and continue straight
    ahead.

14. Jane: **Je vous remercie.°**
    Thank you.

*Au rayon des robes.*    In the dress department.

15. Vendeuse: **Madame désire?**
    What would you like, madam?

16. Jane: **Je cherche une robe de soie vert clair—à
    manches courtes, et pas trop décolletée.**
    I'm looking for a light-green silk dress—with short
    sleeves and not cut too low.

17. Vendeuse: **Ce modèle-ci, madame, c'est la nou-
    velle mode, et une véritable occasion à 1250 (mille
    deux cents cinquante) francs.**
    This model is the latest style, madam, and a real
    bargain at 1.250 francs.

18. Jane: **Oh, c'est vraiment trop cher!** *N'auriez-vous*
    **rien d'autre, à meilleur marché?°**
    Oh, that's really too expensive! Don't you have any-
    thing else, less expensive?

19. Vendeuse: **Il y a** *celle-ci* **à 500 (cinq cents) francs.
    Voyez comme la coupe est élégante. Mais quelle
    est votre taille, madame?**

There's this one at 500 francs. See how elegant the cut is. But what's your size, madam?

20. Jane: **Eh bien, aux États-Unis c'est le dix . . .**
    Well, in the United States it's ten . . .

21. Vendeuse: **Cette robe-ci est pour vous alors. Passons au salon d'essayage . . .**
    This dress is for you, then. Let's go into the fitting room . . .

22. Jane: **Je la° trouve un peu large aux épaules, et trop longue aussi.**
    I find it a little wide in the shoulders, and also too long.

23. Vendeuse: **Essayons la taille en dessous alors. Ah, madame, vous êtes ravissante! Cette robe vous va à merveille!**
    Let's try the next smaller size, then. Ah, madam, you look lovely! This dress suits you wonderfully!

24. Jane: **En effet, elle est très chic . . . Bon, je la prends!**
    Yes, it's really very stylish . . . Okay, I'll take it!

25. Vendeuse: **C'est un excellent choix, madame. Veuillez me suivre à la caisse.**
    It's an excellent choice, madam. Will you come with me to the cashier's desk, please?

26. Jane: (*à la caisse*) **Est-ce que vous acceptez les chèques de voyage?°**
    (at the cashier's desk) Do you accept traveler's checks?

27. Caissier: **Certainement, madame. Si vous ne désirez pas l'emporter, nous pouvons vous l'expédier.°**

Cashier: Certainly, madam. If you don't want to take it with you, we can send it to you.

28. Jane: **Oui, cela vaudrait mieux. Merci beaucoup.**
Yes, that would be better. Thank you very much.

*Au comptoir des mouchoirs.*    At the handkerchief counter.

29. Vendeur: **Qu'est-ce que vous désirez, madame?**
What do you wish, madam?

30. Jane: **Je cherche des mouchoirs pour mon mari.**
I'm looking for some handkerchiefs for my husband.

31. Vendeur: **Il aimera beaucoup *ceux-ci,* j'en suis sûr. Ils sont en coton, à 150 (cent cinquante) francs la douzaine.**
He'll like these very much, I'm sure. They're cotton, at 150 francs a dozen.

32. Jane: ***Auriez-vous* quelque chose de meilleure qualité?**
Would you have something of a better quality?

33. Vendeur: ***Ceux-ci* sont en lin, madame. Ils coûtent 30 (trente) francs la pièce.**
These are linen, madam. They cost 30 francs apiece.

34. Jane: **Oui, je les aime mieux. *Donnez-m'en* une demi-douzaine,° s'il vous plaît.**
Yes, I like these better. Give me a half-dozen of them, please.

35. Vendeur: **Très bien, madame ... Et voici votre monnaie.°**
Very good, madam ... And here's your change.

36. Jane: **Merci beaucoup, monsieur.**
Thank you very much, sir.

37. Vendeur: **À votre service, madame.**
At your service, madam.

## B. NOTES

Title: *grand magasin* has two equivalents: a big store (of any kind) and, more commonly, a department store. In Paris, most of these are on the Right Bank.

2. *en cuir: en* generally precedes the noun for a fabric or material. Examples: *en coton* (in cotton); *en laine* (in wool).

5. *pointure:* the term used to indicate sizes for socks, shoes, stockings, hats, and gloves. To indicate sizes of dresses, suits, coats, and shirts, the term *taille* is used. Some sizes are the same as in the United States, but most are different.

8. *Ils me vont:* They fit me. From *aller* (to fit, to suit), used in connection with clothes, etc. See also 23 in the text.

12. *Les toilettes* refers to the room where the toilet is. There is usually also a small sink (*un lavabo*). *La salle de bains* refers to the bathroom where you take a bath; and the shower is *la douche.*

14. *Je vous remercie:* lit.: I thank you. This expression is a little more formal than *merci,* but is frequently used.

18. *bon marché:* inexpensive. *meilleur marché:* less expensive.

22. *la:* refers to the dress (*la robe*).

26. Traveler's checks are accepted almost everywhere in France.

27. Purchases are delivered—and graciously—if the customer so desires.

34. *une demi-douzaine:* when *demi* precedes the word it modifies, it is invariable.

35. *monnaie:* (small) change or currency. *Argent* is the word for money in general, and *pièces* are coins.

## C. GRAMMAR AND USAGE

### 1. The Present Conditional

The conditional of verbs with irregular future stems:

| 1st Conjugation | 2nd Conjugation | 3rd Conjugation |
|---|---|---|
| (future stem = infin.) | (future stem = infin.) | (future stem = infin. minus final e) |
| *arriver* | *choisir* | *attendre* |
| *j'arriverais* (I'd come, I would come) | *je choisirais* (I'd choose, I would choose) | *j'attendrais* (I'd wait, I would wait) |
| *tu arriverais* | *tu choisirais* | *tu attendrais* |
| *il elle* } *arriverait* | *il elle* } *choisirait* | *il elle* } *attendrait* |
| *nous arriverions* | *nous choisirions* | *nous attendrions* |
| *vous arriveriez* | *vous choisiriez* | *vous attendriez* |
| *ils elles* } *arriveraient* | *ils elles* } *choisiraient* | *ils elles* } *attendraient* |

Note:
- The conditional is formed by adding the endings *-ais, -ais, -ait, -ions, -iez, -aient* to the future stem.

The conjugation of verbs with irregular future stems:

| avoir | être | aller |
|---|---|---|
| future stem = *aur-* | future stem = *ser-* | future stem = *ir-* |
| *j'aurais* (I'd have, I would have) | *je serais* (I'd be, I would be) | *j'irais* (I'd go, I would go) |
| *tu aurais* | *tu serais* | *tu irais* |
| *il elle* } *aurait* | *il elle* } *serait* | *il elle* } *irait* |
| *nous aurions* | *nous serions* | *nous irions* |
| *vous auriez* | *vous seriez* | *vous iriez* |
| *ils elles* } *auraient* | *ils elles* } *seraient* | *ils elles* } *iraient* |

Note:
- For additional examples of the conditional, both regular and irregular verbs, see both the Regular and Irregular Verb Charts.
- The conditional in French is generally used in much the same way as it is in English. Study these sentences:

a. *Il a dit qu'il arriverait demain.* — He said he would arrive tomorrow.
b. *Si j'avais l'argent, j'irais au théâtre.* — If I had the money, I would go to the theater.

See Lesson 16 for additional examples of the conditional used in "if" sentences.

- Notice this special use of the conditional of *devoir:*

a. *Il devrait payer.* — He ought to pay. (He should pay.)

- The conditional is commonly used in expressions of courtesy. Notice the following examples:

a. *Que voudriez-vous?*     What would you like?

b. *Pourriez-vous nous aider?*     Could you help us? (lit.: Would you be able to help us?)

c. *Auriez-vous le temps?*     Would you have the time?

2. Possessive Pronouns

Notice these examples:

a. *Mon père est plus jeune que le tien.*     My father is younger than yours.

b. *J'ai perdu mon dictionnaire. Donnez-moi le vôtre.*     I lost my dictionary. Give me yours.

c. *Ces gants sont jolis. Je n'aime plus les miens.*     These gloves are pretty. I no longer like mine.

d. *Tu t'occupes de ton travail. Je m'occupe du[1] mien.*     You take care of your work. I take care of mine.

Study these forms:

|  | SINGULAR | | PLURAL | |
|---|---|---|---|---|
|  | Masc. | Fem. | Masc. | Fem. |
| mine | *le mien* | *la mienne* | *les miens* | *les miennes* |
| yours | *le tien* | *la tienne* | *les tiens* | *les tiennes* |
| his, hers | *le sien* | *la sienne* | *les siens* | *les siennes* |
| ours | *le nôtre* | *la nôtre* | *les nôtres* | *les nôtres* |
| yours | *le vôtre* | *la vôtre* | *les vôtres* | *les vôtres* |
| theirs | *le leur* | *la leur* | *les leurs* | *les leurs* |

[1] *de + le = du*. See Lesson 7 for contracted forms.

Note:

- In French, all possessives agree with the thing possessed and not the possessor. Example: *Son père est venu* could mean either "His father has come" or "Her father has come." Since *père* is masculine, it takes the masculine possessive in either case.

## 3. Demonstrative Pronouns

Notice these examples:

a. *Je n'aime pas cette robe-ci. Donnez-moi celle-là.*
   I don't like this dress. Give me that one.

b. *Je ne veux pas ce complet-ci. Je prendrai celui-là.*
   I don't want this suit. I'll take that one.

c. *Ces boucles d'oreille? Je ne les aime pas. Je préfère celles de ma soeur.*
   Those earrings? I don't like them. I prefer my sister's.

d. *Ces gants? Je ne les aime pas. Je préfère ceux que vous portez.*
   These gloves? I don't like them. I prefer the ones you are wearing.

Study these forms:

| Singular | | Plural | |
|----------|------|--------|-------|
| Masc. | Fem. | Masc. | Fem. |
| *celui* | *celle* | *ceux* | *celles* |

Note:

- Demonstrative pronouns can only be followed by:

1. *-ci* or *-là*
2. a preposition
3. *qui, que, dont,* or *où*

Examples:

|  | a. *Celle-ci est moins belle.* |
|  | This one is less beautiful. |
|  | b. *Celle de mon ami est épatante.* |
|  | My friend's (the one of my friend) |
|  | is terrific. |
| *La peinture?* | c. *Celle qui est à gauche est plus jolie.* |
| The painting? | The one on the left is prettier. |
|  | d. *Celle que je veux est trop chère.* |
|  | The one that I want is too expensive. |
|  | e. *Celle dont vous parlez ne me plaît pas.* |
|  | The one of which you are speaking |
|  | doesn't please me. |

(See Lesson 9 for explanation of *dont.*)

4. Double Object Pronouns

|  | a. *Il me le donne.* | He gives it to me. |
|  | b. *Il nous le montre.* | He shows them to us. |
| ✗ | c. *Il le lui a prêté.* | He loaned it to him. |
| ✓ | d. *Il les leur a prêtés.* | He loaned them to them. |
|  | e. *Donnez-le-moi.* | Give it to me. |
|  | f. *Ne me le donnez pas.* | Don't give it to me. |
|  | g. *Il m'en donne.* | He gives some to me. |
|  | h. *Donnez-m'en.* | Give me some. |
|  | i. *Ne m'en donnez pas.* | Don't give me any. |
| ✗ | j. *Je l'y mets.* | I'm putting it there. |

Note:

- Study the forms of direct and indirect objects in the Summary of French Grammar.

- The following are possible combinations of word order in all sentences except affirmative imperative.

| Indirect | Direct | Indirect | y | en |
|---|---|---|---|---|
| me | | | | |
| te | le | lui | | |
| nous } precedes | la } precedes | leur } precedes y precedes *en* | | |
| vous | les | | | |

- The order of double object pronouns in affirmative imperative is as follows:

| Direct | | Indirect | | *y* | | *en* |
|--------|---|----------|---|-----|---|------|
| | | *moi* | | | | |
| | | *toi* | | | | |
| *le* | | *lui* | | | | |
| *la* } | precedes | *nous* } | precedes | *y* | precedes | *en* |
| *les* | | *vous* | | | | |
| | | *leur* | | | | |

- *Me* and *te* become *moi* and *toi* after *le, la, les.* Example: *Donnez-le moi!*


## EXERCISES


A. Substitute each of the words or expressions in parentheses for the underlined word or expression in the model sentence. Write the complete sentence and say it aloud.

1. *Pourriez-vous le faire?* (*lire, demander, choisir, contrôler, payer*)
2. *J'aime le mien.* (*le tien, le sien, le nôtre, le vôtre, le leur*)
3. *Je m'occuperai des miens.* (*des tiens, des siens, des nôtres, des vôtres, des leurs*)


B. Replace the underlined adjective-noun combination with the pronoun.

Example: *Je ne veux pas cette robe-ci./Je ne veux pas celle-ci.*

1. *Donnez-moi ce crayon-ci.*
2. *Je préfère ces livres-là.*
3. *Regardez ces tables-ci.*
4. *Prenez ces numéros-ci.*

C. Expand the following by placing *Celui dont je vous ai parlé* in front of each of the following. Write the entire sentence, say it, and give the English equivalent.

1. _____ *a été vendu.*
2. _____ *coûte trop cher.*
3. _____ *ne me plaît pas.*
4. _____ *est excellent.*
5. _____ *est le frère de Michel.*
6. _____ *est venu me voir.*

D. Replace the object nouns with object pronouns, and translate them.

Example: *Il me donne les livres./Il me les donne.*

1. *Il lui donne le paquet.*
2. *Il nous montre les robes.*
3. *Ne me donnez pas ce verre.*
4. *Il me montre des cahiers.*
5. *J'y mets le livre.*

E. Make the following sentences negative. Translate the negative sentences.

Example: *Donnez-le-moi./Ne me le donnez pas.*

1. *Montrez-la-leur.*
2. *Vendez-les-lui.*
3. *Donnez-m'en.*
4. *Racontez-la-nous.*
5. *Prête-le-moi.*

F. Translate the following into French. Then say them aloud.

1. *Un chapeau?* I prefer that one in silk.
2. *Une robe?* I like this one in rayon.

3. *Des gants?* He likes those in wool.
4. *Des chaussures?* She likes those in leather.
5. *Des chemises?* We prefer these in cotton.
6. *Des bas?* She prefers these in nylon.
7. (for hats, shoes, gloves) What is your size?
8. (for coats, dresses, suits) What is your size?
9. I'd like this one (masc.) in pink.
10. I'd like that one (fem.) in navy blue (*bleu marine*).
11. I'd like these (masc.) in white.
12. I'd like those (masc.) in red.
13. I'd like these (fem.) in yellow.
14. He'd like those (fem.) in gray.
15. The dress with the long sleeves.
16. This one (masc.) suits you wonderfully.
17. That one (fem.) suits you (fam.) perfectly.
18. Here is something (*quelque chose de*) beautiful.
19. There is nothing else (*rien d'autre*) here.
20. He's going to send them to you.
21. He's going to wrap them for him.
22. Give them to me.
23. Don't tell them about it. (Lit.: Don't tell it to them.)
24. Could you tell me where the bus is?
25. Would you know the name of that gentleman?
26. I would like to see him.
27. Would you have the kindness to tell me (to indicate to me) the time?

G. From among the three choices, select the best translation for the English word or phrase given at the beginning of each sentence. Write the complete sentence, and translate.

1. (every day) *Je voudrais des gants pour* _____.
   (a) *toujours*
   (b) *toutes les jours*
   (c) *tous les jours*

2. (quite) *Ceux-là sont _____ jolis.*
   - (a) *aussi*
   - (b) *assez*
   - (c) *assis*

3. (sizes) *Les _____ pour les gants sont les mêmes.*
   - (a) *points*
   - (b) *tailles*
   - (c) *pointures*

4. (a silk dress) *Je cherche _____.*
   - (a) *une soie robe*
   - (b) *une robe soie*
   - (c) *une robe de soie*

5. (bargain) *C'est une _____.*
   - (a) *occasion*
   - (b) *opportunité*
   - (c) *marché*

6. (in the shoulders) *Je la trouve large _____.*
   - (a) *dans l'épaule*
   - (b) *aux épaules*
   - (c) *sur les épaules*

7. (What) *_____ vous désirez, madame?*
   - (a) *Que*
   - (b) *Qu'est-ce que*
   - (c) *Quoi*

8. (I'm looking for) *_____ des mouchoirs.*
   - (a) *Je regarde pour*
   - (b) *Je cherche*
   - (c) *Je cherche pour*

9. (a dozen) *Ils se vendent à 100 francs _____.*
   - (a) *la douzaine*
   - (b) *une douzaine*
   - (c) *par douzaine*

10. (change) *Voici votre _____.*
    - (a) *change*
    - (b) *monnaie*
    - (c) *argent*

# LESSON 7

## ON SE FAIT COIFFER
## WE GET OUR HAIR DONE

A. DIALOGUE

*Chez le coiffeur.* At the hairdresser's.

1. Coiffeur: **Ah, bonjour, monsieur. Qu'est-ce que nous pouvons faire pour vous aujourd'hui?**
Good day, sir. What can we do for you today?

2. Charles: **Une coupe de cheveux, d'abord. J'ai l'impression qu'ils poussent *plus vite que jamais* ces jours-ci.**
First a haircut. I have the feeling that my hair is growing faster than ever these days.

3. Coiffeur: **Comment voulez-vous que je vous les coupe?°**
How would you like me to cut it for you?

4. Charles: **Pas trop longs sur le dessus, et assez courts sur les côtés et sur la nuque. Employez la tondeuse, s'il vous plaît.**
Not too long on top, and rather short on the sides and on the nape of the neck. Use the clippers, please.

5. Coiffeur: **Très bien, monsieur ... Voilà! Je fais la raie à droite ou à gauche?**
Very well, sir. There! Shall I part it on the right or on the left?

6. Charles: **À gauche, s'il vous plaît.**
On the left, please.

7. Coiffeur: **Bien. Encore un coup de° peigne ... Et voilà, monsieur!**
Good. Another combing ... And there you are, sir!

8. Charles: **Et maintenant, pourriez-vous me raser? Mais attention—j'ai la barbe dure.**
And now, could you give me a shave? But be careful—I have a tough beard.

9. Coiffeur: **Ne vous inquiétez pas, monsieur. Ce sera vite fait.**
Don't worry, sir. It will be done quickly.

10. Charles: **Quel luxe que de *se faire raser* de temps en temps!**
What a luxury to get shaved by someone else from time to time!

11. Coiffeur: **À votre service, monsieur. Maintenant, une serviette chaude ...**
At your service, sir. Now, a hot towel ...

12. Charles: **Ah! Mais vraiment, vous me gâtez!**
Ah! But you are really pampering me!

13. Coiffeur: **C'est un plaisir, monsieur. On vous reverra la semaine prochaine?**
It's a pleasure sir. Will we see you again next week?

14. Charles: **Oui, je vais prendre rendez-vous à la caisse.**
Yes, I'll make an appointment at the cashier's desk.

15. Coiffeur: ***Vous pourrez le faire* quand vous paierez.°**
You can do it when you pay the bill.

16. Charles: **Très bien. Et voilà quelque chose pour vous.°**
Fine. And here's something extra for you.

17. Coiffeur: **Merci beaucoup, monsieur. À la semaine prochaine.**
Thank you very much, sir. See you next week.

*Dans le rue.* In the street.

18. Charles: **Tiens,° te voilà, chérie!° Je venais justement te chercher.**
Well, there you are, dear. I was just coming to get you.

19. Jane: **Je vois que *tu t'es fait couper les cheveux.***
I see that you got your hair cut.

20. Charles: **Et *je me suis fait raser* aussi. Et toi?**
And I got a shave too. And you?

21. Jane: **Un shampooing° et une coupe, et puis *je me suis fait faire* un brushing comme toujours.**
A shampoo and cut, and then I had my hair blow-dried as usual.

22. Charles: **Est-ce que tu t'es fait faire des U.V.?**
Did you use the tanning bed?

23. Jane: **Oui, tu as raison.**
Yes, you're right.

24. Charles: **La beauté, c'est tellement compliqué! Et cher, d'ailleurs. Est-ce qu'il nous reste de l'argent pour aller dîner quelque part?**
Beauty is so complicated! And expensive, too. Do we have any money left to go have dinner somewhere?

25. Jane: **Ça° dépend où tu veux manger!**
    That depends on where you want to eat!

26. Charles: **Si on allait à la Tour d'Argent?°**
    How about going to the Tour d'Argent?

27. Jane: **À la Tour d'Argent? Tu veux frimer, chéri. Tu veux que tout le monde te voie. Et en plus, c'est trop cher.**
    The Tour d'Argent? You want to show off, dear. You want everyone to see you. And anyway, it's too expensive.

28. Charles: **As-tu une meilleure idée?**
    Do you have a better idea?

29. Jane: **Oui. Nous allons manger des crêpes rue Mouffetard.° Et après nous allons nous installer dans un café sur la Place de la Contrescarpe, boire quelque chose, regarder les passants, et bavarder un peu. Qu'est-ce que tu en penses?**
    Yes. We'll go eat crepes in the rue Mouffetard. And afterward we'll settle down in a café on the Place de la Contrescarpe to have something to drink, watch people passing by, and chat a bit. What do you think of that?

30. Charles: **C'est parfait, chérie. Tu as toujours des idées géniales.**
    Perfect, honey. You always have great ideas.

## B. NOTES

3. *je vous les coupe:* Note the use of the present tense, whereas in English we would use the future. In general, use the present tense when referring to an action in the immediate future. In this phrase, *les* refers to *les cheveux.* Lit.: Do I cut them (*les cheveux*) for you?

7. *un coup de:* a blow or stroke of or with something. Used in expressions such as *un coup de pied* (a kick), *un coup de coude* (a nudge), *un coup de téléphone* (a phone call).

15. Notice the use of the future tense in *quand vous paierez.* In many instances where the future is only implied in English, it is used in French.

16. A tip of approximately 15 percent is usually given to persons who have performed some service.

18. *Tiens!:* a commonly used expression to introduce sentences or thoughts; similar to the English "Well!" However, *Tiens* always expresses mild and usually pleasant surprise.
*chérie:* a common term of endearment similar to the English "darling." The masculine is *chéri.*

21. *un shampooing:* an example of "franglais"; that is, English words that are invading the French language more and more.

25. *ça:* a common abbreviated form for *cela.*

26. *La Tour d'Argent:* one of the most chic and expensive restaurants in Paris, located near Notre-Dame. It is noted especially for its pressed duck, which is first chosen by the diner and then prepared to his or her taste.

29. *La rue Mouffetard* is a picturesque street near the Latin Quarter. It is lined with a great variety of restaurants, cafés, and markets. It passes through the *Place de la Contrescarpe,* whose bars and cafés are popular after dark.

## C. GRAMMAR AND USAGE

1. *Que jamais* ("than ever") in comparisons

|  | *plus/moins* | Adj./Adv. | *que* | *jamais* |
|---|---|---|---|---|
| a. *Ils parlent* | *plus* | *vite* | *que* | *jamais.* |
| b. *Tu es* | *plus* | *jolie* | *que* | *jamais.* |
| c. *Il est* | *moins* | *aimable* | *que* | *jamais.* |

a. They are speaking faster than ever.
b. You are prettier than ever.
c. He is less likeable than ever.

2. *Pouvoir* + infinitive

| *pouvoir* | Pronoun Object | Infinitive | Complement |
|---|---|---|---|
| a. *Je peux* | *vous* | *faire* | *autre chose.* |
| b. *Vous pouvez* | *le* | *voir* | *plus tard.* |
| c. *Nous pourrions* | *lui* | *parler.* | |

a. I can do something else for you.
b. You can see it later.
c. We could talk to him.

Note:
- Notice that the pronoun object comes after *pouvoir* and immediately before the infinitive.

3. *Se faire* + infinitive

| Subject | Reflex. Pron. | *faire* | Infinitive | Complement |
|---------|---------------|---------|------------|------------|
| a. *Je* | *me* | *fais* | *couper* | *les cheveux.* |
| b. *Nous* | *nous* | *ferons* | *bâtir* | *une maison.* |
| c. *Il* | *s'* | *est fait* | *raser.* | |
| d. *Je* | *me* | *suis fait* | *faire* | *les ongles.* |

a. I am having my hair cut.
b. We will have a house built.
c. He got shaved.
d. I had my nails done.

Note:
- The auxiliary *être* must be used when *se faire* + infinitive are used in the *passé composé*. (See c. and d. below.)
- The past participle of *faire* does not agree; i.e., it is invariable when followed by the infinitive. (See c. and d.)

4. The definite article with parts of the body

| | Def. Art. | Part of Body | |
|---|-----------|--------------|---|
| a. *Elle a* | *les* | *yeux* | *bleus.* |
| b. *Tu t'es fait couper* | *les* | *cheveux.* | |
| c. *Je me suis coupé* | *le* | *doigt.* | |
| d. *J'ai* | *la* | *tête* | *qui tourne.* |
| e. *J'ai mal* | *aux* | *dents.* | |

a. She has blue eyes.
b. You got your hair cut.

 c. I cut my finger.
 d. My head is spinning.
 e. I have a toothache.

Note:

- À and *les* become *aux*; à + *le* become *au*. See section 5.
- In general, correct French uses the definite article (*le, la, les*) with parts of the body, instead of the possessive adjective (*mon, ton,* etc.) You will, however, hear the possessive adjective in colloquial speech.

5. Contractions: The prepositions *à* and *de*, when used with the masculine or plural definite article, are contracted. Study the following:

| at the, to the, in the | of the, about |
| --- | --- |
| *à + le = au* | *de + le = du* |
| *à + les = aux* | *de + les = des* |
| *à + la* not contracted | *de + la* not contracted |
| *à + l'* used if noun begins with vowel | *de + l'* used if noun begins with vowel |

Examples:

 a. *Le patron du magasin est allé aux Halles.*
  The owner of the store went to Les Halles.
 b. *L'histoire des pays d'Europe commence à la fin de l'empire romain.*
  The history of the countries of Europe begins at the end of the Roman Empire.
 c. *Au début de la pièce, les comédiens chantent ensemble.*
  At the beginning of the play, the actors sing together.

6. *Chez* ("at the place of")

| Subject | Verb | chez | Complement | |
|---------|------|------|-----------|---|
| a. *Je* | *vais* | *chez* | *lui.* | |
| b. | *Venez* | *chez* | *moi* | *demain.* |
| c. *Il* | *a été* | *chez* | *le médecin.* | |
| d. *Nous* | *l'avons vu* | *chez* | *Dupont* | *hier soir.* |

a. I am going to his place/his home.
b. Come to my house tomorrow.
c. He has been to the doctor's.
d. We saw him at Dupont's yesterday evening.

Note:
- *Chez* + noun or pronoun complement encompasses the meanings of "at the home of," "at the place of," "at the place of work of," "at the location of" someone.

## EXERCISES

A. Write each of the following sentences in full, say aloud, and translate.

*Elle parle*  (1) *au garçon qu'elle a recontré à la banque.*
(2) *de l'arbre qui est en fleurs.*
(3) *aux enfants qui se rendent à l'épicerie.*
(4) *constamment du petit truc[1] qu'elle a vu au magasin.*
(5) *souvent de la petite-fille du professeur.*

B. Substitute each word in parentheses for the underlined word in the model sentence. Say and write the entire new sentence.

1. *Vous pouvez le voir plus tard.* (*faire, demander, dire, chercher, manger, boire, lire*)

[1] *truc:* thing, gadget, etc.

2. *Nous pourrions vous le montrer.* (*donner, demander, dire, expliquer, recommander*)

C. Transform each sentence below to indicate that the subject is having somebody else perform the action.
Example: *Je me coupe les cheveux. Je me fais couper les cheveux.*

1. *Je me lave les cheveux.*
2. *Je me teins² les cheveux.*
3. *Je me rase.*
4. *Je me fais un brushing.*
5. *Je me fais les ongles.*

D. Transform each sentence below from present to passé composé. Say and translate each.
Example: *Je me fais faire des tresses./ Je me suis fait faire des tresses.*

1. *Je me fais raser.*
2. *Elle se fait faire les ongles.*
3. *Il se fait couper les cheveux.*

E. Translate the following sentences into French. Then say them aloud.

1. What can we do for you, madame?
2. How can I help you, sir?
3. What does monsieur [madame] desire?
4. She wants to have a shampoo.
5. He wants to have his hair cut.
6. She wants to have her nails done.
7. She wants to have her hair lightened (*éclaircir*).
8. Don't cut it too short at the nape of the neck (*la nuque*).
9. What luxury to be at the hairdresser's!

² From *teindre*—to dye, to tint

10. What luxury to go to Paris!
11. I'd like a haircut.
12. She'd like a shampoo.
13. Do it as usual (*d'habitude*).
14. Do it as always.
15. Do it as you wish.
16. She will have a long wait. ⃗

*Elle en aura pour longtemps.*

17. Will I have a long wait? (use *Est-ce que*)
18. The terrace of the café is always open to the public.
19. Do you (polite) want to go with him to the library in order to (*pour*) speak to the students?
20. The critic from *Le Monde* spoke to me about the films of today.
21. Come (fam.) with me to the school of agriculture.
22. At our place, you'll find a lot of books.

E. From among the three choices given, select the best translation for the English word or phrase given at the beginning of each sentence. Write the complete sentence, and translate.

1. (faster) *Ils poussent* _____ *que jamais.*
   (a) *vite*
   (b) *plus vite*
   (c) *plus rapide*
2. (as usual) *Je vous les coupe* _____ .
   (a) *comme jamais*
   (b) *comme d'habitude*
   (c) *comme d'habit*
3. (a long time) *Vous en aurez pour* _____ .
   (a) *un long temps*
   (b) *un longtemps*
   (c) *longtemps*
4. (next door) *Ma femme est* _____ .
   (a) *à côté*
   (b) *du côté*
   (c) *à la porte*

5. (once in a while) *Quel luxe de se faire raser* _____.
   (a) *une fois*
   (b) *de temps en temps*
   (c) *de quelque temps*
6. (next week) *On vous reverra* _____.
   (a) *prochaine semaine*
   (b) *la semaine prochaine*
   (c) *une semaine prochaine*
7. (something extra) *Voilà* _____ *pour vous.*
   (a) *quelque chose plus*
   (b) *quelque chose mais*
   (c) *quelque chose en plus*
8. (There you are) _____, *chérie!*
   (a) *Voilà toi*
   (b) *Voilà vous*
   (c) *Te voilà*
9. (something different) *Il y a* _____.
   (a) *quelque chose de différent*
   (b) *quelque chose différent*
   (c) *chose différente*
10. (this time) *Pas de manucure* _____?
    (a) *cette fois-ci*
    (b) *ce temps-ci*
    (c) *cette heure-ci*

# LESSON 8

## AU THÉÂTRE
## AT THE THEATER

A. DIALOGUE

*Au bureau de location.*   At the ticket office.

'. Charles: **Est-ce que vous avez quatre places pour
   ce soir?** *Des fauteuils* **d'orchestre, de préférence,
   et pas trop sur le côté.**

Do you have four seats for this evening? Orchestra seats, preferably, and not too far to the side.

2. Employée: **Voyons ...** *je n'ai que*° *des places sé-parées* **à l'orchestre, sauf quelques-unes qui sont sur le côté. Mais j'ai encore** *de bonnes places* **au balcon, au centre.**
Let's see ... I have only separate seats left in the orchestra, except for a few on the side. But I still have good seats in the balcony, in the center.

3. Charles: **Très bien, alors; je les prends.**
Fine, then; I'll take them.

4. Employée: **Cela fait cent cinquante francs,**° **mon-sieur.**
That's one hundred and fifty francs, sir.

5. Charles: **À quelle heure commence la représenta-tion, s'il vous plaît?**
At what time does the performance begin, please?

6. Employée: **À 21 heures**° **précises, monsieur.**
At nine o'clock exactly, sir.

*Au Théâtre Français.*   At the Théâtre Français.

7. Charles: **Tiens, voilà Nicole et Michel! Nicole, Michel, quel plaisir de vous revoir!**
Look, there are Nicole and Michel. Nicole, Michel, what a pleasure to see you again!

8. Michel: **Vous êtes si gentils de nous avoir invités ce soir.**
You are so kind to invite us this evening.

9. Nicole: **Votre robe est ravissante, Jane. La couleur vous va à merveille.**

Your dress is gorgeous, Jane. The color looks great on you.

10. Jane: **Vous êtes très aimable. Je viens de l'acheter. Ici, à Paris, naturellement.**
You're very kind. I've just bought it. Here in Paris, of course.

11. Michel: **Le rideau va bientôt se lever.**
The curtain will be going up soon.

12. Le Vendeur de Programmes: **Un programme, messieurs?**
Program, gentlemen?

13. Michel: **Permettez-moi, Charles. Deux programmes, s'il vous plaît.**
Permit me, Charles. Two programs, please.

14. Nicole: (*à Jane en aparté*) **En France il faut acheter le programme. On donne aussi un pourboire à l'ouvreuse.**
(to Jane, aside) In France you have to buy the program. You also give a tip to the usherette.

15. L'Ouvreuse: **Vos billets, messieurs? Par ici, s'il vous plaît. Troisième rang, les quatre premières places.**
Your tickets, gentlemen? This way, please. Third row, the first four seats.

16. Michel: **Merci, madame. Et voici quelque chose pour vous.**
Thank you, madam. And here's something for you.

17. Charles: **Avec les jumelles, nous verrons très bien la scène.**
With the opera glasses, we'll see the stage very well.

18. Nicole: **Que de monde! Cette pièce fait toujours salle comble.**
What a crowd! This play always draws a full house.

19. Michel: **Chut! ... Les trois coups;° la pièce va commencer.**
Shh! ... The three knocks. The play is about to begin.

*À l'entracte, dans l'entrée.*   During the intermission, in the foyer.

20. Nicole: **Un grand succès, à en juger par les applaudissements! Vous les avez entendus?**
A great success, judging by the applause! Did you hear it?

21. Charles: **Les comédiens° sont tout à fait extraordinaires. Ils vous font vraiment éprouver les sentiments des personnages. Voilà pourquoi j'adore les pièces en France.**
The actors are quite extraordinary. They really make you feel the emotions of the characters. That's why I adore plays in France.

22. Nicole: **Je trouve aussi que les décors et l'éclairage illustrent parfaitement l'action.**
I also think that the sets and the lighting bring out the action perfectly.

23. Jane: **Même mon mari, qui est un fanatique du cinéma, avouera qu'un film n'est pas souvent si fort, si émouvant ...**
Even my husband, who's a movie fan, will admit that a film is not often so powerful, so moving ...

24. Michel: **À vrai dire, je trouve qu'une intrigue me paraît toujours moins intense à l'écran.**

Truthfully, I find that a plot always seems to me to be less intense on the screen.

25. Charles: **Je voudrais bien revoir cette pièce, mais nous n'en aurons pas le temps.**
I'd very much like to see this play again, but we won't have the time to do it.

26. Nicole: **Cette pièce passe souvent à la télévision. Vous aurez sûrement l'occasion de la revoir.**
This play is often shown on television. You'll surely have the chance to see it again.

27. Jane: **Vraiment? Sur quelle chaîne?**
Really! On what channel?

28. Nicole: **Je crois que c'est la deuxième.° Mais vous le trouverez certainement dans un journal.**
I think it's channel two. But you'll certainly find it in the newspaper.

29. Charles: **Et il y a toujours *des troupes françaises*° qui font des tournées aux États-Unis.**
And there are always French companies that go on tour in the United States.

30. Michel: **À propos de spectacles, *êtes-vous déjà allés* à l'Opéra Bastille? Les interprétations sont toujours excellentes.**
Speaking of entertainment, have you been to the Bastille Opera yet? The performances are always excellent.

31. Nicole: **Et si vous aimez les œuvres symphoniques ou la musique de chambre, il y a aussi plusieurs salles de concert à Paris.**
And if you like symphonic works or chamber music, there are also several concert halls in Paris.

32. L'Ouvreuse: **Reprenez vos places, mesdames et messieurs. Le quatrième acte commence.**
Return to your seats, ladies and gentlemen. The fourth act is beginning.

33. Charles: *Dépêchons-nous,* **alors! Nous ne voulons pas manquer le dénouement!**
Let's hurry, then! We don't want to miss the ending!

## B. NOTES

2. *je n'ai que:* In this context, the idea might also be expressed as *il ne reste que* or *il n'y a que.*

4. The theater and opera are generally subsidized by the government. Seats are therefore relatively inexpensive.

6. Official time is given on the 24-hour clock in announcements of starting, ending, departure, and arrival times for activities related to public entertainment, transportation, private invitations, and many formal events. For example, a 2:00 P.M. train will be listed in the schedule as leaving at *14 h.* (*heures*). But the 12-hour clock will also be heard in everyday conversation.

19. *trois coups:* To announce the fact that the curtain is about to rise, three knocks are sounded.

21. *Les comédiens:* Actors of any kind.

28. French television has five channels available to the public, two of which are owned and operated by the government. There is also a private channel, called *Canal +,* that is available by paid subscription and only at certain times of the day. The

French also have access to many cable and satellite channels.

29. Excellent French theater groups (called *troupes*) such as those of the Comédie Française and the Théâtre National Populaire have delighted American audiences in recent years.

## C. GRAMMAR AND USAGE

1. *Ne* + verb + *que* = only

| Subject | *ne* | Verb | *que* | Object |
|---------|------|------|-------|--------|
| a. *Je* | *n'* | *ai* | *que* | *des places séparées.* |
| b. *Nous* | *n'* | *avons* | *que* | *dix francs.* |
| c. *Elle* | *ne* | *fait* | *que* | *parler.* |
| d. *Je* | *ne* | *veux* | *que* | *ton bonheur.* |

a. I have only separate seats.
b. We have only ten francs.
c. She only talks. (She does nothing but talk.)
d. I want only your happiness.

2. The partitive article. In English, we express the concept of partition by the words "some" or "any." For example, "I have some apples." This indicates that, of all the apples in the world, I have only a part. This concept of partition is expressed in French by the use of *de* + the definite article (*le, la, les*). Notice that "some" or "any" may be merely implied in English, whereas it is always expressed in French.

Study the material below, and particularly notice the contrasts in meaning between the sentences using the definite article alone, and those using the partitive article.

Before masculine singular nouns:

|       | Def. Article | Noun | | Part. Article | Noun |
|-------|------|------|------|------|------|
| a. *Voici* | *le* | *café.* | *Voulez-vous* | *du* | *café?* |
| b. *Voici* | *le* | *vin.* | *Voulez-vous* | *du* | *vin?* |
| c. *Voici* | *le* | *fromage.* | *Elle veut* | *du* | *fromage.* |

a. Here's the coffee. Do you want (some/any) coffee?
b. Here's the wine. Do you want (some/any) wine?
c. Here's the cheese. She wants (some) cheese.

Note:
- "Some" or "any" before a masculine singular noun is *du* (contraction of *de + le*).

Before feminine singular nouns:

|       | Def. Article | Noun | | Part. Article | Noun |
|-------|------|------|------|------|------|
| a. *Voici* | *la* | *craie.* | *Voulez-vous* | *de la* | *craie?* |
| b. *Voilà* | *la* | *viande.* | *Nous mangerons* | *de la* | *viande.* |
| c. *Voici* | *la* | *monnaie.* | *Vous avez* | *de la* | *monnaie.* |

a. Here's the chalk. Do you want (some/any) chalk?
b. There's the meat. We'll eat (some) meat.
c. Here's the change. You have (some) change.

Note:
- "Some" or "any" before a feminine singular noun is *de + la*.

Before singular nouns beginning with a vowel:

|   | | Def. Article | Noun | | Part. Article | Noun |
|---|---|---|---|---|---|---|
| a. | *Voici* | *l'* | *argent.* | *Il me faut* | *de l'* | *argent.* |
| b. | *Voici* | *l'* | *eau.* | *Il me faut* | *de l'* | *eau.* |
| c. | *Voilà* | *l'* | *essence.* | *Il nous faut* | *de l'* | *essence.* |

- a. Here's the money.  I need (some) money.
- b. Here's the water.  I need (some) water.
- c. There's the gas.  We need (some) gas.

Note:
- "Some" or "any" before all singular nouns beginning with a vowel is *de l'*.

Before all plural nouns:

|   | Def. Article | Noun | | Part. Article | |
|---|---|---|---|---|---|
| a. | *Les* | *places?* | *Je vais chercher* | *des* | *places à l'orchestre.* |
| b. | *Les* | *programmes?* | *J'achèterai* | *des* | *programmes pour tous.* |
| c. | *Les* | *acteurs?* | *Vous allez voir* | *des* | *acteurs qui sont excellents.* |

- a. The seats? I'm going to get some seats in the orchestra.
- b. The programs? I'll buy (some) programs for everybody.
- c. The actors? You are going to see (some) actors who are excellent.

Note:
- "Some" or "any" before most plural nouns either masculine or feminine, is *des* (contraction of *de* + *les*). Exceptions to this rule are discussed below.

In negative sentences:

| Subject | Negative Verb | Partitive Article | Noun |
|---|---|---|---|
| a. | *Ne veut-elle pas* | *de* | *fromage?* |
| b. *Non, elle* | *ne veut pas* | *de* | *fromage.* |
| c. *Nous* | *ne mangeons pas* | *de* | *viande.* |
| d. *Il* | *ne nous faut pas* | *d'* | *essence.* |
| e. *Je* | *n'achèterai pas* | *de* | *programmes.* |

a. Doesn't she want any cheese?
b. No, she doesn't want any cheese.
c. We don't eat (any) meat.
d. We don't need any gas.
e. I won't buy (any) programs.

Note:
- "Some" or "any" in a negative sentence is *de* (*d'*) alone, without a definite article. Notice that this holds true before *all* nouns, masculine and feminine, singular and plural.

Plural partitive nouns preceded by adjectives:

| | *de* + article | Noun | Contrast | *de* | Adjective | Noun |
|---|---|---|---|---|---|---|
| a. *J'ai* | *des* | *places.* | *J'ai* | *de* | *bonnes* | *places.* |
| b. *Elle a* | *des* | *robes.* | *Elle a* | *de* | *belles* | *robes.* |
| c. *J'ai* | *des* | *amis.* | *J'ai* | *d'* | *autres* | *amis.* |
| d. *J'ai lu* | *des* | *livres.* | *J'ai lu* | *de* | *bons* | *livres.* |

| | |
|---|---|
| a. I have (some) seats. | I have (some) good seats. |
| b. She has (some) dresses. | She has (some) beautiful dresses. |
| c. I have (some) friends. | I have (some) other friends. |
| d. I've read (some) books. | I've read (some) good books. |

Note:

- If the noun, of whatever gender or number, is preceded by an adjective, use only *de* or *d'*.

3. Imperative forms with pronouns

### Affirmative

| | |
|---|---|
| a. *Permettez-moi.* | Permit me. |
| b. *Excuse-toi.* | Excuse yourself. |
| c. *Pardonnez-moi.* | Pardon me. |
| d. *Excusez-nous.* | Excuse us. |
| e. *Parlons-lui.* | Let's speak to him. |

### Negative

| | |
|---|---|
| a. *Ne me permettez pas . . .* | Don't permit me . . . |
| b. *Ne t'excuse pas.* | Don't excuse yourself. |
| c. *Ne me pardonnez pas.* | Don't pardon me. |
| d. *Ne nous excusez pas.* | Don't excuse us. |
| e. *Ne lui parlons pas.* | Let's not speak to him. |

Note:

- The object pronoun always precedes the verb except in the positive imperative.

4. Verbs conjugated with *être*

| Auxiliary *être* | Past Participle |
|---|---|
| a. *Êtes-vous* | *allés?* |
| b. *Est-elle* | *partie?* |
| c. *Sont-ils* | *arrivés?* |
| d. *Sont-elles* | *restées?* |

a. Did you go? (Have you gone?)
b. Did she leave? (Has she left?)
c. Did they arrive? (Have they arrived?)
d. Did they stay? (Have they stayed?)

Note:
- About fifteen intransitive verbs are conjugated with *être* instead of *avoir* in compound tenses. The most important are (a) verbs of motion: *aller,* to go; *venir,* to come; *arriver,* to arrive; *partir,* to leave; *entrer,* to enter; *sortir,* to go out; *monter,* to go up; *descendre,* to go down; *tomber,* to fall; *retourner,* to return; and (b) verbs that express a change of state: *naître,* to be born; *mourir,* to die; *rester,* to remain; *devenir,* to become.
- Compounds of verbs above, e.g., *rentrer,* to come back or go in again, and *revenir,* to come back, are also conjugated with *être.*
- These verbs agree with the subject in number (singular and plural) and gender (masculine or feminine). Remember that *vous* may be singular or plural and masculine or feminine. Examples:
  *Ah, vous êtes arrivée, Mme. Lewis.*
  *Ah, vous êtes arrivés, messieurs.*

Study these contrasts:

| | |
|---|---|
| a. *Elle est montée.* | She went up. |
| *Elle a monté les bagages.* | She took up the bags. |
| b. *Elle est sortie.* | She went out. |
| *Elle a sorti le chien.* | She took the dog out. |

Verbs conjugated with *avoir* agree only with a preceding direct object. Contrast:

| | |
|---|---|
| a. *Elle a acheté les livres.* | She bought the books. |
| b. *Elle les a achetés.* | She bought them. |
| c. *Elle lui a donné les livres.* | She gave him the books. |

## EXERCISES

A. Replace *seulement* by *ne . . . que* in each of the following sentences. Write the complete sentence, say it aloud, and translate.

Example: *J'ai seulement des places séparées./Je n'ai que des places séparées.*

1. *Elle a seulement deux sœurs.*
2. *Ils ont seulement quatre pièces.*
3. *Elle veut seulement ton bonheur.*
4. *Nous avons seulement un peu d'argent.*

B. Expand the following sentences by placing *bons* or *bonnes* before the noun. Make the necessary change in the form *des*. Say and translate.

Example: *J'ai des amis./J'ai de bons amis.*

1. *Vous avez des idées.*
2. *J'ai lu des livres.*
3. *Nous avons vu des films.*
4. *J'ai mangé des frites.*
5. *Elle a écrit des lettres.*

C. Transform the following to the negative.

Example: *Parlez-moi./Ne me parlez pas.*

1. *Pardonne-lui.*
2. *Regardons-les.*
3. *Écoutez-nous.*
4. *Excusez-la.*
5. *Lève-toi.*

D. Substitute each of the words or expressions in parentheses for the underlined word in the model sentence. Write and say each new sentence.

1. *Nous sommes <u>entrés</u>.* (*partis, arrivés, venus, restés, tombés*)
2. *Elle est <u>sortie</u>.* (*partie, devenue riche, restée, née, montée*)

E. Transform the following sentences to the past. (Make sure the past participle agrees with the subject.) Say and translate the new sentences.

Example: *Nous arrivons/Nous sommes arrivés.*

1. *Elle descend.*
2. *Ils viennent.*
3. *Elles partent.*
4. *Nous restons.*
5. *Vous entrez.*

F. Translate the following sentences into French, then say them aloud.

1. We only want seats in the center.
2. There are some seats at the café.
3. We have good plays in Paris.
4. We have some other seats.
5. Don't show me the program.
6. Introduce us to Michel.
7. Give us the money. Don't give him the money.
8. Today he is leaving at nine o'clock.
   Yesterday he left at nine o'clock also.
9. She stayed at the office until eight o'clock.
10. She is pleased to see the actors.
11. I'll have the time to do it.
12. Will they have the chance (*l'occasion*) to do it?
13. What interests me is the setting (*le décor*).
14. What interests him is the action.
15. Give me some sugar.
16. He has money.
17. We would like some apples.
18. Go to the market, because we don't have any milk.
19. He bought very good shoes.

G. From among the three choices, select the best translation for the English word or phrase given at the beginning of each sentence. Write the complete sentence, and translate.

1. (on the side) *Quatre places, pas trop* _____.
   (a) *à côté*
   — (b) *sur le côté*
   (c) *du côté*
2. (good seats) *J'ai encore* _____.
   (a) *bonnes places*
   (b) *des bonnes places*
   (c) *de bonnes places*

3. (to) *Quel plaisir* _____ *vous revoir.*
   (a) *de*
   (b) *à*
   (c) *pour*

4. (suits) *La couleur vous* _____ *à merveille.*
   (a) *suit*
   (b) *complète*
   (c) *va*

5. (Permit me) _____, *Charles.*
   (a) *Me permet*
   (b) *Permettez-me*
   (c) *Permettez-moi*

6. (This way) _____, *s'il vous plaît.*
   (a) *Ce chemin*
   (b) *Cette route*
   (c) *Par ici*

7. (Truthfully) _____, *il me plaît.*
   (a) *Le vrai*
   (b) *À vrai dire*
   (c) *Vraiment dire*

8. (It's) _____ *la deuxième chaîne.*
   (a) *C'est*
   (b) *Elle est*
   (c) *Est*

9. (Let's hurry) _____, *alors!*
   (a) *Laissons vite*
   (b) *Passons rapide*
   (c) *Dépêchons-nous*

# LESSON 9

## AU MUSÉE DU LOUVRE
## AT THE LOUVRE MUSEUM

A. DIALOGUE

1. Employée: **Quarante francs° chacun, s'il vous plaît.**
   Forty francs each, please.

2. Charles: **Voici, madame.** (*En aparté à Jeanne*) **Nous aurions dû venir dimanche. L'entrée est moins chère le dimanche.**
   Here you are, ma'am. (Aside to Jane) We should have come Sunday. Admission is cheaper on Sundays.

3. Guide: **Monsieur, puis-je vous suggérer une visite guidée ou une visite-conférence?**
   Sir, may I suggest a guided tour or a lecture tour?

 4. Jane: **Moi, j'aimerais une visite guidée. Mon mari s'y connaît en peinture, mais ...**
   *I'd* like a guided tour. My husband is knowledgeable about painting, but ...

5. Charles: **Je ne suis qu'un peintre amateur.**
   I'm only an amateur painter.

6. Guide: **Vous trouverez ici bien de l'inspiration. Le Louvre° est probablement le musée d'art le plus riche du monde. L'édifice est l'ancienne demeure des rois de France.**
   You will find plenty of inspiration here. The Louvre is probably the richest art museum in the world. The building is the former residence of the kings of France.

7. Jane: **Quelles sont les choses les plus inté-ressantes à voir?**
   What are the most interesting things to see?

8. Guide: *Je vous ferai voir* **rapidement les anti-quités, les sculptures, et les objets d'art ...**
   I'll show you the antiquities, the sculptures, and the art objects quickly ...

9. Jane: **Regardez! Enfin je vois de près la Vénus de Milo. C'est ma statue préférée.**
   Look! At last I'm seeing the *Venus de Milo* at close range. It's my favorite statue.

10. Guide: **Vous n'êtes pas la seule à l'admirer. Re-gardez à droite, et vous verrez la Victoire de Samothrace, qui est également bien connue.**
    You are not the only one to admire it. Look on the right, and you will see the *Winged Victory,* which is equally well known.

11. Charles: **C'est formidable. On voit dans ces salles toute l'histoire de l'antiquité grecque et romaine.**
    It's magnificent. You see the entire history of Greek and Roman antiquity in these rooms.

12. Jane: **En effet—bustes et statues, sarcophages, frises, bas-reliefs ...**
    That true—busts and statues, sarcophagi, friezes, bas-reliefs ...

13. Guide: **On voit des sculptures de toutes les grandes époques. On voit représentés le Moyen-Age, la Renaissance, le dix-septième siècle ...**
    You can see sculptures of all the great periods. The Middle Ages, the Renaissance, the seventeenth cen-tury are represented ...

14. Charles: **Les meubles anciens sont aussi à voir.**
    The antique furniture is also worth seeing.

15. Guide: **Oui, on peut admirer les chefs d'œuvre du mobilier, de l'orfèvrerie, de la tapisserie. Regardez aussi les bronzes, les ivoires, et les bijoux de la couronne de France.**
Yes, you can admire the masterpieces of furniture, goldsmiths' work, tapestry. Look at the bronzes, the ivories, and the French crown jewels, also.

16. Jane: **Que de richesses! Mais où sont les peintures?**
What riches! But where are the paintings?

17. Guide: **Par ici. Comme vous allez le voir, *il y a des peintures* classiques et modernes, gouaches, aquarelles, huiles, ainsi que des gravures, des eaux-fortes . . .**
This way. As you will see, there are classical and modern paintings, gouaches, watercolors, oils, as well as engravings, etchings . . .

18. Charles: **Et de tous les genres aussi—paysages, natures-mortes, nus . . .**
And of all kinds too—landscapes, still lifes, nudes . . .

19. Guide: **Suivez-moi, s'il vous plaît, dans la Grande Galerie. *Je vous ferai voir* une toile que vous reconnaîtrez . . .**
Follow me, please, into the Great Gallery. I'll show you a canvas that you will recognize . . .

20. Charles: **Ah! La Joconde° de Léonard de Vinci!**
Ah! The Mona Lisa, by Leonardo da Vinci!

21. Guide: **C'est une des œuvres maîtresses de tous les temps. *Il y a des gens* qui restent émerveillés devant cette peinture pendant des heures entières.**
This is one of the greatest works of all time. Some people stay in front of this painting for hours filled with wonder.

22. Jane: **Mais où sont les tableaux de l'école impres-
    sionniste? Je ne les vois nulle part.**
    But where are the pictures of the Impressionist
    School? I don't see them anywhere.

23. Guide: **Pour les impressionistes, il faudra aller au
    musée d'Orsay.°**
    For the Impressionists, you will have to go to the
    Musée d'Orsay.

24. Jane: *Allons-y un autre jour.*
    Let's go there another day.

25. Charles: **D'accord. Je voudrais voir les tableaux
    des pointillistes.**
    Okay. I'd like to see the paintings of the Pointillists.

26. Jane: **Moi, je n'aime pas beaucoup les poin-
    tillistes. Mais, où est-ce qu'on trouve les
    Toulouse-Lautrec,° les Degas,° les Matisse,° et** *les
    autres peintres dont on entend toujours parler?*
    *I* don't like the Pointillists very much. But where
    can we see the Toulouse-Lautrecs, the Degas, the
    Matisses, and the other painters about whom we
    hear so much?

27. Charles: **Il doit y en avoir quelque part. Mais ne
    les cherchons pas maintenant. J'en ai assez des
    musées pour le moment.**
    There must be some somewhere. But let's not look
    for them now. I've had enough of museums for the
    time being.

B. NOTES

1. There is a small admission fee to museums, often
   reduced on Sunday and for students.

6. The Louvre Museum, one of the largest in the world, is on the Right Bank. As will be noted in the dialogue, it is known to most people for its painting of the *Mona Lisa* and the statues of the *Venus de Milo* and the *Winged Victory,* or *Nike.*

20. The Mona Lisa is known as *La Joconde* (in Italian, *La Gioconda*), because of her famous enigmatic smile.

23. The *Musée d'Orsay,* formally a train station, houses the city's Impressionist art.

26. Toulouse-Lautrec: a nineteenth-century painter noted for his colorful portrayals of Parisian night life. Degas: Impressionist painter of the late nineteenth and early twentieth century, noted for his paintings of ballet dancers.
    Matisse: twentieth-century French artist famous for his decorative paintings and use of color.

## C. GRAMMAR AND USAGE

1. *Faire* + infinitive

| Subject | Indirect Obj. Pro. | *faire* | Infinitive | Complement |
|---------|--------------------|---------|------------|------------|
| a. *Je* | *vous* | *ferai* | *visiter* | *le musée.* |
| b. *Je* | *lui* | *ferai* | *voir* | *La Joconde.* |
| c. *Il* | *nous* | *a fait* | *connaître* | *ses amis.* |
| d. *Nous* | *leur* | *avons fait* | *savoir* | *la nouvelle.* |

a. I'll show you around the museum. (I'll have you visit the museum.)
b. I'll show him the *Mona Lisa.* (I'll have him see the *Mona Lisa*).
c. He had us meet his friends.

d. We told them the news. (We had them informed of the news.)

Note:

- The indirect object pronoun is used when the subject is not having something done to himself. (Refer to Lesson 7 on the *"Coiffeur"* for contrasting use of the reflexive *se faire* followed by an infinitive.)
- Remember that the reflexive verb *se faire* uses *être* in compound tenses, whereas nonreflexive *faire* takes *avoir*.

a. *Elle s'est fait couper les cheveux.* — She got her hair cut.

b. *Elle lui a fait peindre la maison.* — She had him paint the house.

2. *Il y a*—there is, there are

| Il y a | Sing. or Pl. Noun | Adjective | Complement |
|--------|-------------------|-----------|------------|
| a. *Il y a* | *des gens* | | *qui restent . . .* |
| b. *Il y a* | *un livre* | *intéressant* | *sur la table.* |
| c. *Il y a* | *une peinture* | | *dans la Grande Galerie.* |

a. There are people who stay . . .
b. There is an interesting book on the table.
c. There is a painting in the Great Gallery.

Note:

- *Il y a* is used for singular and plural nouns as an equivalent for "there is" or "there are" in an unstressed statement of fact. Contrast with *voilà* (there is/there are), which is used to point to something or someone. Contrast:

a. *Il y a un livre sur la table.*
   There's a book on the table.
b. *Il y a deux comédiens dans la pièce.*
   There are two actors in the play.

c. *Voilà le livre de M. Lewis.*
There's Mr. Lewis's book.
d. *Voilà les deux comédiens.*
There are the two actors.

3. *Aller + y*

CONTRAST

| Verb-*y* | *N'y* | Verb | *pas* |
|---|---|---|---|
| a. *Allons-y.* | *N'y* | *allons* | *pas.* |
| b. *Vas-y.* | *N'y* | *vas* | *pas.* |
| c. *Allez-y.* | *N'y* | *allez* | *pas.* |

a. Let's go there.                Let's not go there.
b. Go there (fam. sing.)          Don't go there.
c. Go there (polite and           Don't go there.
   pl.)

Note:
• *Vas-y* and *allez-y* are used collectively as equivalents
  of "go ahead" and "go to it."

4. *Dont*—about whom, of whom, whose, of which, about
   which

| Noun (Sing. or Pl.) | *dont* | Subject | Clause |
|---|---|---|---|
| a. *Les autres peintres* | *dont* | *on* | *entend parler* ... |
| b. *Le tableau* | *dont* | *je* | *t'ai parlé* ... |
| c. *La femme* | *dont* | *j'* | *ai fait la connaissance* ... |
| d. *La femme* | *dont* | *le fils* | *est dans la classe* ... |

a. The other painters whom we hear about (about
   whom we hear people speak) ...
b. The picture about which I spoke to you ...

   c. The woman whose acquaintance I made (lit.: of
      whom I made the acquaintance) . . .

   d. The woman whose son is in the class . . .

Note:

- *Dont* precedes the subject of the subordinate clause.
- It is invariable.
- *Dont* may be replaced by *de qui* (for persons) or *de*
  plus the appropriate form of *lequel* (for persons or
  things). *Dont,* however, is more commonly used.
  Compare the following sentences with the examples
  given in the chart above.

   a. *Les autres peintres de qui/desquels on . . .*

   b. *L'homme de qui/duquel je . . .*

   c. *La femme de qui/de laquelle . . .*

- *Lequel* and its variants should be used to avoid ambi-
  guity when it is not clear which person is referred to.
  Study the forms and variants of *lequel* and contrast the
  two examples.

|  | which, whom | to which, whom | of which, whom, whose |
|---|---|---|---|
| masc. | *lequel* | *auquel* | *duquel* |
| fem. | *laquelle* | *à laquelle* | *de laquelle* |
| plu. | *lesquel(le)s* | *auxquel(le)s* | *desquel(le)s* |

   a. *Le fils de la femme auquel j'ai parlé.*

      The son of the woman to whom I spoke. (The mas-
      culine *auquel* indicates you spoke to the son.)

   b. *Le fils de la femme à laquelle j'ai parlé.*

      The son of the woman to whom I spoke. (The fem-
      inine *à laquelle* indicates you spoke to the woman.)

## EXERCISES

A. Substitute each of the words or expressions in parentheses for the underlined word or expression in the model sentence. Write the complete sentence and say it aloud.

1. *Il me fera visiter le Louvre.* (*te, lui, nous, vous, leur*)
2. *Nous vous avons fait voir le livre.* (*lire, acheter, comprendre, connaître, apprécier*)
3. *Il y a un livre sur la table.* (*un stylo, un cahier, un crayon, des assiettes, des fourchettes*)
4. *L'homme dont j'ai entendu parler . . .* (*la femme, les garçons, le livre, la pièce, la peinture, le musée*)

B. Expand the expressions below by placing *Il y a* in front of each. Say the entire sentence, then write it.

Example: *une femme à la porte/il y a une femme à la porte.*

1. *quatre peintures au mur*
2. *vingt personnes dans la salle*
3. *des garçons devant l'école*
4. *de la bonne viande chez le boucher*
5. *du sucre dans le placard*

C. Transform the following sentences from affirmative to negative, say, and write out their translations.

1. *Vas-y.*
2. *Allez-y.*
3. *Il y va.*
4. *Il y est allé.*
5. *Nous y sommes allés.*
6. *Elles y sont allées.*

D. Replace *de* + the relative pronoun by *dont* in the following sentences, and translate.

1. *L'homme de qui je t'avais parlé est arrivé.*
2. *La femme de laquelle j'avais fait la connaissance hier s'appelle Mme. Dupont.*

3. *Les hommes desquels j'avais entendu parler sont partis pour Paris.*
4. *Les femmes desquelles vous connaissez les fils ont aussi des filles.*
5. *Le livre duquel vous avez besoin n'est pas à la bibliothèque.*

E. Translate the following sentences into French. Then say them aloud.

1. She'll have you visit the Louvre.
2. We'll have him see the paintings.
3. I'll have them look at the statues.
4. There's the Opera! There's also a beautiful (*un bel*) Opera in Milan.
5. There's the Place de la Concorde! There's also a beautiful square (*une belle place*) in Rome.
6. There's the Louvre! There's also a beautiful museum in New York.
7. Here are the *objets d'art* of which he spoke to you.
8. Here are the sculptures of which they spoke to him.
9. Here are the paintings of which she spoke to them.
10. Here are the masterpieces of which we spoke to you.
11. There are the painters whom we always hear about.
12. There are the Impressionists whom I always hear about.
13. My wife is knowledgeable about music.
14. I am knowledgeable about books.

F. Translate the following dialogue:

I'd like to go to the Louvre.
Let's go there right away.
Where are the paintings?
I'd also like to see the statues.
Look! There are the masterpieces!

**G.** From among the three choices, select the best translation for the English word or phrase given at the beginning of each sentence. Write the complete sentence, and translate.

1. (each) *Vingt francs* _____, *s'il vous plaît.*
   - (a) *l'un*
   - (b) *chacun*
   - (c) *chaque*

2. (We should have) _____ *venir dimanche.*
   - (a) *Nous devons*
   - (b) *Nous avons dû*
   - (c) *Nous aurions dû*

3. (knows about) *Mon mari* _____ *peinture.*
   - (a) *s'y connaît en*
   - (b) *se connaît autour*
   - (c) *sait de*

4. (One can admire) _____ *les chefs-d'œuvre.*
   - (a) *On doit admirer*
   - (b) *On sait admirer*
   - (c) *On peut admirer*

5. (Follow me) _____, *s'il vous plaît.*
   - (a) *Conduisez-moi*
   - (b) *Venez-moi*
   - (c) *Suivez-moi*

6. (How well displayed it is!) _____ (*la peinture*)
   - (a) *Comment bien exposée elle est!*
   - (b) *Qu'elle est bien exposée!*
   - (c) *Qu'elle est bien exposé!*

7. (nowhere) *Je ne les vois* _____.
   - (a) *dans aucun lieu*
   - (b) *partout*
   - (c) *nulle part*

8. (right away) *Allons-y* _____.
   - (a) *tout de suite*
   - (b) *à droit*
   - (c) *toute suite*

9. (I prefer) _____ le cubisme.
   (a) *Je préfére*
   (b) *Je préfère*
   (c) *Je prefer*

10. (Let's not look for them) _____ *maintenant.*
    (a) *Ne laissons chercher*
    (b) *Ne les regardons pas*
    (c) *Ne les cherchons pas*

# LESSON 10

## LES PRODUITS DE L'ARTISANAT;
## LA PEINTURE
## HANDICRAFTS; PAINTING

### A. DIALOGUE

*On décide d'aller au Marché aux Puces.*   We decide to go to the Flea Market.

1. Jane: **Nous avons si souvent entendu parler du Marché aux Puces.° Qu'est-ce que c'est?**
   We've heard about the Flea Market so often. What is it?

2. Michel: **C'est un grand marché en plein air; c'est-à-dire,° *ce sont plusieurs petits marchés qui se suivent . . . où l'on° peut acheter* des objets d'occasion,° comme des meubles, des bibelots, ou des antiquités.**
   It's a large open-air market, that is, several markets one after the other . . . where you can buy second-hand things like furniture, knicknacks, or antiques.

3. Jane: **Il y aura donc *des choses qui pourraient nous intéresser,* et peut-être même *quelque chose***

*que nous pourrions* acheter, n'est-ce pas,
Charles? Tu t'y connais en objets d'art. Si on y
allait, tous les trois?°
Then there will be things that could interest us, and
perhaps even something we could buy, right,
Charles? You know art objects. Suppose the three of
us went?

4. Charles: **Volontiers! Allons-y!**
   Gladly! Let's go!

*On arrive au Marché aux Puces.*   We arrive at the Flea
Market.

5. Jane: **Ah! Voilà** *une cafetière qui est bien jolie.*
   **C'est combien, madame?**
   Oh! There's a coffeepot that's very pretty. How
   much is it, ma'am?

6. Marchande: **Cent cinquante francs. C'est du
   Limoges,° madame.**
   One hundred fifty francs. It's Limoges porcelaine,
   madam.

7. Michel: (*En aparté*) **N'oubliez pas qu'il ne faut
   pas tout croire, et qu'il faut marchander.**°
   (*Aside*) Don't forget that you mustn't believe everything, and that you must bargain.

8. Jane: **Oui, en effet, c'est du Limoges. Je vous en
   offre cent francs.**
   Yes, as a matter of fact, it is Limoges. I'll give you
   one hundred francs for it.

9. Marchande: **Madame,** *c'est la plus jolie cafetière*
   **sur l'étagère ... Remarquez cette jolie bordure
   faite à la main ...**

Madam, it's the prettiest coffeepot on the shelf . . .
Notice this beautiful handmade border design . . .

10. Jane: **Vous me la laissez à cent vingt francs?**
Will you give it to me for one hundred twenty
francs?

11. Marchande: **Va pour° cent vingt francs! Allez!
Prenez-la!**
Sold for one hundred twenty francs. Go on! Take it!

12. Jane: **Michel,** *je me demande où se trouvent* **les
stands de bibelots et de faïence . . .**
Michel, I wonder where the knickknack and pottery
stands are . . .

13. Michel: **Là, au bout de cette allée, à gauche, je
crois . . .**
There, at the end of the passage, to the left, I
think . . .

14. Jane: **Attendez! Regardez en face! Les beaux
meubles de style!**
Wait! Look across the way! The beautiful antique
furniture!

15. Charles: **Regardez cette magnifique bergère Louis
XV . . .** *celle qui est recouverte* **de tapisserie Au-
busson.°** *Elle est de loin la plus belle* **de toutes . . .**
Look at that magnificent Louis XV easy chair . . .
the one that is upholstered in Aubussson tapestry.
It's by far the most beautiful of all . . .

16. Jane: **De toutes les bergères, peut-être. Mais moi,
je préfère ce canapé Louis XVI,** *celui qui est
sculpté et doré* **. . .**
Of all the easy chairs, maybe. But I prefer the Louis
XVI sofa, the one that is carved and gilded . . .

17. Charles: **Si on achetait les deux?**
How about buying both of them?

18. Jane: **Ne sois pas trop impulsif, Charles. Nous avons à peine assez d'argent pour en acheter une!°**
Don't be too impulsive, Charles. We have hardly enough money to buy one of them!

*Dans une galerie d'art.*    In an art gallery.

19. Charles: **Pardon, madame. Est-ce que vous exposez en ce moment les toiles de Paillac?**
Pardon me, ma'am. Are you showing the canvases of Paillac at present?

20. Marchande: **Celui qui a exposé à Beaubourg° l'année dernière?**
The one who showed at Beaubourg last year?

21. Charles: **C'est ça.**
That's the one.

22. Marchande: **Oui, monsieur. Il nous en reste encore quelques-unes. Des peintures à l'huile, seulement. Des gouaches ... eh bien, nous n'en avons pas.**
Yes, sir. We still have a few left. Oil paintings only. Gouaches ... well, we haven't any at all.

23. Charles: **Nous cherchons un assez grand tableau.**
We're looking for a rather large picture.

24. Marchande: **Comme grands tableaux, nous n'avons que des natures mortes. Veuillez m'accompagner au fond de la galerie pour que je puisse vous les montrer.**

In a large size, we have only still lifes. Please come with me to the rear of the gallery so that I can show them to you.

25. Charles: **En voilà une aux couleurs brillantes. Le bleu du premier plan contraste avec le rouge du fond.**
Here is one with brilliant colors. The blue of the foreground contrasts with the red of the background . . .

26. Marchande: **La toile de gauche est plus belle que celle de droite. Il y a une harmonie dans le mouvement qui me plaît beaucoup.**
The canvas at the left is more beautiful than the one at the right; there is a harmony of movement which I like very much.

27. Charles: **Et** *celle du milieu est la meilleure* **de toutes, à mon avis. Elle doit être très chère.**
And the one in the middle is the best of all, in my opinion. It must be very expensive.

28. Marchande: **Les tableaux de Paillac, de cette grandeur, se vendent à sept mille cinq cents (7500) francs.**
The pictures by Paillac, in this size, sell for 7500 francs.

29. Charles: **Ah, oui? C'est bien trop cher pour moi.**
Oh, really? That's much too expensive for me.

30. Marchande: **Vous savez bien, dès qu'un peintre est reconnu . . . Je vous conseille d'aller à Montmartre.° Vous y trouverez certainement un peintre encore inconnu qui sera content de vous vendre quelque chose à meilleur marché.**
You know how it is, as soon as a painter is recognized . . . I advise you to go to Montmartre. You'll

certainly find a painter there who is still unknown and who'll be happy to sell you something cheaper.

31. Charles: **Merci, madame. Vous avez été bien aimable.**
Thank you, ma'am. You've been very kind.

## B. NOTES

1. *Marché aux Puces:* a flea market where one can find antiques and bric-a-brac of all kinds.

2. *c'est-à-dire:* lit.: "that is to say." Another equivalent might be "I mean."
*où l'on:* This expression is used in fairly formal French usage. In colloquial French, you will more often hear *où on*.
*occasion:* may also mean "on sale"; when referring to new things, a "bargain."

3. *Si on y allait, tous les trois!* could also be translated as "How about the three of us going?"

6. *Limoges:* the name of a famous expensive porcelain made in the city of Limoges, about 200 miles southwest of Paris. The city of Sèvres, near Versailles, is also well known for porcelain.

7. *marchander:* "Bargaining" is part of the fun and is expected.

11. *Va pour:* an expression to indicate that something (usually a selling price) has been agreed upon or settled for.

15. *Aubusson:* the name of the town well known for the manufacture of tapestries. Other fine tapestries are made at Beauvais and at the Manufacture des Gobelins in Paris.

18. Note that *en* is used here with a number. This can be translated as "of them," as in: *Il a trouvé trois amis au café,* which becomes *Il en a trouvé trois.* See Lesson 11 for more uses of *en*.

20. *Beaubourg* is another name for the *Centre Pompidou,* named for the president who conceived it. (Georges Pompidou was president of France from 1969 to 1973.) It contains an art museum, a library, a cinema, art studios, and a restaurant. It is particularly known for its bold contemporary architectural style and the lively colors of its exterior pipes and stairways.

30. *Montmartre:* a hill on the Right Bank in Paris. The top of the hill is the Butte Montmartre. It is the site of the Sacre Cœur Basilica as well as a favorite haunt and working place of amateur artists. When people refer to art or artists, they generally use the terms *La Butte* and *Montmartre* interchangeably.

## C. GRAMMAR AND USAGE

1. Relative pronoun—*qui:* who, which, that—used as subject

| Sing. or Pl. | *Qui* as subject | Verb | Complement | |
|---|---|---|---|---|
| a. *La dame* | *qui* | *vend* | *la cafetière* | *veut trop d'argent.* |
| b. *La bergère* | *qui* | *est* | *recouverte de soie* | *est jolie.* |
| c. *Les hommes* | *qui* | *arrivent* | | *sont mes cousins.* |
| d. *Les bateaux* | *qui* | *traversent* | *l'océan* | *sont grands.* |
| e. *Je connais la dame* | *qui* | *vend* | *la cafetière.* | |

a. The lady (who is) selling the coffeepot wants too
   much money.
b. The easy chair (which is) covered with silk is
   pretty.
c. The men (who are) arriving are my cousins.
d. The boats which cross the ocean are big.
e. I know the lady (who is) selling the coffeepot.

Note:
  • The relative clause may be embedded in a sentence (a.
    to d.) or it may come at the end of the sentence (e.).
  • The relative pronoun must be expressed in French
    even though it is often omitted in English.

2. Relative pronoun—*que:* whom, which, that—used as
   objects

|  | *Que* as Object | Sub. | Verb |  |
| --- | --- | --- | --- | --- |
| a. *Le marchand* | *que* | *vous* | *voyez* | *est aveugle.* |
| b. *Le canapé* | *que* | *je* | *voudrais acheter* | *est trop cher.* |
| c. *Les toiles* | *que* | *j'* | *aime* | *sont toutes de Degas.* |
| d. *Les hommes* | *que* | *j'* | *ai connus* | *sont tous à la retraite.* |
| e. *Je voudrais acheter les choses* | *que* | *j'* | *ai vues* | *hier.* |

a. The merchant (whom) you see over there is blind.
b. The sofa (which) I'd like to buy is too expensive.
c. The canvases (which) I like are all by Degas.

    d. The men (whom) I knew are all retired.

    e. I'd like to buy the things (that) I saw yesterday.

Note:

- The past participle of the relative clause agrees with the antecedent of *que* in number and gender. (Study the last two examples above.)

3. Relative pronoun—*où:* on which, in which, at which, where

|  | *où* | Subject, etc. |
|---|---|---|
| a. *Le stand* | *où* | *on vend la porcelaine* . . . |
| b. *La maison* | *où* | *je suis né(e)* . . . |

    a. The stand at which (where) they sell porcelain . . .

    b. The house in which (where) I was born . . .

4. Superlatives

|  | Determiner | *plus/moins* | Adjective | *de* |  |
|---|---|---|---|---|---|
| a. *C'est*[1] | *mon* | *plus* | *grand* |  | *souci.* |
| b. *C'est* | *la* | *moins* | *jolie* |  | *robe.* |
| c. *Elle est de loin* | *la* | *plus* | *chère* | *de* | *toute la boutique.* |
| d. *C'est* | *le* | *plus* | *vieux* | *de* | *tous les hommes.* |

    a. It's my biggest worry.

    b. It's the least pretty dress.

    c. It's by far the most expensive in the whole store.

    d. He's the oldest of all the men.

[1] The contrast between *c'est* and *il* (*elle*) *est* is discussed in Lesson 20.

|  | Noun | Deter-miner | plus/moins | Adjective |
|---|---|---|---|---|
| a. *C'est* | *la peinture* | *la* | *plus* | *intéressante.* |
| b. *C'est* | *l'artiste* | *le* | *moins* | *reconnu du groupe.* |
| c. *Ce sont* | *mes amies* | *les* | *plus* | *riches.* |

a. It's the most interesting painting.
b. He's the least recognized painter in the group.
c. They are my richest friends.

Note:

- The superlative of the adjective is formed by placing a determiner (definite article: *le, la, les*) or possessive (*mon, notre,* etc.) before *plus* or *moins*.
- *De* is placed after the superlatives and in front of a noun or pronoun to express "in, of, among."
  See second example above.
- Irregular adjectives are:

|  | Comparative | Superlative |
|---|---|---|
| *bon* (good) | *meilleur* | *le meilleur* |
| *mauvais* (bad) | *pire* | *le pire* |
| *petit* (small—in importance) | *moindre* | *le moindre* |

Note:

- Remember that in the superlative, the determiner agrees with the noun in number and gender.
- As we know, adjectives agree with the nouns they describe (see below, however).
- *Pire* is used primarily in a moral sense.

Colors modified by other adjectives or nouns

|  | Color | Modifier |
|---|---|---|
| a. *Elle avait les yeux* | *bleu* | *ciel.* |
| b. *Elle avait un manteau* | *jaune* | *paille.* |
| c. *Elle portait une jupe* | *vert* | *foncé.* |
| d. *Elle avait deux robes* | *bleu* | *vert.* |
| e. *Elle a acheté une robe* | *marron* | *clair.* |

a. She had sky-blue eyes.
b. She had a straw-colored coat.
c. She was wearing a dark green skirt.
d. She had two blue-green dresses.
e. She bought a light brown dress.

Note:

- Adjectives of color modified by another adjective or noun do not agree with the nouns they modify or describe; they are invariable.

### EXERCISES

A. Substitute each word in parentheses for the underlined word in the model sentence. Write the complete sentence and say it aloud.

1. *Ce tableau est le plus beau de l'exposition.* (*reconnu, abstrait, surréaliste, remarquable, original, réaliste*)
2. *Nous voulons acheter vos toiles les plus récentes.* (*originales, brillantes, coûteuses, chères*)
3. *Sur un fond bleu, le peintre a mis des fleurs bleues.* (*blanches, jaunes, rouges, roses, violettes*)
4. *L'homme qui arrive est mon père.* (*frère, cousin, fils, ami, oncle, grand-père*)
5. *La porcelaine que j'ai achetée est belle.* (*vue, admirée, remarquée*)

6. *Le magasin où je vais est près d'ici.* (*l'école, la maison, l'église, la bibliothèque, le cinéma*)

B. In the sentence *La maison que j'ai vendue est belle*, replace *je* by the other subject pronouns (*tu, il, elle, nous, vous, ils, elles*). Make all necessary verb changes.

C. Translate the following sentences into French; then say them aloud.

1. The merchant who sells the coffeepot is nice.
2. The lady who is buying the furniture is my wife.
3. The merchant (whom) you see is nice.
4. The lady (whom) we like is here.
5. The clothes (which) I'm wearing are old.
6. The rings (which) you have are beautiful.
7. It's the longest passage in the market.
8. It's the richest canvas in the gallery.
9. He's the most recognized painter in Paris.
10. It's the best design in the collection.
11. It's the oldest picture in the collection.
12. There will be (some) furniture at the market.
13. There will be (some) paintings at the gallery.
14. It will be necessary to bargain.
15. It will be necessary to wear old clothes.
16. She looks (*a l'air*) elegant.
17. Do I look rich? (use *Est-ce que*)
18. They don't look nice.
19. I wonder if he has a sofa.
20. One wonders if they have any paintings.
21. We wonder if you have any *objets d'art*.
22. I'd like to see it close up.
23. I'd like to see it from afar.
24. She wants to see it from here.
25. You'll find it at the end of the passage.
26. You'll find it opposite the gallery.
27. Will I find it at the corner of the street? (use *Est-ce que*)

28. Show me a sky-blue easy chair.
29. There's a dark green sofa.
30. I'd like a light red tapestry.
31. Do you prefer the tapestry on the right?
32. I prefer the canvas in the middle.
33. She prefers the canvas on the left.

D. From among the three choices, select the best translation for the English word or phrase given at the beginning of each sentence. Write the complete sentence, and translate.

1. (heard) *Nous avons si souvent _____ du Marché aux Puces.*
   (a) *entendu*
   (b) *écouté parler*
   (c) *entendu parler*
2. (all three of us) *Si on y allait _____?*
   (a) *tous trois de nous*
   (b) *les trois nous*
   (c) *tous les trois*
3. (that we could buy) *Il y aura quelque chose _____.*
   (a) *que nous pourrions acheter*
   (b) *que nous pouvions acheter*
   (c) *que nous avons pu acheter*
4. (bargain) *Il faut _____*
   (a) *marchander*
   (b) *marcher*
   (c) *acheter*
5. (across the way) *Regardez _____*
   (a) *à travers le chemin*
   (b) *en face*
   (c) *en traversant la route*
6. (Don't be) *_____ trop impulsif.*
   (a) *N'êtes pas*
   (b) *Ne soyez pas*
   (c) *Ne faites pas être*

7. (the one who) [masc.] _____ *a exposé à Beau-bourg* . . .
   (a) *Le qui*
   (b) *Il qui*
   (c) *Celui qui*
8. (a few) [*toiles*] *Il nous en reste encore* _____ .
   (a) *un quelque*
   (b) *quelques-uns*
   (c) *quelques-unes*
9. (must be) *La toile* _____ *très chère.*
   (a) *doit être*
   (b) *peut être*
   (c) *faut être*


# LESSON 11

## ON PREND DES PHOTOS
## WE TAKE PICTURES


A. DIALOGUE


*On se prépare.*    Getting ready.

1. Charles: **Tu es prête? Rapelle-toi, c'est aujour-d'hui que nous avons décidé de revoir nos en-droits préférés et** *de prendre des photos.*°
   Are you ready? Remember, it's today that we de-cided to see our favorite places again and to take some pictures.

2. Jane: **Mais bien sûr!** *Tu as assez de pellicules*°
   **pour les appareils?**°
   Of course! Do you have enough film for the cam-eras?

3. Charles· **Oui, je crois, mais je voudrais passer chez le photographe** *pour en° acheter d'autres* **et** *pour demander quelques conseils.°*
Yes, I think so, but I'd like to stop by a camera store to buy more and to ask for some advice.

4. Jane: **Rappelle-toi qu'il nous faut des pellicules pour les diapos° et quelques vidéocassettes pour le caméscope.**
Remember that we need some film for the slides and some cassettes for the camcorder.

5. Charles: **Tu as raison. Je voudrais me souvenir° des couleurs vives des cafés du Marais.**
You're right. I'd like to remember the bright colors of the cafés in the Marais.

6. Jane: **Et moi, je voudrais immortaliser pour toujours les toiles des artistes sur la Place du Tertre.° Je voudrais des vidéocassettes, des diapos, et quelques photos de tous les endroits que nous aimons.**
And I'd like to capture forever the canvases of the artists on the Place du Tertre. I'd like some videocassettes, some slides, and a few snapshots of all the places we like.

*Chez le photographe.* In the camera store.

7. Charles: **Je voudrais deux pellicules pour cet appareil.**
I would like two rolls of film for this camera.

8. Employé: **Voici. C'est un très bon appareil que vous avez là.**
Here they are. That's a very good camera you have there.

9. Charles: **Oui.** *J'en suis très satisfait.* **Donnez-moi aussi deux pellicules-diapo pour cet appareil, s'il vous plaît.**
Yes. I'm very happy with it. Let me also have two rolls of slide film for this camera, please.

10. Employé: **Vingt-quatre ou trente-six poses?**
Twenty-four or thirty-six exposures?

11. Charles: **Trente-six, s'il vous plaît. Est-ce que vous pourriez aussi donner un coup d'œil° à cet autre appareil?**
Thirty-six, please. Would you also please take a look at this other camera?

12. Employé: *Qu'est-ce qui* **ne vas pas?°**
What's the trouble?

13. Charles: **Quelquefois, quand j'appuie sur le déclencheur, il reste engagé.°**
Sometimes, when I press on the release, it sticks.

14. Employé: **Je connais bien ce modèle. Il ne faut jamais appuyer sur le bouton trop longtemps. Enlevez tout de suite votre doigt.**
I know this model well. You must never press the button for too long. Take your finger off it right away.

15. Charles: **Ah! Merci beaucoup, monsieur.**
Ah! Thank you very much, sir.

16. Employé: **Vous désirez autre chose? Non? Alors, je vous mets tout cela dans un sac. Bonne chance!**
Is there anything else? No? Then I'll put all this in a bag for you. Good luck!

*À l'Arc de Triomphe.* At the Arch of Triumph.

17. Jane: **Nous voici à l'Arc de Triomphe.° Je voudrais une vue panoramique de l'Étoile. N'oublie pas de retirer le cache.**
Here we are at the Arch of Triumph. I'd like a panoramic view of the Etoile. Don't forget to uncap the lens.

18. Charles: *Ne t'en fais pas.°* **Je reviens tout de suite. Mets-toi là devant le Drugstore.° Ainsi on te verra sur la photo.**
Don't worry. I'll be right back. Stand over there, in front of the Drugstore. That way, you'll be in the picture.

*Sur la Place de la Concorde.* At the Place de la Concorde.

19. Jane: **Prends maintenant quelques vues des Champs-Elysées de l'autre bout. Attention! Ne prends pas les voitures. Attends que le feu passe au rouge.**
Now take some shots of the Champs-Élysées from the other end. Watch out! Don't get the cars in. Wait until the light turns red.

20. Charles: **C'est magnifique. Je vois parfaitement tous les cafés, les kiosques et les arbres jusqu'à l'Arc de Triomphe.**
This is wonderful. I see perfectly all the cafés, the newspaper stands, and the trees up to the Arch of Triumph.

*Sur la Place du Tertre.* At the Place du Tertre.

21. Jane: **Charles, mets-toi ici. Je voudrais le Sacré-Cœur° et ces deux restaurants.**

Charles, stand here. I'd like the Sacré-Cœur and these two restaurants.

22. Charles: **Bien. Mais attends que je change la pellicule. Ah! La lumière commence à changer. Je ferais mieux de changer l'ouverture.**
Fine. But wait until I reload the camera. Oh! The light is beginning to change. I'd better enlarge the aperture.

23. Jane: **Tu ne l'as pas fait pour les autres photos?**
You didn't do that for the other shots?

24. Charles: **Ne t'en fais pas. Il y a quinze ans que° je prends des photos, et je les ai toujours réussies.**
Don't worry. I've been taking pictures for fifteen years, and I've always had them turn out well.

25. Jane: **Surtout n'oublie pas de prendre ces artistes. J'aime bien leurs peintures à l'huile.**
Be sure to get these artists into the picture. I like their oil paintings.

26. Charles: **Moi aussi. Et j'espère que nous pourrons faire developper les photos pendant que nous sommes en voyage.**
So do I. And I hope we'll be able to have the photos developed while we're traveling.

27. Jane: **Et nous ferons faire plusieurs épreuves des meilleures *pour les envoyer* à nos amis.**
And we'll have several prints made of the best ones to send our friends.

28. Charles: **Peut-être même des agrandissements.**
Maybe even some enlargements.

29. Jane: **Pourvu que tu n'aies pas raté les photos.**
Provided you haven't spoiled the pictures.

30. Charles: **Allons donc! Tu sais bien que je suis un bon photographe.**
Come on! You know very well that I'm a good photographer.

## B. NOTES

1. *La photo* is the customary short form of *la photographie* and means "photograph." Be careful of the false cognate *photographe*, which means "photographer."

2. Note that *une pellicule* is the film used in a camera, and *un film* is what is seen on TV or at the movies. *appareil:* the general term for *appareil photographique*, any still camera.

3. *en:* of it; of them. In this case, *en* refers to *pellicules*. *conseils:* Notice that "advice," which is always used in the singular in English, can be plural in French.

4. *Diapositives,* or simply *diapos,* are slides.

5. *me souvenir: se souvenir* and *se rappeler* both mean "to remember." When you use *se souvenir* you must use *de* before the object. Example: *Je me souviens de votre nom.* (I remember your name.) But: *Je me rappelle votre nom.*

6. *la Place du Tertre:* a celebrated and lively colorful square in Montmartre where restaurants, painters, and tourists abound.

11. *un coup d'œil:* a glance. *Donner un coup d'œil à* or *jetter un coup d'œil sur* means "to glance at."

12. *ne va pas: aller* and *marcher* are used colloquially for "to work," "to run," "to function." Example: *Mon horloge ne marche pas.* My clock isn't working.

13. *engagé:* or . . . *il reste bloqué.*

17. *Arc de Triomphe:* Arch of Triumph. A large arch in
    the center of the Place de l'Étoile, under which is
    found the Tomb of the Unknown Soldier.

18. *ne t'en fais pas:* lit.: "don't make anything of it."
    *S'en faire* is used casually for "to worry."
    *le Drugstore:* an elegant French fantasy of what an
    American drugstore is like, located on the Champs-
    Elysées. There are now several American-type drug-
    stores in Paris. Before the influx of American
    influence, *les pharmacies* sold only drugs.

21. *Sacré-Cœur:* This basilica is a spectacular example
    of Byzantine style architecture. It dominates Mont-
    martre and can be seen from almost anywhere in
    Paris.

24. *Il y a quinze ans que:* lit.: "It is fifteen years
    that . . ." This very common time expression is dis-
    cussed in Lesson 19.

## C. GRAMMAR AND USAGE

1. *En*—some of it; some of them; of it; of them

CONTRAST:

a. *J'ai acheté des robes.*         *J'en ai acheté.*
b. *Je voudrais de la viande.*      *J'en voudrais.*
c. *J'ai beaucoup d'argent.*        *J'en ai beaucoup.*
d. *Il m'a donné trois livres.*     *Il m'en a donné trois.*
e. *Ne me donnez pas de*            *Ne m'en donnez pas.*
   *pommes.*
f. *Donnez-moi des pommes.*         *Donnez-m'en.*

| a. I bought some dresses. | I bought some (of them). |
| b. I'd like some meat. | I'd like some (of it). |
| c. I have a lot of money. | I have a lot (of it). |
| d. He gave me three books. | He gave me three (of them). |
| e. Don't give me any apples. | Don't give me any (of them). |
| f. Give me some apples. | Give me some (of them). |

Note:

- The partitive construction (*de* + definite article + noun), discussed in Lesson 8, is replaced by *en* when the "partitioned" noun is not specifically mentioned, but only implied. See examples a., b., c., f. above. Study the position of *en* in these sentences.
- When the sentence ends with a number or an adverb of quantity, the sentence must contain *en*. (See c. and d. above.)
- *En* is never omitted in French, but in many expressions, *en* need not be translated into English, particularly when the word or expression to which it refers is clear. Examples:

| *Combien de livres avez-vous?* | How many books do you have? |
| *J'en ai trois.* | I have three. |
| *Il n'en reste que des natures mortes.* | There are only still lifes left. |

- *En* is invariable: Even when the noun to which *en* refers is feminine or plural, there is no agreement of the past participle. (See examples a. and d. above.)
- *En* precedes the verb of which it is the object, except in affirmative requests, e.g., *Donnez-en à Charles.* Give some to Charles.

2. *Assez de*—enough

|  | *assez* | *de* | Noun (Sing. or Pl.) |
|---|---|---|---|
| a. *J'ai* | *assez* | *de* | *pellicules.* |
| b. *Il a mangé* | *assez* | *de* | *pain.* |
| c. *Nous n'avons pas* | *assez* | *d'* | *argent.* |

a. I have enough film.
b. He ate enough bread.
c. We don't have enough money.

3. *Qu'est-ce qui*—what (lit.: What is it that)

| *Qu'est-ce qui* | Verb |
|---|---|
| a. *Qu'est-ce qui* | *ne va pas?* |
| b. *Qu'est-ce qui* | *arrive?* |
| c. *Qu'est-ce qui* | *s'est passé?* |

a. What's wrong?
b. What's happening? } Notice the two French equiva-
c. What happened? } lents of "What's happening?"
                    } or "What's going on?"

Note:
- The interrogative form *qu'est-ce qui* is used as a *sub-ject.*
- It refers only to things.
- It always begins a sentence.

4. *Pour* + infinitive = to; in order to

|  | *pour* | Pron. | Infinitive |
|---|---|---|---|
| a. *Il faut manger* | *pour* |  | *vivre.* |
| b. *On doit prendre le train* | *pour* | *y* | *aller.* |
| c. *Je suis arrivé* | *pour* | *les* | *voir.* |
| d. *Allez au magasin* | *pour* | *en* | *acheter.* |

a. It is necessary to eat (in order) to live.

b One must take the train (in order) to go there.

c. I arrived (in order) to see them.

d. Go to the store (in order) to buy some.

## EXERCISES

A. Substitute each of the words in parentheses for the underlined word in the model sentence. Write the complete sentence and say aloud, and translate.

1. *J'en ai acheté.* (*demandé, cherché, trouvé, mangé, regardé*)
2. *Il a assez de films.* (*pellicules, appareils* [*watch the d'*], *vidéo-cassettes, diapos, photos*)
3. *Allez au magasin pour en acheter.* (*voir, trouver, chercher, admirer, essayer*)

B. Expand the expressions below by placing *Qu'est-ce qui* in front of each. Write the complete sentence and say it aloud.

1. _____ *se passe?*
2. _____ *ne marche pas?*
3. _____ *vous ennuie?*
4. _____ *est arrivé?*
5. _____ *l'inquiète?*

C. Replace the underlined expression by *en*. Say and write the entire new sentence and translate. Example: *Il faut faire du travail./Il faut en faire.*

1. *J'ai acheté des robes.*
2. *Je voudrais du pain.*
3. *Nous avons assez de viande.*
4. *Il m'a donné quatre livres.*
5. *Prêtez-moi des chaussettes.*

D. Translate the following sentences into French. Then say them aloud.

1. Photos? He took several of them.
2. I'd like four of them.
3. Don't give me any film; I have enough.
4. Do you have enough film for the camera?
5. Yes, but there's not enough light.
6. What's on the table?
7. What's going to happen?
8. What's bothering you? (*ennuyer*)
9. In order to learn, one must understand.
10. I don't have enough money to buy this camcorder.
11. Do you have to take a plane to get there?

E. From among the three choices, select the best translation for the English word or phrase given at the beginning of each sentence. Write the complete sentence, and translate.

1. (enough) *Tu as* _____ *pellicules-diapo?*
   (a) *assez*
   (b) *assez de*
   (c) *assez des*
2. (maybe even) _____ *des agrandissements aussi.*
   (a) *Même certain*
   (b) *Même peut-être*
   (c) *Peut-être même*
3. (at least) *Il nous en faudra* _____ *deux.*
   (a) *à moins.*
   (b) *moins*
   (c) *au moins*
4. (remember) *Je voudrais* _____ *des couleurs.*
   (a) *se souvenir*
   (b) *me souvenir*
   (c) *rappeller-moi*

5. (Here they are) _____.
   (a) *Voici les sont*
   (b) *Les voici*
   (c) *Ici ils sont*
6. (in the) *Je l'ai acheté* _____ *États-Unis.*
   (a) *dans les*
   (b) *dans l'*
   (c) *aux*
7. (a glance) *Veuillez aussi jeter* _____ *à cet appareil?*
   (a) *un cherche*
   (b) *un regard*
   (c) *un coup d'oeil*
8. (anything else) *Y a-t-il* _____?
   (a) *autre chose*
   (b) *quoi d'autre*
   (c) *rien d'autre*
9. (up to) *Je vois* _____ *l'Arc de Triomphe.*
   (a) *haut à*
   (b) *jusqu'à*
   (c) *mont à*
10. (I'd better) _____ *de changer l'ouverture.*
    (a) *Je mieux*
    (b) *Je fais meilleur*
    (c) *Je ferais mieux*

# LESSON 12

## AGENCE DE VOYAGES
## TRAVEL AGENCY

### A. DIALOGUE

*On demande des renseignements.*   Asking for information.

   1. Employée: **Bonjour, messieurs'dames. En quoi puis-je vous être utile?**
      Good day, sir, madam. How can I help you?

2. Charles: **Nous voudrions explorer la France, *en dehors de Paris*. Pourriez-vous suggérer quelques itinéraires?**
   We'd like to explore France, outside of Paris. Could you suggest some itineraries?

3. Employée: **Avec plaisir. Où voudriez-vous aller?**
   With pleasure. Where would you like to go?

4. Charles: **Nous pensions faire d'abord quel-ques petites excursions aux alentours de Paris. À Fontainebleau,° par exemple.**
   We were thinking of taking a few little trips in the areas surrounding Paris first. To Fontainebleau, for example.

5. Employée: **Je vous conseille de louer une voiture. Sinon il y a un très bon autocar° qui part pour Fontainebleau plusieurs fois par jour.**
   I advise you to rent a car. Or otherwise there is a very good bus that leaves for Fontainebleau several times a day.

6. Jane: **Et pour Chartres° et Versailles?°**
   And for Chartres and Versailles?

7. Employée: **Vous pouvez y aller *en train*. Il n'y aura pas de problèmes pour les billets. Et ensuite?**
   You can go there by train. There will be no problem with the tickets. And what else?

8. Charles: **Nous voudrions voir la Bretagne,° les châteaux de la Loire,° ou peut-être la Côte d'Azur.**
   We'd like to see Brittany, the châteaux of the Loire, or maybe the Riviera.

9. Jane: **C'est un choix difficile entre un peu de campagne, un peu de plage, et quelques beaux monuments historiques.**

It's a difficult choice between a little country, a little beach, and some fine historic monuments.

10. Employée: **Où que vous alliez, vous devriez prendre le T.G.V.° C'est rapide, pratique, et très agréable.**
Wherever you go, you should take the T.G.V. It's fast, practical, and very comfortable.

11. Jane: **Nous voulions aussi voyager *en Italie et dans la Suisse française.*° Mais mon mari préfère aller d'abord *en Espagne* et *au Portugal.***
We also wanted to travel in Italy and French-speaking Switzerland. But my husband would rather go to Spain and Portugal first.

12. Employée: **Vous ferez ces voyages *en avion,* sans doute. Vous gagnerez° ainsi beaucoup de temps.**
You'll probably make those trips by plane. You will save a lot of time that way.

13. Charles: **Oui, je crois que c'est une bonne idée.**
Yes, I think that's a good idea.

14. Employée: **Voulez-vous que je vous réserve une place? Nous pouvons faire votre itinéraire maintenant.**
Do you want me to reserve a place for you? We can arrange your itinerary now.

15. Jane: **Si vous permettez, nous allons y réfléchir ce soir, et nous reviendrons demain.**
If you don't mind, we'll think about it this evening, and we'll come back tomorrow.

*Le lendemain.* The next day.

16. Employée: **Ah, bonjour. Alors, qu'est-ce que vous avez décidé?**
Oh, hello. So, what have you decided?

17. Charles: **Voyons. Nous voudrions deux billets d'autocar pour Fontainebleau pour demain matin.**
Let's see. We'd like two bus tickets for Fontainebleau for tomorrow morning.

18. Jane: **Et deux billets de train pour Versailles pour dimanche matin. On nous a dit qu'on peut voir les Grandes Eaux seulement le dimanche.**
And two railway tickets for Versailles for Sunday morning. We were told that we can see the fountains playing only on Sundays.

19. Employée: **Oui, c'est juste. On peut les voir aussi tous les jours de fête.**
Yes, that's correct. You can also see them on all holidays.

20. Charles: **Nous avons décidé de prendre le T.G.V. pour aller visiter les châteaux de la Loire et aussi pour aller sur la Côte d'Azur.**
We've decided to take the T.G.V. to go visit the châteaux of the Loire and also to go to the Riviera.

21. Jane: **Voudriez-vous nous retenir des chambres d'hôtel? J'ai ici la liste des villes que nous voulons visiter.**
Would you please reserve hotel rooms for us? I have a list here of the cities that we want to visit.

22. Employée: **Vous avez bien choisi. Je vois ici Chambord,° Chenonceaux,° et Amboise.° Où préférez-vous passer la nuit? Tours° serait pratique. Vous pourriez y louer une voiture pour visiter les châteaux.**
You've made a good choice. I see here Chambord, Chenonceaux, and Amboise. Where do you prefer to spend the night? Tours would be practical. You could rent a car there to visit the châteaux.

23. Jane: **On passera la nuit à Tours, alors.** *Pensez-vous que nous puissions aller* **directement** *à Arles?*
We'll spend the night in Tours, then. Do you think we can go directly to Arles?

24. Employée: **Si vous y tenez absolument, vous pourriez le faire, mais c'est un peu long.**
If you insist on it, you could do it, but it's a little far.

25. Charles: **Qu'est-ce que vous suggérez à la place?**
What do you suggest instead?

26. Employée: **Vous pourriez passer un jour** *à Lyon.*° **Ainsi vous verriez les paysages aux bords du Rhône.° La campagne là est une des plus belles de toute la France, à mon avis.**
You could spend a day in Lyons. That way you'd see the scenery in the Rhone Valley. The country-side there is one of the most beautiful in all of France, in my opinion.

27. Charles: **J'ai entendu dire qu'il y avait de très bons vins** *dans cette région.*
I've heard that there are some very good wines in that region.

28. Jane: **Les vins ne m'intéressent pas, mais la plage, si. Nous voudrions passer au moins trois jours** *à Cannes.*
Wines don't interest me, but the beach does. We'd like to spend at least three days in Cannes.

29. Charles: **Et comme nous voulons passer la plupart de notre temps sur la plage, nous voudrions un hôtel qui donne sur la mer.**
And since we want to spend most of our time on the beach, we'd like a hotel facing the sea.

30. Employée: **Je vais m'occuper de tout cela cet après-midi. J'ai des collègues à Cannes qui vous**

**trouveront tout ce qu'il vous faut ... Et pour le voyage *en Espagne?***

I'll take care of all that this afternoon. I have colleagues in Cannes who will find you everything you need. And for the trip to Spain?

31. Jane: **Nous pensons le faire aussi *en voiture.***
    We intend to do it by car also.

32. Charles: **Comme cela, on verra d'autres régions de France.**
    In that way, we'll see other regions of France.

## B. NOTES

4. *Fontainebleau:* a small town near Paris noted for its beautiful château, built by François I as a hunting lodge, and its surrounding large forests. The art school in Fontainebleau is highly regarded.

5. *Un autocar,* or simply *un car,* is an intercity bus. *Un bus* is a bus used for public transportation within a city.

6. *Chartres:* a small town near Paris with a Gothic cathedral whose stained-glass windows are considered among the most beautiful in the world.
   *Versailles:* the former palace of French kings, built by Louis XIV, noted particularly for its formal gardens, its fountains, and its Hall of Mirrors. The treaty ending World War I was signed there.

8. *Bretagne* (Brittany) is the province that occupies the rugged peninsula in the northwestern corner of France. It is a region rich in history and culture, with neolithic *menhirs* and *dolmens* (megaliths), charming fishing villages, and a Celtic heritage complete with its own language (Breton), which has begun to regain popularity and importance.

*Les châteaux de la Loire:* The banks of the Loire River—the longest river in France—are lined with Renaissance castles. The most famous are Chenonceaux, Amboise, Chambord, and Azay-le-Rideau.

10. The *T.G.V.,* or *train à grande vitesse,* is France's high-speed train.

11. *Suisse française:* French-speaking Switzerland is also referred to as *la Suisse romande.*

12. *gagnerez: gagner,* to win, to gain. Also "to earn," as in *gagner de l'argent,* to earn money; *gagner sa vie,* to earn one's living.

22. *Chambord* is the immense château built by François I. Begun in 1519, it comprises 440 rooms, 365 chimneys, and a famous double-helix staircase.
   *Chenonceaux* is a graceful château that actually spans the River Cher.
   The *Château d'Amboise* overlooks the city of Amboise, and aside from a large tower, a Gothic chapel, and some apartments, little of the original structure remains.
   *Tours* is a modern city with a very active student population. Attractions of the city itself include a charming old quarter and a Gothic cathedral, and the surrounding region is home to some of France's most spectacular châteaux.

26. *Lyon:* a large city (the third largest in France) about 300 miles southeast of Paris, noted for silk and related industries.
   *le Rhône:* a river in southeastern France, which the Saône River joins at Lyons. It flows into the Mediterranean.

## C. GRAMMAR AND USAGE

1. Prepositions *en, à, dans* with place names

|  | *en* | Feminine Countries, Provinces, Continents |
|---|---|---|
| a. *Je voudrais voyager* | *en* | *France.* |
| b. *Je voudrais voyager* | *en* | *Bretagne.* |
| c. *Je voudrais voyager* | *en* | *Suisse.* |
| d. *Je voudrais voyager* | *en* | *Amérique.* |

a. I'd like to travel to France.
b. I'd like to travel to Brittany.
c. I'd like to travel to Switzerland.
d. I'd like to travel to America.

|  | *à* + Art. | Masculine Countries and Provinces |
|---|---|---|
| a. *Il habite* | *au* | *Portugal.* |
| b. *Il ira* | *au* | *Canada.* |
| c. *Il habite* | *au* | *Languedoc.* |
| d. *Il ira* | *aux* | *États-Unis.* |

a. He lives in Portugal.
b. He will go to Canada.
c. He lives in Languedoc.
d. He will go to the United States.

|  | *à* | Cities |
|---|---|---|
| a. *Nous voudrons aller* | *à* | *Fontainebleau.* |
| b. *Nous resterons* | *à* | *Chartres.* |
| c. *Nous voudrons aller* | *à* | *New-York.* |
| d. *Nous resterons* | *à* | *Londres.* |

a. We'll want to go to Fontainebleau.
b. We'll stay in Chartres.
c. We'll want to go to New York.
d. We'll stay in London.

|  | *dans* | Place | Modifier |
|---|---|---|---|
| a. *Il va* | *dans* | *l'Amérique* | *du Sud.* |
| b. *Il travaille* | *dans* | *la Suisse* | *française.* |
| c. *Il voyage* | *dans* | *le Canada* | *français.* |

a. He is going to South America.
b. He is working in French Switzerland.
c. He is traveling in French Canada.

Note:
- All continents are feminine.
- Place names ending in *e* are feminine except for *le Mexique.*
- Cities are preceded by *à* alone. Notable exceptions are *au* Havre (*to* Le Havre), *au Mans* (to Le Mans), and *à la Nouvelle Orléans* (to New Orleans).
- *En* is used instead of *au* for masculine countries beginning with a vowel. Example: *Nous allons en Israël.* We are going to Israel.
- *Dans* is used when a region or country is qualified by another adjective or phrase.

2. Preposition *de* with place names

|  | *de* | Feminine Countries, Provinces, Continents |
|---|---|---|
| a. *Il vient* | *de* | *France.* |
| b. *Christelle vient* | *de* | *Bretagne.* |
| c. *Ils viennent* | *d'* | *Amérique.* |

a. He comes from France.
b. Christelle comes from Brittany.
c. They come from America.

|  | *de* | Cities |
|---|---|---|
| a. *Nous arriverons* | *de* | *New York.* |
| b. *Ils viennent* | *de* | *Paris.* |
| c. *Elle arrivera* | *de* | *Londres.* |

a. We'll arrive from New York.
b. They come from Paris.
c. She'll arrive from London.

|  | *de* + Art. | Masculine Countries and Provinces |
|---|---|---|
| a. *Il revient* | *du* | *Portugal.* |
| b. *Tu reviens* | *du* | *Danemark.* |
| c. *Il vient* | *du* | *Japon.* |
| d. *Ils viennent* | *du* | *Languedoc.* |
| e. *Nous revenons* | *des* | *États-Unis.* |

a. He is coming back from Portugal.
b. You're coming back from Denmark.
c. He comes from Japan.
d. They come from Languedoc.
e. We're coming back from the United States.

|  | *de* + Art. | Place | Modifier |
|---|---|---|---|
| a. *Elle est arrivée* | *de l'* | *Amérique* | *du Nord.* |
| b. *Solange vient* | *du* | *Canada* | *français.* |
| c. *Vous reviendrez* | *de la* | *Suisse* | *française.* |

a. She arrived from North America.
b. Solange comes from French Canada.
c. You will come back from French Switzerland.

Note:
- *Il revient du Havre.*   He returns from Le Havre.
  *Il revient du Mexique.* He returns from Mexico.

3. Prepositions with means of transportation

|  | *en* |  |
|---|---|---|
| a. *Il voyage* | *en* | *autobus.* |
| b. *Nous voyagerons* | *en* | *avion.* |
| c. *J'y suis allé* | *en* | *voiture.* |
| d. *Ils sont allés* | *en* | *train.* |
| e. *Vous êtes venus* | *en* | *bateau.* |

a. He travels by bus.
b. We'll travel by plane.
c. I went there by car.
d. They went by train.
e. You came by boat.

|  | *à* |  |
|---|---|---|
| a. *Il aime se promener* | *à* | *pied.* |
| b. *Nous irons* | *à* | *bicyclette.* |
| c. *Ils venaient* | *à* | *cheval.* |

a. He likes to take a walk (to go on foot).
b. We'll go by bike.
c. They used to come on horseback.

4. Subjunctive after the interrogative or negative of *croire* and *penser*

| Interrogative of *croire* and *penser* | *que* | Subjunctive | Complement |
|---|---|---|---|
| a. *Croyez-vous* | *qu'* | *il soit* | *intelligent?* |
| b. *Pensez-vous* | *qu'* | *elle soit arrivée?* | |

a. Do you believe (that) he's intelligent?
b. Do you think (that) she has arrived?

| Negative of *croire* and *penser* | *que* | Subjunctive | Complement |
|---|---|---|---|
| a. *Je ne crois pas* | *qu'* | *il soit arrivé.* | |
| b. *Je ne pense pas* | *qu'* | *elle soit* | *riche.* |
| c. *Il ne croit pas* | *que* | *nous ayons* | *de l'argent.* |

a. I don't believe (that) he has arrived.
b. I don't think (that) she is rich.
c. He doesn't believe (that) we have any money.

## EXERCISES

A. Substitute each of the words or expressions in parentheses for the underlined word or phrase in the model sentence. Write the complete sentence and say it aloud.

1. *Il voudrait aller en France.* (*Amérique, Afrique, Provence, Asie, Europe, Angleterre*)
2. *Il doit aller à Paris.* (*Londres, New-York, Madrid, Buenos Aires, Genève*)
3. *Elle va toujours dans l'Amérique du Sud.* (*l'Amérique du Nord, l'Amérique Centrale, la Suisse française, l'Afrique du Sud*)
4. *Il est revenu hier de New York.* (*Paris, Londres, France, Bretagne, Provence*)
5. *Elle aime voyager en avion.* (*autobus, voiture, train, bateau*)

B. Replace *je* by the other subject pronouns (*tu, il, elle, nous, vous, ils, elles*). Make the necessary changes in the verb forms. Say and write the new sentences.

1. *Croit-il que je sois stupide?*
2. *Il ne pense pas que j'aie de l'argent.*

C. Translate the following sentences into French; then say them aloud.

    1. They went to Italy last year.
    2. There is a beautiful cathedral in Chartres.
    3. In France, people (*on*) speak French.
    4. We received a letter from Québec.
    5. She came back from Paris yesterday.
    6. This wine comes from Portugal.
    7. They always travel by car.
    8. I returned home on foot.
    9. I don't think they are very expensive.
    10. Do you believe that he came yesterday?

D. From among the three choices, select the best translation for the English word or phrase given at the beginning of each sentence. Write the complete sentence, and translate.

    1. (outside of) *Je voudrais voyager _____ Paris.*
       (a) *hors*
       (b) *en dehors de*
       (c) *loin de*

    2. (anywhere) *Vous pouvez aller _____.*
       (a) *n'importe où*
       (b) *de tout*
       (c) *toujours*

    3. (by train) *Vous pouvez y aller _____.*
       (a) *à train*
       (b) *au train*
       (c) *en train*

    4 (road map) *J'ai besoin d' _____.*
       (a) *une route carte*
       (b) *une carte route*
       (c) *une carte routière*

    5. (a lot of time) *Vous gagnerez ainsi _____.*
       (a) *grand temps*
       (b) *un lot de temps*
       (c) *beaucoup de temps*

6. (What) _____ vous avez décidé?
   (a) Qu'est-ce que
   (b) Que
   (c) Quoi

7. (on Sundays) On peut voir les Grandes Eaux seulement _____.
   (a) dimanche
   (b) sur dimanche
   (c) le dimanche

8. (hotel rooms) Voudriez-vous bien nous retenir des _____?
   (a) hôtel chambres
   (b) chambres d'hôtel
   (c) pièces d'hôtel

9. (If you insist) _____ , vous pourrez le faire.
   (a) Si vous tenez
   (b) Si vous en tenez
   (c) Si vous y tenez

# LESSON 13

## VOITURES—LOCATION
## CARS—RENTAL

### A. DIALOGUE

*Location d'une voiture.*   Renting a car.

1. Employé: **Bonjour, messieurs'dames. Qu'est-ce que vous désirez?**
   Good day, sir, ma'am. May I help you?

2. Charles: *Nous voudrions louer une voiture. Quels sont les tarifs?*
   We would like to rent a car. What are the rates?

3. Employé: **Cela dépend du modèle que vous choisissez, monsieur. C'est pour vous deux?**
That depends on the model you choose, sir. It's for the two of you?

4. Jane: **Oui, mais nous avons beaucoup de bagages.**
Yes, but we have a lot of baggage.

5. Employé: **Une Renault° 19 fera votre affaire, alors. Quatre places, cinq portières . . .**
A Renault 19 will meet your needs, then. Four seats, four doors, plus the trunk . . .

6. Charles: **Est-ce qu'une galerie sera fournie gratuitement?**
Will a luggage rack be furnished free of charge?

7. Employé: **Oui, monsieur. Et pour la location, vous pouvez payer *par jour* ou *par semaine*.**
Yes, sir. And as for the rental, you can pay by the day or by the week.

8. Jane: **Qu'est-ce qui est inclus dans le tarif?**
What's included in the rate?

9. Employé: **L'huile, le graissage, les frais d'entretien normal—aussi l'assurance tous risques et toutes les taxes.**
The oil, the lubrication, the costs of normal upkeep—also full insurance and all the taxes.

10. Jane: **L'essence et le kilométrage° ne sont pas compris?**
Gas and mileage are not included?

11. Employé: **Le kilométrage est illimité, madame. Quant à l'essence, le super ne coûte que cinq francs cinquante (5,50) le litre.°**

Mileage is unlimited, ma'am. As for gas, "super" costs only 5 francs 50 (centimes) a liter.

12. Charles: **Nous payerons quand nous rendrons la voiture, n'est-ce pas?**
We pay when we return the car, don't we?

13. Employé: **Non, monsieur. Le montant est payable à l'avance et une caution est déduite de votre carte de crédit.**
No, sir, the total amount is payable in advance and a deposit is deducted from your credit card.

14. Charles: **Et pour la livraison de la voiture?**
And what about the delivery of the car?

15. Employé: **À Paris, il n'y a qu'un petit supplément de 20 francs. On vous la livre directement à l'hôtel.**
In Paris, there's only a small supplementary charge of 20 francs. We deliver it to you right at the hotel.

16. Jane: **Mais si on la laisse ailleurs?**
But if we leave it somewhere else?

17. Employé: **Dans ce cas-là, les frais de retour dépendent de la distance entre l'endroit où vous prenez la voiture et celui où vous la déposez.**
In that case, the charge for returning the car depends on the distance between the place you take the car and the place you leave it.

18. Charles: *Qu'est-ce qu'il nous faut* **comme papiers?**
What do we need in the way of documents?

19. Employé: *Il ne vous faut qu'*un permis de conduire valable, monsieur. Nous fournissons tous les autres documents.

You need only a valid driver's license, sir. We furnish all the other documents.

20. Charles: **Très bien. Nous allons y réfléchir ce soir, et si nous décidons de louer une voiture au lieu d'en emprunter une, nous reviendrons demain.**
Very good. We'll think about it tonight, and if we decide to rent a car we'll come back tomorrow.

21. Jane: **Nous avons un ami qui nous a dit qu'il pourrait nous prêter sa nouvelle voiture.**
We've got a friend who told us that he could lend us his new car.

22. Employé: **Je comprends. Alors, à demain peut-être.**
I understand. Then, maybe I'll see you tomorrow.

*Sur la route.* On the road.

23. Charles: **Nous aurions dû rester sur l'autoroute. Nous sommes complètement perdus! Et on va se retrouver en panne° d'essence!**
We should have stayed on the highway. We're completely lost! And we're going to be out of gas!

24. Jane: **Mais tu m'as dit que tu voulais avoir un aperçu de la campagne française. On y est! Je ne vois que des arbres, des champs . . .**
Well, you told me that you wanted to see a little bit of the French countryside. We're here! I don't see anything but trees, fields . . .

25. Charles: **Et quelqu'un qui fait du vélo!**
And someone on a bike!

26. Jane: **Heureusement. Pourvu qu'elle connaisse la région!**
Luckily. Let's hope that she knows the area.

27. Charles: **Excusez-moi, mais nous sommes** *à quelle*
    *distance* **de la station-service la plus proche?**
    Excuse me, but how far are we from the nearest gas
    station?

28. Cycliste: **Vous avez de la chance. Elle n'est qu'à**
    **environ dix minutes d'ici.**
    You're in luck. It's only about ten minutes from
    here.

29. Jane: **Il faut continuer tout droit?**
    Do we keep going straight ahead?

30. Cycliste: **Non, non. Faites demi-tour et allez jus-**
    **qu'aux premiers feux. Là vous tournez à droite et**
    **au prochain carrefour, vous tournez à gauche.**
    **La station-service est juste là, sur la gauche.**
    No, no. You make a U-turn and continue until the
    first traffic light. There you turn right and at the next
    intersection turn left. The gas station is right there,
    on the left.

31. Charles: **Vous nous avez sauvé la vie!**
    You've saved our lives!

32. Jane: **Merci, Madame.**
    Thank you, ma'am.

33. Cycliste: **De rien. Bonne journée!**
    Don't mention it. Have a good day!

34. Jane: **Charles, l'autoroute est peut-être moins in-**
    **téressante, mais c'est beaucoup plus difficile de**
    **s'y perdre.**
    Charles, maybe the highway is less interesting, but
    it's much more difficult to get lost there.

## B. NOTES

5. *Renault* is a brand of French car. Some others are Citroën and Peugeot. In France, cars are generally designated not only by the name, but also by the model number (e.g., *une Renault 19*).

10. *kilométrage:* Distances are measured in kilometers. A kilometer is five-eighths of a mile.

11. *litre:* a measure of liquid capacity, a little over a quart. Gasoline is sold by the liter and is considerably more expensive than in the U.S.

23. *en panne* is a useful expression when describing problems:
    *être en panne*—to be stuck, to be out of order
    *être en panne de*—to be out of (*essence,* etc.)
    *laisser quelqu'un en panne*—to leave someone in a bind
    *tomber en panne*—to break down

## C. GRAMMAR AND USAGE

1. The interrogative pronoun *quel*

| Quel | être | |
|------|------|------|
| a. *Quel* | *est* | *votre projet?* |
| b. *Quelle* | *est* | *sa nationalité?* |
| c. *Quels* | *étaient* | *ses conseils?* |
| c. *Quelles* | *sont* | *tes intentions?* |

a. What is your plan?
b. What is his nationality?
c. What were his/her suggestions? (What was his/her advice?)
d. What are your intentions?

2. The interrogative adjective *quel*

| *Quel* | Noun | Verb |
|---|---|---|
| a. *Quel* | *âge* | *avez-vous?* |
| b. *Quelle* | *heure* | *est-il?* |
| c. *Quels* | *livres* | *avez-vous lus?* |
| d. *Quelles* | *maisons* | *aimez-vous?* |

a. How old are you?
b. What time is it?
c. What books have you read?
d. What houses do you like?

Note:
  • In c., the past participle agrees with *livres,* which is
    the preceding direct object. See Lesson 15.

The interrogative pronoun *quel* after prepositions:

| Preposition | *quel* | Noun | |
|---|---|---|---|
| a. *À* | *quel* | *moment* | *est-il arrivé?* |
| b. *Pour* | *quelle* | *raison* | *est-elle partie?* |
| c. *Avec* | *quels* | *amis* | *êtes-vous sortis?* |
| d. *De* | *quelles* | *histoires* | *parlez-vous?* |

a. At what moment did he arrive?
b. For what reason did she leave?
c. With what friends did you go out?
d. Of what stories are you speaking?

3. *Par* in expressions of time

| Expression | *par* | Unit of time |
|---|---|---|
| a. *Il y va deux fois* | *par* | *semaine.* |
| b. *Nous mangeons trois fois* | *par* | *jour.* |
| c. *Il paie les impôts une fois* | *par* | *an.* |

a. He goes there twice a week.
b. We eat three times a day.
c. He pays taxes once a year.

4. Forms of *falloir* with indirect object pronoun

|        | Ind. Obj. Pron. | *falloir* | Noun as Dir. Obj.     |
|--------|-----------------|-----------|-----------------------|
| a. *Il* | *me*           | *faut*    | *un livre.*           |
| b. *Il* | *me*           | *faudra*  | *deux billets.*       |
| c. *Il* | *vous*         | *faudra*  | *de l'argent.*        |
| d. *Il* | *lui*          | *fallait* | *une nouvelle voiture.* |

a. I need a book.
b. I'll need two tickets.
c. You'll need some money.
d. He needed a new car.

5. *Penser* + infinitive—to think of, to consider, to intend

|         | *penser*      | Infinitive |                |
|---------|---------------|------------|----------------|
| a. *Que* | *pensez-vous* | *faire*    | *demain?*      |
| b.      | *Je pense*    | *voyager*  | *en Italie.*   |
| c. *Nous* | *pensions*  | *louer*    | *des chambres.* |

a. What do you intend to do (are you thinking of doing) tomorrow?
b. I intend to travel (am considering traveling) to Italy.
c. We intended to rent (thought of renting) some rooms.

EXERCISES

A. Substitute each of the words in parentheses for the underlined word in the model sentence. Write each new
sentence and say it aloud.

1. *Quelle est votre ambition?* (*idée, profession, natio-
nalité, adresse, préférence*)
2. *Quels livres as-tu lus?* (*a-t-il, a-t-elle, avez-vous, ont-
ils, ont-elles*)
3. *Elle pense partir demain.* (*rentrer, sortir, venir, téléphoner, commencer*)

B. Complete the sentences below by placing *par jour* at the
end of each one, and translate.

1. *Il mange trois fois.*
2. *Ils se voient deux fois.*
3. *Elles sortent une fois.*
4. *Il me téléphone plusieurs fois.*
5. *Nous les changeons une fois.*

C. Transform each of the following sentences according to
the model:
*J'ai besoin de cent francs./Il me faut cent francs.*

1. *Nous avons besoin de trois livres.*
2. *Il a besoin d'un ami.*
3. *Ils ont besoin d'argent.*[1]
4. *Vous avez besoin de conseils.*[1]
5. *Elle a besoin de sommeil.*[1]

---

[1] Remember that *de* is not followed by the definite article in *avoir
besoin de* unless the noun is qualified. However, *de* requires the
article after *Il faut.*
Contrast: *Il a besoin de médicament.* } He needs medicine.
        *Il lui faut du médicament.*
But: *Il a besoin du médicament que j'ai acheté.*
    He needs the medicine that I bought.

D. Translate the following sentences into French. Then say them aloud.

1. What's her question?
2. What's your problem?
3. What were his reasons?
4. Which dress do you prefer?
5. Which car did he buy?
6. What trip will they take?
7. I see her once a year.
8. Children go to school five days a week.
9. How many times a day do you eat?
10. I need a car for my work.
11. He needed money.
12. Do you need a new car?
13. She intended to work last night.
14. What do you intend to do Saturday?
15. I intend to go to the movies.

E. From among the three choices, select the one that correctly renders the English word or phrase given at the beginning of each sentence, write the complete sentence, and translate.

1. (the two of you) *C'est pour* _____.
   (a) *les deux de vous*
   (b) *deux de vous*
   (c) *vous deux*
2. (were thinking about) *Nous* _____ *aller en Espagne.*
   (a) *allons croire de*
   (b) *avons pensé de*
   (c) *pensions*
3. (depends on) *Cela* _____ *tarif.*
   (a) *vaut le*
   (b) *dépend sur le*
   (c) *dépend du*

4. (will meet your needs) *Une Peugeot 504* _____.
   (a) *rencontrera vos besoins*
   (b) *vous le fera*
   (c) *fera votre affaire*
5. (What) _____ *est inclus dans le tarif?*
   (a) *Quel*
   (b) *Quoi*
   (c) *Qu'est-ce qui*
6. (As for) _____ *l'essence, c'est trop cher.*
   (a) *Comme pour*
   (b) *Quant à*
   (c) *Quant pour*
7. (return) *Nous payerons quand nous* _____ *la voiture.*
   (a) *rendrons*
   (b) *rendons*
   (c) *retournons*
8. (elsewhere) *Mais si on la laisse* _____?
   (a) *autre place*
   (b) *d'ailleurs*
   (c) *ailleurs*
9. (out of) *Nous sommes* _____ *essence.*
   (a) *hors d'*
   (b) *pannés d'*
   (c) *en panne d'*
10. (Fill it up) _____ *du super, s'il vous plaît.*
    (a) *Remplissez-le*
    (b) *Faite le plein*
    (c) *Prendez-la pleine*

# LESSON 14

## À LA STATION-SERVICE
## AT THE SERVICE STATION

A. DIALOGUE

1. Mécanicien: **Bonjour, monsieur, 'dame. Vous désirez?**
   Hello. What can I do for you?

2. Jane: **Le plein, s'il vous plaît.**
   Fill it up, please.

3. Mécanicien: **De l'ordinaire ou du super?**
   With regular or with super?

4. Jane: **Quand j'appuie sur l'accélerateur, il y a un drôle de bruit° dans le moteur. Faites le plein du super, s'il vous plaît.**
   When I step on the gas, there's a strange noise in the motor. Fill it with super, please.

5. Mécanicien: **Très bien, madame.**
   Okay.

6. Charles: **Voudriez-vous aussi vérifier la pression des pneus? Nous allons faire un long voyage.**
   Could you also check the pressure in the tires? We're going to take a long trip.

7. Jane: **Et par moments sur la route, je sentais la voiture qui dérapait un peu.**
   And every now and then on the road I felt the car skid a little.

8. Mécanicien: **Volontiers. Mais, votre pneu avant est crevé,° semble-t-il.**
   Gladly. But, your front tire seems to be flat.

9. Jane: **Comment! J'ai un pneu crevé?**
   What? I've got a flat?

10. Mécanicien: **C'était probablement causé par un clou ou par un morceau de verre. C'est sans aucun doute° à cause de ça que la voiture dérapait.**
    It was probably caused by a nail or by a piece of glass. It's certainly because of that that the car was skidding.

11. Charles: **Il y a une roue de secours dans le coffre.**
    There's a spare tire in the trunk.

12. Mécanicien: **Ah, bon! Je vais vous le remplacer, alors. Et comme vous faites un long voyage, je vais vérifier les bougies et la batterie.**
    Good. I'll change it for you, then. And since you're taking a long trip, I'll check the spark plugs and the battery.

13. Jane: **Mettez un peu d'eau dans le radiateur. Le moteur chauffait tout à l'heure.**
    Also, put a little water in the radiator. The motor was heating up a little while ago.

14. Mécanicien: **Très bien, madame. Et si vous voulez faire le graissage, et faire changer l'huile . . .**
    No problem, ma'am. And if you'd like to have a lube job done and the oil changed . . .

15. Jane: **D'accord. C'est la voiture de notre ami et on veut être sûr que tout marche bien.**
    Yes, let's do it. It's our friend's car and we want to be sure that everything is okay.

16. Charles: **Oui, il vient de l'acheter il y a quelques mois.**
    Yes, he just bought it a few months ago.

17. Mécanicien: **Je vois qu'il y a plusieurs choses à réparer.**
I see that there are several things to be repaired.

18. Charles: **Plusieurs choses à réparer? On a abimé° la voiture de Michel!**
Several things to be repaired? We've ruined Michel's car!

19. Mécanicien: **Pas du tout, monsieur. On a souvent ces petits ennuis, même au début.**
Not at all. People often have these little annoyances, even in the beginning.

20. Charles: **Vous avez raison. Faudra-t-il qu'on la laisse au garage?**
You're right. Will we have to leave it in a garage?

21. Mécanicien: **Pendant quelques heures, au moins, si vous voulez que je fasse une remise en état. Et comme vous faites un voyage, je peux la commencer tout de suite.**
For a few hours at least, if you want me to put it into shape. And since you're taking a trip, I can start it right away.

22. Jane: **Excellent! Mais j'espère qu'il ne faudra pas commander des pièces de rechange.**
Great! But I hope it won't be necessary to order spare parts.

23. Charles: **Faites seulement le strict nécessaire.**
Do only what's absolutely necessary.

24. Mécanicien: **Très bien, alors. Si vous voulez repasser dans quelques heures, tout sera prêt.**
Very good. If you would like to come back in a few hours, everything will be ready.

25. Jane: **C'est parfait, alors. Vous êtes très gentil.**
That's perfect. You're very kind.

26. Mécanicien: **Nous faisons toujours de notre mieux pour satisfaire nos clients.**
We always do our best to satisfy our clients.

27. Charles: **À plus tard, monsieur.**
We'll see you later.

28. Mécanicien: **À plus tard, monsieur, 'dame.**
See you later.

29. Jane: **C'est une bonne chose qu'il ne soit pas trop occupé. On a vraiment de la chance!**
It's a good thing that he's not too busy. We're really lucky.

30. Charles: **Oui, tu as raison. Mais qu'est-ce qu'on va faire dans ce petit village pendant qu'il répare la voiture?**
Yes, you're right. But what are we going to do in this little village while he repairs the car?

31. Jane: **Voyons. Il est midi et demi, il doit y avoir une boulangerie au centre, et en arrivant j'ai vu un beau champ à côté d'une rivière.**
Let's see. It's half past noon, there must be a bakery in the center, and on our way here I saw a beautiful field next to a stream.

32. Charles: **Un pique-nique, alors?**
A picnic, then?

## B. NOTES

4. *un drôle de bruit:* a funny (kind of) noise. In the expression *un drôle de,* or *une drôle de* for feminine nouns, the word *drôle* means "strange" or "peculiar." However, when *drôle* follows the noun it describes, it means "funny." Compare *une histoire drôle,* "a funny story" with *une drôle d'histoire,* "a strange story."

8. The verb *crever* means "to burst" or "to split," but it also has many idiomatic usages. Study the following examples:

   | | |
   |---|---|
   | *J'ai un pneu crevé.* | I have a flat tire. |
   | *Nous sommes crevés!* | We're exhausted! |
   | *Je crève de faim!* | I'm starving to death! |
   | *Elle m'a crevé le coeur.* | She broke my heart. |
   | *Ils se crèvent au travail.* | They're working themselves to death. |
   | *Tu as crevé de rire.* | You burst out laughing. |

10. Be careful of the expression *sans doute*. It does not mean "without doubt." *Sans doute* means "probably," and *sans aucun doute* means "without a doubt" or "assuredly."

18. *Abîmé*, from the verb *abîmer*, is a useful expression when describing things that are ruined, damaged, or in poor condition.

## C. GRAMMAR AND USAGE

1. *Y*—there; in it; in there; about it; etc. (The equivalent depends on the context.)

|  | Prep. of Place | Place |  | y | Verb | Object |
|---|---|---|---|---|---|---|
| a. *Je vais* | *à* | *Paris.* | *J'* | *y* | *vais.* |  |
| b. *Nous sommes* | *à* | *l'école.* | *Nous* | *y* | *sommes.* |  |
| c. *Je mettrai 2 litres* | *dans* | *le réservoir.* | *J'* | *y* | *mettrai* | *2 litres* |
| d. *Il est resté* | *chez* | *moi.* | *Il* | *y* | *est resté.* |  |
| e. *J'ai mis le livre* | *sur* | *le bureau.* | *J'* | *y* | *ai mis* | *le livre* |

a. I'm going to Paris.          I'm going there.
b. We are at school.            We are there.
c. I'll put two liters in       I'll put 2 liters in it.
   the tank.
d. He stayed at my house.       He stayed there (in it).
e. I put the book on the        I put the book on it.
   desk.

| *Imperative* | Prep. | Place | Imperative | y |
|---|---|---|---|---|
| a. *Va* | *à* | *l'école.* | *Vas-* | *y.* |
| b. *Allez* | *au* | *magasin.* | *Allez-* | *y.* |

a. *Go to school.*          Go there.
b. *Go to the store.*       Go there.

Note:

• The pronoun *y* is placed before the verb except in positive imperative sentences. Contrast:

| *Allons-y!* | Let's go there! |
| *N'y allons pas!* | Let's not go there! |
| *Nous y allons.* | We're going there. |

Study the following contrasts:

a.
| *Je pense à Jean.* | *Je pense à lui.* |
| *Je pense à mon travail.* | *J'y pense.* |

b.
| *Je réponds à Marie.* | *Je lui réponds.* |
| *Je réponds à la lettre.* | *J'y réponds.* |

c.
| *J'obéis à ma mère.* | *Je lui obéis.* |
| *J'obéis à la loi.* | *J'y obéis.* |

a. I'm thinking of John.          I'm thinking of him.
   I'm thinking of my             I'm thinking of it.
   work.
b. I answer Marie.                I answer her.
   I answer the letter.           I answer it.
c. I obey my mother.              I obey her.
   I obey the law.                I obey it.

Note:
- Use *y* to replace *à* + an inanimate object. With animate beings, use the indirect object pronoun.

2. *Aller* + infinitive—going to; will and shall future; immediate future.

|  | *aller* | Infinitive |  |
|---|---|---|---|
| a. *Il* | *va* | *venir* | *demain.* |
| b. *Nous* | *allons* | *sortir* | *plus tard.* |
| c. *Elles* | *vont* | *acheter* | *des robes.* |

a. He's going to come tomorrow. (He'll come tomorrow. He's coming tomorrow.)
b. We're going to go out later. (We'll go out later.)
c. They're going to buy some dresses. (They'll buy some dresses.)

3. Forms of irregular adjectives.
   Study these contrasts:

| Feminine | Masculine |
|---|---|
| a. *une longue promenade* | *un long voyage* |
| b. *Elle est gentille.* | *Il est gentil.* |
| c. *Elle est heureuse.* | *Il est heureux.* |
| d. *Elle est active.* | *Il est actif.* |
| e. *Elle est neuve.* | *Il est neuf.* |
| f. *Elle est fière.* | *Il est fier.* |
| g. *Elle est étrangère.* | *Il est étranger.* |
| h. *Elle est belle.* | *Il est beau.* |
| i. *Elle est italienne.* | *Il est italien.* |
| j. *Elle est sèche.* | *Il est sec.* |

| | |
|---|---|
| a. a long walk | a long trip |
| b. She is nice. | He is nice. |
| c. She is happy. | He is happy. |
| d. She is active. | He is active. |
| e. It is new. | It is new. |
| f. She is proud. | He is proud. |
| g. She is foreign. | He is foreign. |
| h. She is beautiful. | He is handsome. |
| i. She is Italian. | He is Italian. |
| j. It is dry. | It is dry. |

Note:

- Remember that all nouns, both animate and inanimate, have gender in French. Therefore, *il* and *elle* are translated as "he" and "she" when they refer to *Paul* and *Marie,* but when they refer to *"un pantalon"* and *"une robe,"* they are translated as "it."

## EXERCISES

A. Replace the underlined phrases in each of the following sentences by *y*, *lui*, or *leur*. Write the complete sentence, say aloud, and translate.

Example: *Je vais à Londres./J'y vais.*

1. *Elle restera à Rome.*
2. *Je passerai mes vacances à la mer.*
3. *Il parle à Jean.*
4. *J'ai trouvé mes chaussettes sous le lit.*
5. *Il est entré dans le magasin.*
6. *Elle lit le roman à l'enfant.*
7. *Il a posé une question aux messieurs.*
8. *Il a passé trois semaines chez sa tante.*

B. Transform the affirmative to the negative.

Example: *J'y vais./Je n'y vais pas.*

1. *J'y suis.*
2. *J'y reste.*
3. *Il y obéit.*
4. *Elle y répond.*
5. *Nous y pensons.*
6. *Allez-y.*
7. *Vas-y.*
8. *Allons-y.*
9. *Répondons-y.*
10. *Entrez-y.*

C. Transform the future sentences below to a verb phrase with *aller*, and translate.

Example: *Il viendra demain./Il va venir demain.*

1. *Elle partira ce soir.*
2. *Ils sortiront plus tard.*
3. *Elles arriveront à sept heures.*
4. *Nous ferons une promenade.*
5. *Elle verra sa sœur demain.*

D. Translate the following sentences into French; then say
   them aloud.

   1. I'm going there in three weeks.
   2. We stayed there for (*pendant*) a month.
   3. Her trip? She thinks about it every day.
   4. We're going to leave tomorrow.
   5. Is she going to come later?
   6. I'm going to replace the flat tire.
   7. It's a long story.
   8. What a beautiful car!
   9. He isn't very happy today.

E. From among the three choices, select the best translation
   for the English word or phrase given. Write the complete
   sentence, and translate.

   1. (exactly) *Je ne sais pas* _____.
      (a) *justement*
      (b) *juste*
      (c) *au juste*
   2. (funny) *Il y a* _____ *bruit.*
      (a) *un étrange*
      (b) *un drôle de*
      (c) *un drôle*
   3. (still) *Je croyais en avoir* _____ *quelques litres.*
      (a) *tranquille*
      (b) *chaque*
      (c) *encore*
   4. (across) *Nous allons faire un voyage* _____ *les
      Alpes.*
      (a) *á travers*
      (b) *en face*
      (c) *par*
   5. (a spare tire) *Il y a* _____ *dans le coffre.*
      (a) *un pneu maigre*
      (b) *une roue de secours*
      (c) *une roue de rechange*

6. (if necessary) *Je vais vérifier les bougies* _____.
   (a) *s'il faut*
   (b) *s'il nécessaire*
   (c) *s'il le faut.*

7. (new) [the car] *Elle est* _____.
   (a) *neuf*
   (b) *nouvelle*
   — (c) *neuve*

8. (Not at all) _____, *monsieur.*
   (a) *Pas du tout*
   (b) *Pas à tout*
   (c) *Pas tout*

9. (I'll need) _____ *la voiture.*
   (a) *J'aurai besoin de*
   (b) *J'aurai faut de*
   (c) *J'aurai besoin*

10. (our best) *Nous faisons* _____.
    (a) *notre meilleur*
    (b) *notre mieux*
    — (c) *de notre mieux*

# LESSON 15

## L'EUROTUNNEL
## THE CHUNNEL

### A. DIALOGUE

*À la Gare du Nord.*   At the Gare du Nord.

1. Charles: **Voilà l'escalier mécanique qui mène au°
   terminal de l'Eurostar.°**
   Here's the escalator that goes to the Eurostar terminal.

2. Jane: **Oui, prenons ce chariot. On peut mettre tous
   nos bagages dessus, et regarde—il s'adapte à l'escalier. On n'a plus besoin de les porter.**

Yes, let's take this cart. We can put all our luggage on it, and look—it fits onto the escalator. We don't need to carry it anymore.

3. Charles: **Ouf! Quel soulagement! Et ils sont gratuits.**
   Whew! What a relief! And they're free.

4. Jane: **Que c'est aéré et lumineux.**
   How airy and bright it is.

5. Charles: **Quelle difference entre cette atmosphère et celle du reste de la gare. Maintenant je sais pourquoi *j'en ai si souvent entendu parler*.**
   What a difference between this atmosphere and the rest of the station's. Now I know why I've heard about it so often.

6. Jane: **Oh là là, regarde la queue. Nous en aurons pour longtemps° sans doute.**
   Wow, look at that line. It'll probably take us a long time.

7. Charles: **Au fait,*j'ai entendu dire que* tout était très rapide et efficace ici.**
   As a matter of fact, I've heard that everything here is quick and efficient.

*Dans le train.*   In the train.

8. Jane: **Tu avais raison. Nous voici bien installé.**
   You were right. Here we are, all settled in.

9. Charles: **Heureusement ... Est-ce que tu te souviens de notre dernier voyage? L'agent d'immigration avait examiné nos passeports comme si nous étions des criminels!**
   Fortunately ... Do you remember our last trip? The

immigration officer examined our passports as if we were criminals!

10. Jane: **Et il *voulait qu'on ouvre* toutes nos valises! J'ai vraiment cru qu'on ne nous laisserait pas partir!**
And he wanted us to open all of our suitcases! I really thought they weren't going to let us leave!

11. Charles: **Oui, et *on les a fouillées* comme si nous étions des contrebandiers.**
Yes, and they searched them as if we were smugglers.

12. Jane: **Et les formalités! On nous a fait remplir tant de fiches et de formulaires. En fin de compte, nous avons mis presque deux heures.°**
And the red tape! They made us fill out so many slips and forms. In the end, it took us almost two hours.

13. Charles: **Avec la C.E.° tout est plus simple. Les Européens ne doivent plus montrer leur passeport puisqu'ils appartiennent tous à la même communauté. Il n'y a que nous autres, les non-Européens, qui devons° les montrer.**
With the European Union, everything is simpler. Europeans no longer have to show their passports, since they all belong to the same union. Only we non-Europeans have to show them.

14. Jane: **Ah, *je vois venir une marchande de journaux.* Madame, je voudrais *Le Monde* s'il vous plaît.**
Ah, I see a newspaper vendor coming. Ma'am, I'd like a copy of *Le Monde*, please.

15. Employée: **Voilà, madame.**
Here you are, ma'am.

16. Jane: **Je vous dois combien?**
How much do I owe you?

17. Employée: **Rien, madame. Les journaux sont gratuits.**
Nothing ma'am. Newspapers are free.

18. Jane: **Ah! Et maintenant, tout ce qu'il me faut c'est un sandwich et je serai au comble du bonheur.**
Ah! And now, all I need is a sandwich and I'll be in heaven.

19. Charles: **Voilà ton côté américain. Moi, un Perrier me suffira si tu me permets de lire** *Le Monde* **après toi.**
There's your American side. I'd be happy with a Perrier if you let me read your copy of *Le Monde* after you.

20. Jane: **Cela va de soi, Charles. Regarde, voici la marchande de sandwichs. Quand on parle du loup, on en voit la queue!**
That goes without saying, Charles. Look, here's the sandwich vendor now. Speak of the devil!

21. Charles: **Madame, s'il vous plaît, je voudrais un Perrier.**
Excuse me, ma'am, I'd like a Perrier.

22. Jane: **Et pour moi, un jambon-beurre, s'il vous plaît. Merci, madame.**
And for me, a ham and butter sandwich, please. Thank you, ma'am.

23. Charles: **Tu sais, Jane, il faut trois heures pour aller de Paris à Londres, mais on sera dans le tunnel même pendant trente minutes seulement!**
You know, Jane, it takes three hours to go from Paris to London, but we'll be in the tunnel itself for only thirty minutes.

24. Jane: **Heureusement pour les claustrophobes!**
Lucky for the claustrophobics.

25. Charles: **Ça alors! Nous sommes arrivés si vite que je n'ai pas pu terminer le journal!**
Wow! We arrived so fast I couldn't even finish the paper!

26. Jane: **C'était si rapide que nous aurons toute la journée pour jouer les touristes. Descendons les valises.**
It was so fast that we'll have the whole day in London to tour the city. Let's get our suitcases.

27. Charles: **Mettons-nous en route!**
Let's hit the road!

## B. NOTES

1. *mener à* is an expression that means "lead to," as in: *Ce chemin mène au jardin.* This path leads to the garden.
*L'Eurostar* is the train that goes from the Gare du Nord in Paris to Waterloo Station in London in three hours. The fastest train in the world, it travels at speeds of up to 180 miles per hour.

6. *En avoir pour longtemps* is a colloquial expression that means "to have a long wait."

12. *Mettre deux heures* means "to take two hours." Study the following example: *Nous avons mis trois heures pour aller en Bretagne.* It took us three hours to travel to Brittany. This can also be said, *Il nous a pris trois heures pour aller en Bretagne.*

13. *La Communauté Européenne,* or *la C. E.,* is the name of the European Union.

*Il n'y a que nous . . . qui devons les montrer:* Note that the verb *devoir* agrees with *nous*, the subject to which it refers. Examples of this construction:

| | |
|---|---|
| *C'est moi qui l'ai dit.* | I'm the one who said that. |
| *C'est toi qui vas au magasin.* | You're the one who's going to the store. |

## C. GRAMMAR AND USAGE

1. *Entendre, voir* + infinitive

| Subject | *entendre/voir* | Infinitive | Complement |
|---|---|---|---|
| a. *J'* | *ai entendu* | *parler* | *de cela.* |
| b. *Il* | *a entendu* | *dire* | *cela.* |
| c. *Elle* | *a entendu* | *dire* | *qu'il était malade.* |
| d. *Nous* | *avons vu* | *venir* | *le marchand.* |
| e. *Nous* | *les entendons* | *jouer.* | |

a. I heard that spoken of
b. He heard that (said).
c. She heard (it said) that he was sick.
d. We saw the vendor come.
e. We hear them playing.

2. *Vouloir* + the subjunctive

| *Vouloir* | *que* | Subject | Subjunctive | Complement |
|---|---|---|---|---|
| a. *Voulez-vous* | *que* | *j'* | *ouvre* | *les valises?* |
| b. *Je veux* | *qu'* | *elle* | *vienne* | *me voir.* |
| c. *Il ne veut pas* | *que* | *vous* | *soyez* | *en retard.* |
| d. *Ne voulez-vous pas* | *qu'* | *il* | *sache* | *la vérité?* |

a. Do you want me to open (lit.: that I open) the bags?
b. I want her to come (lit.: that she come) to see me.

    c. He doesn't want you to be (lit.: that you be) late.
    d. Don't you want him to know (lit.: that he know) the truth?

Note:

- The infinitive (not the subjunctive) is used when the subject of the main verb and of the subordinate verb are the same. Contrast the following:

| | |
|---|---|
| *Je veux venir vous voir.* | I want to come to see you. |
| *Je veux qu'il vienne vous voir.* | I want him to come to see you. |

3. Agreement of the past participle

With *avoir:*

| | |
|---|---|
| a. *Nous avons vu les hommes.* | We saw the men. |
| b. *Nous les avons vus.* | We saw them. |
| c. *Les hommes que nous avons vus sont nos frères.* | The men whom we saw are our brothers. |
| d. *Les femmes que nous avons vues sont nos sœurs.* | The women whom we saw are our sisters. |
| e. *Quels hommes avez-vous vus?* | What men have you seen? |
| f. *Quelles femmes avez-vous vues?* | What women have you seen? |
| g. *Combien d'hommes avez-vous vus?* | How many men have you seen? |
| h. *J'en ai vu trois.* | I've seen three of them. |
| i. *Combien de femmes avez-vous vues?* | How many women have you seen? |
| j. *J'en ai vu trois.* | I've seen three of them. |
| k. *Je les lui ai donné(e)s.* | I gave them to him. |

Note:

- Past participles of verbs conjugated with *avoir* agree
  in number and gender with the direct object only when
  it precedes the verb. There is never any agreement
  with *en,* however.

With *être:*

a. ***Nous sommes arrivés***     We arrived yesterday.
***hier.***

b. ***Elles étaient sorties***     They had gone out very
***de très bonne heure.***     early.

c. ***Ils sont restés***     They stayed a long time.
***longtemps.***

Note:

- Past participles of verbs conjugated with *être* (except
  reflexive verbs) agree in number and gender with the
  subject. Refer to Lesson 8 to review material on use of
  *être.*

  Reflexive and reciprocal verbs:

a. ***Nous nous sommes***     We washed ourselves.
***lavés.***

b. ***Nous nous sommes***     We washed our hands.
***lavé les mains.***

c. ***Nous nous sommes***     We saw each other.
***vus.***

d. ***Nous nous sommes***     We spoke to each other.
***parlé.***

Note:

- Past participles of reflexive and reciprocal verbs agree
  with the ~~direct~~ object only, and only when it precedes
  the verb. In example b., *les mains* is the direct object,
  but it follows the verb. In example d., there is no
  agreement because *nous* is an indirect object pronoun.

4. Verbs ending in *-cer*

| | |
|---|---|
| *je commence* | *nous commençons* |
| *tu commences* | *vous commencez* |
| *il* ⎫ *commence* | *ils* ⎫ *commencent* |
| *elle* ⎭ | *elles* ⎭ |

Note:
- For other tenses, see Regular Verb Charts.
- *commencer à*—to begin to
- Similarly conjugated are: *avancer, menacer, annoncer, placer, prononcer, remplacer.*

5. Verbs ending in *-ger*

| | |
|---|---|
| *je mange* | *nous mangeons* |
| *tu manges* | *vous mangez* |
| *il* ⎫ *mange* | *ils* ⎫ *mangent* |
| *elle* ⎭ | *elles* ⎭ |

Note:
- For other tenses, see Regular Verb Charts.
- Similarly conjugated are: *arranger, corriger, songer, changer, nager, partager.*

## EXERCISES

A. Substitute each of the words in parentheses for the word or expression in the model sentence. Write the complete sentence and say aloud.

1. *Nous avons entendu parler de cela. (Jean, Marie, cette pièce, ce film, ces livres, ces histoires, ceux-là, M. Dupont)*
2. *Il a vu venir l'agent (le mécanicien, l'employé, le professeur, la femme, les ouvreuses)*
3. *Il ne veut pas que vous soyez en retard. (malade, paresseuse, fatiguée, triste, malheureuse, active)*
4. *Ils sont partis hier. (rentrés, arrivés, venus, sortis, tombés, retournés, morts)*

5. *(les livres) Nous les avons lus.* *(vus, écrits, achetés, regardés, cherchés, admirés)*
6. *(les femmes) Il les a vues.* *(regardées, cherchées, admirées, aimées)*

B. Expand the clauses listed below as indicated:

- Place *J'ai entendu dire* in front of each of the following, write, say, and translate:

1. *qu'elle était arrivée.*
2. *que vous étiez malade.*
3. *qu'ils étaient très pauvres.*
4. *que tu étais parti hier.*
5. *qu'il ne voulait pas venir*

- Place *Il ne veut pas* in front of each of the following, write, say, and translate.

6. *que vous dormiez en classe.*
7. *qu'elle sache la vérité.*
8. *que nous parlions trop fort.*
9. *que je fasse ce voyage.*
10. *qu'ils aillent à Paris.*
11. *que je finisse ce travail.*
12. *qu'elles apprennent cette nouvelle*

C. Translate the following sentences into French. Then say them aloud.

1. Have you heard of this book?
2. I heard that she will leave tomorrow.
3. I see the vendor coming.
4. He doesn't want me to be sad.
5. Do you want me to come at three o'clock?
6. I want you to leave immediately!
7. The books I read were excellent.
8. I read them last year.
9. She arrived late.
10. We met each other, but we didn't write to each other.

11. Let's eat together.
12. I was beginning to read when he came in.
13. We are beginning to get tired (lit.: to tire ourselves).
14. She was eating slowly.

D. From among the three choices, select the best translation for the English word or phrase given, write the complete sentence, and translate.

1. (line) *Regarde cette _____!*
   (a) *ligne*
   (b) *queue*
   (c) *quelle*

2. (between) *C'est le tunnel _____ la France et l'Angleterre.*
   (a) *entre*
   (b) *contre*
   (c) *à travers*

3. (leads) *C'est l'escalier qui _____ au terminal.*
   (a) *va*
   (b) *guide*
   (c) *mène*

4. (heard) *J'ai _____ qu'ils sont efficaces.*
   (a) *entendu*
   (b) *entendu dire*
   (c) *entendu parler*

5. (settled) *Nous voici déjà _____.*
   (a) *settlés*
   (b) *installés*
   (c) *arrangés*

6. (a long time) *Nous en aurons pour _____.*
   (a) *un longtemps*
   (b) *longtemps*
   (c) *beaucoup de temps*

7. (How) _____ *lumineux!*
   (a) *Comment*
   (b) *Que*
   (c) *Qu'est-ce qui*

8. (It took us) _____ *trois heures pour y aller.*
   (a) *Nous avons mis*
   (b) *Il nous a mis*
   (c) *Il nous avons pris*

9. (Do you remember) _____ *notre dernier voyage?*
   (a) *Te souviens-tu de*
   (b) *Te souviens-tu*
   (c) *Souviens-toi*

10. (searched) [*les valises*] *On les a* _____.
    (a) *cherchées*
    (b) *fouillé*
    (c) *fouillées*

# LESSON 16

## À LA BANQUE
## AT THE BANK

A. DIALOGUE

*Au guichet de change.*   At the exchange window.

1. Charles: **Est-ce que je peux changer ici un chèque de voyage° de cent dollars?**
   Can I change a hundred-dollar traveler's check here?

2. Caissier: ***Certainement,* monsieur. Vous n'avez qu'à le contresigner.**
   Certainly, sir. You only have to countersign it.

3. Charles: **Quel est le taux du dollar,° monsieur?**
   How much is the dollar, sir?

4. Caissier: **Le taux est cinq francs dix aujourd'hui. Et maintenant, votre passeport, s'il vous plaît.**

The exchange rate is five francs ten today. And now, your passport, please.

5. Charles: **Mon passeport? Pour quoi faire?**
   My passport? What for?

6. Cassier: **Il me faut le numéro de votre passeport, votre nom, et votre adresse pour pouvoir remplir cette fiche.**
   I need the number of your passport, your name, and your address in order to fill out this form.

7. Charles: **Ah! Je comprends! Le voici, monsieur.**
   Ah! I understand! Here it is, sir.

8. Caissier: **Je vous les donne en coupures de 100F?**
   Would you like it in 100-franc bills?

9. Charles: **Donnez-moi des grosses coupures avec quelques petites coupures aussi, s'il vous plaît.**
   Give it to me in large bills with a few small ones too, please.

10. Caissier: **Voilà, monsieur, quatre cent quatre-vingt-neuf francs soixante. Et n'oubliez pas de garder cette fiche.**
    Here you are, sir. Four hundred eighty-nine francs sixty. And don't forget to keep this form.

11. Charles: **Mais ce n'est pas le taux de change. Vous m'avez dit cinq francs dix.**
    But that's not the exchange rate. You told me five francs ten.

12. Caissier: **Oui, Monsieur, mais il y a aussi une commission° de quatre pour cent.**
    Yes, sir, but there's also a four percent commission.

13. Charles: **Ah, oui, d'accord. Et pour un transfert de devises à l'étranger, à qui dois-je m'adresser?°**
    Oh yes, of course. And for a transfer of funds to a foreign account, to whom should I speak?

14. Caissier: **Adressez-vous au Service International, monsieur.**
Go to International Service, sir.

*Au Service International.* At International Service.

15. Mme. Lemaître: **Que puis-je faire pour vous, monsieur?**
How can I help you?

16. Charles: **Je voudrais transférer des devises des États-Unis, et je voudrais faire payer les frais par ma banque à New York.**
I would like to transfer some funds from the United States, and I'd like to have the fees paid by my bank in New York.

17. Mme. Lemaître: *Avant de faire le transfert,* **vous avez deux choses à régler. La première concerne le type de devises que vous voulez envoyer, le franc ou le dollar. Si vous voulez envoyer des francs, il vous faudra payer une commission aux États-Unis. Sinon, vous la paierez ici. La deuxième question concerne les renseignements sur votre banque aux États-Unis.**
Before making the transfer, you have two matters to consider. The first is what currency you want to send—the French franc or the dollar. If you want to send francs, you will have to pay a commission in the United States. If not, you will pay it here. The second matter is information on your bank in America.

18. Charles: **Comment l'argent sera-t-il envoyé?**
How will the money be sent?

19. Mme. Lemaître: **Toutes les transactions sont informatisées ces jours-ci. Vous aurez votre argent dès demain matin.**

All transactions are computerized these days. You'll have your money as early as tomorrow morning.

20. Charles: **Excellent! Et, autre chose encore, en cas de besoin,** *pourrais-je louer un coffre-fort,* **ou bien ouvrir un compte ici?**
Excellent! And, another thing. If I needed to, could I rent a safe-deposit box or open an account here?

21. Mme. Lemaître: **Bien sûr. Nous sommes à votre disposition.**
Of course. We are at your service.

22. Charles: **Qu'est-ce que je dois faire?**
What do I have to do?

23. Mme. Lemaître: **Pour ouvrir un coffre-fort, il suffit de nous donner votre adresse permanente ainsi que votre passeport et vos références bancaires complètes.**
In order to open a safe-deposit box, all you have to do is give us your permanent address as well as your passport and all your bank references.

24. Charles: **D'accord. Et pour le compte en banque?**
All right. And for the bank account?

25. Mme. Lemaître: **Il nous faut les mêmes renseignements mais, en plus, vous devrez déposer une somme d'argent minimum.**
We need the same information but, on top of that, you will have to make a minimum deposit.

26. Charles: **Je vais simplement faire le transfert aujourd'hui.**
I'll just make the transfer today.

27. Mme. Lemaître: *Après avoir rempli le formulaire,* **adressez-vous au guichet 4. Notre représentant s'occupera de° votre transfert.**

After filling out this form, go to window 4. Our representative will take care of your transfer.

28. Charles: **Merci beaucoup, madame. Dois-je m'adresser à vous demain?**
Thank you very much, ma'am. Should I ask for you tomorrow?

29. Mme. Lemaître: **Oui, venez me voir directement.**
Yes, come see me directly.

30. Charles: **Alors, à demain!**
Until tomorrow, then!

## B. NOTES

1. *chèques de voyage:* Traveler's checks are accepted nearly everywhere in the world. They can be changed in banks and in many other stores and commercial establishments. Note that the English-derived term *le traveler's check* is often used in French.

3. *le taux du dollar:* The exchange rate, or *le taux de change,* is posted in all banks and in many newspapers. The rate fluctuates daily, but it also varies from place to place on any given day. Therefore, when exchanging large amounts of money, it is important to look around and compare rates.

12. On top of the fluctuating exchange rate, most establishments will charge a commission for exchanging your currency. This varies from place to place, and again, it is wise to compare.

13. The verb *s'adresser à* means "to go to," "to report to," "to inquire at," or "to see" when referring to official capacities or situations. The expression *adresser la parole à quelqu'un* means "to address someone."

27. The verb *s'occuper de* means "to handle," "to deal with," "to take care of," or "to be responsible for."

## C. GRAMMAR AND USAGE

1. *Avant de* + infinitive = before —ing

|  | *avant de* | Infinitive |  |
|---|---|---|---|
| a. *Mangez* | *avant de* | *partir.* | |
| b. | *Avant de* | *décider,* | *vous devriez réfléchir.* |
| c. *Réfléchissez* | *avant de* | *décider* | *de partir.* |

    a. Eat before leaving.
    b. Before deciding, you should think.
    c. Think before deciding to leave.

Note:
  • *Avant de* + infinitive may start or end a sentence or
    may be embedded in a sentence (Example c., above).

2. Perfect infinitive

$$après + \begin{Bmatrix} avoir \\ \text{or} \\ être \end{Bmatrix} + \begin{matrix} \text{past} \\ \text{participle} \end{matrix} = \begin{cases} \text{after —— ing} \\ \text{after having } \dots \\ \text{after being } \dots \end{cases}$$

| *après* | Obj. Pron. | *avoir/* *être* | Past Part. |  |
|---|---|---|---|---|
| a. *Après* |  | *avoir* | *reçu* | *le chèque, il est parti.* |
| b. *Après* |  | *avoir* | *encaissé* | *le chèque, elle est sortie.* |
| c. *Après* | *les* | *avoir* | *vues,* | *je m'en suis allé(e).* |
| d. *Après* |  | *être* | *rentré,* | *il est venu me voir.* |
| e. *Après* |  | *être* | *arrivés,* | *ils ont dit, "Bonjour."* |
| f. *Après* |  | *être* | *arrivées,* | *elles ont changé de robe.* |
| g. *Après* | *s'* | *être* | *lavée,* | *elle s'est habillée.* |
| h. *Après* | *m'* | *être* | *levé(e),* | *je me suis lavé(e).* |

    a. After receiving the check, he left.
    b. After cashing the check, she went out.

   c. After having seen them (fem.), I went away.

   d. After having returned home, he came to see me.

   e. After arriving (masc. pl.), they said, "Good day."

   f. After arriving (fem. pl.), they changed their dresses.

   g. After getting washed, she got dressed.

   h. After getting up, I got washed.

3. The conditional perfect

The conditional perfect is formed by using the conditional of *avoir* or *être,* plus the past participle of the verb. Cond. of *avoir* + past part. of *faire* + complement = I would have done that, etc.

| *J'aurais* | *fait* | *cela.* |
|---|---|---|
| *Tu aurais* | *fait* | *cela.* |
| *Il aurait* | *fait* | *cela.* |
| *Elle aurait* | *fait* | *cela.* |
| *Nous aurions* | *fait* | *cela.* |
| *Vous auriez* | *fait* | *cela.* |
| *Ils auraient* | *fait* | *cela.* |
| *Elles auraient* | *fait* | *cela.* |

Cond. of *être* + past part. of *entrer* = I would have entered, etc.

| *Je serais* | *entré(e).* |
|---|---|
| *Tu serais* | *entré(e).* |
| *Il serait* | *entré.* |
| *Elle serait* | *entrée.* |
| *Nous serions* | *entré(e)s.* |
| *Vous seriez* | *entré(e)(s).* |
| *Ils seraient* | *entrés.* |
| *Elles seraient* | *entrées.* |

Note:
- The conditional perfect is generally used in French as it is in English. Examples:
  *Je serais parti(e) à l'heure.*
  I would have left on time.
  *Elle aurait acheté deux robes.*
  She would have bought two dresses.
- For the use of the conditional perfect in sentences with "if" clauses, see Section 4 in this lesson.
- Note the special use of the conditional perfect of *devoir: Il aurait dû payer l'addition.*
  He should have paid the check.

4. Sentences with "if"

| If | Present | | Present/Imperative/Future |
|---|---|---|---|
| a. *Si* | *vous avez* | *de l'argent,* | *vous le dépensez.* |
| b. *Si* | *vous avez* | *de l'argent,* | *dépensez-le.* |
| c. *Si* | *vous avez* | *de l'argent,* | *vous le dépenserez.* |

a. If you have some money, you spend it.
b. If you have some money, spend it.
c. If you have some money, you will spend it.

| If | Imperfect | | Conditional |
|---|---|---|---|
| a. *Si* | *elle avait* | *de l'argent,* | *elle achèterait une robe.* |
| b. *Si* | *nous avions* | *le temps,* | *nous viendrions vous voir.* |

a. If she had some money, she would buy a dress.
b. If we had the time, we would come to see you.

| If | Past Perfect | | Past Conditional |
|---|---|---|---|
| a. *Si* | *j'avais eu* | *le temps,* | *je serais allé(e) au cinéma.* |
| b. *Si* | *vous étiez sorti,* | | *vous auriez vu l'accident.* |

a. If I had had the time, I would have gone to the movies.
b. If you had gone out, you would have seen the accident.

5. Forms of adverbs

| Feminine form of adjective | Adverb | English |
| --- | --- | --- |
| *heureuse* | *heureusement* | fortunately |
| *certaine* | *certainement* | certainly |
| *réelle* | *réellement* | really, actually |

| Feminine form of adjective | Adverb (with added accent) | English |
| --- | --- | --- |
| *précise* | *précisément* | precisely |
| *énorme* | *énormément* | enormously |
| *profonde* | *profondément* | profoundly |

| Masc. adjective ending in vowel | Adverb | English |
| --- | --- | --- |
| *poli* | *poliment* | politely |
| *vrai* | *vraiment* | really |
| *absolu* | *absolument* | absolutely |
| *véritable* | *véritablement* | truly |
| *instantané* | *instantanément* | immediately at once |

| Masc. adjective ending in *ent* or *ant* | Adverb | English |
| --- | --- | --- |
| *constant* | *constamment* | constantly |
| *suffisant* | *suffisamment* | sufficiently |

| prudent | prudemment | prudently |
|---|---|---|
| évident | évidemment | evidently |
| intelligent | intelligemment | intelligently |

## EXERCISES

A. Substitute each of the words or expressions in parentheses for the underlined word or expression in the model sentence. Write the complete sentence and say it aloud.

1. *Mangez avant de partir. (sortir, travailler, commencer, téléphoner, boire, y aller [Note: d'])*
2. *Après avoir mangé, elle est partie. (étudié, travaillé, changé de robe, lu le livre, dit ''Au revoir'')*
3. *Après être rentrée, elle m'a téléphoné. (arrivée, revenue, retournée, entrée, descendue, montée)*
4. *Si nous avons de l'argent, nous achèterons une voiture. (un rouleau de film, une maison, un canot, une télévision)*
5. *S'il avait une voiture, il vous la donnerait. (une plume, une cigarette, une allumette, une radio)*
6. *S'il avait fait beau (temps), je serais sorti. (allé à la plage, parti plus tôt, resté encore trois jours, arrivé à l'heure)*

B. Expand the following expressions by placing *avant de commencer* in the position indicated by the line. Say, write, and translate.

1. *Reposez-vous _____.*
2. *Il faut réfléchir _____.*
3. *Vous devez manger _____.*
4. *_____ je viendrai vous voir.*
5. *_____ elle a téléphoné à son amie.*
6. *Pensez bien _____ ce travail.*
7. *Réfléchissez bien _____ ce que vous allez faire.*

C. Expand the following by placing *Il parle* in front of each. Say and write each sentence.

1. _____ *constamment.*
2. _____ *prudemment.*
3. _____ *poliment.*
✗ 4. _____ *intelligemment.*
5. _____ *suffisamment.*

D. Translate the following sentences into French, then say them aloud.

1. She said good-bye before leaving.
2. Before saying no, make an effort.
3. I wash my hands before eating.
4. After reading them, I returned [*rendre*] the books to Mary.
5. After returning home, she went to bed.
6. After showing my passport, I opened a bank account.
7. If she gives him enough information, he will be able to fill out the form.
8. I'd write to you more often if I had the time.
9. If it had snowed, I'd have stayed home.
10. Fortunately, we have enough money.
11. She's evidently very intelligent.
12. You're absolutely right.
13. I should have spoken to him.
14. They would have left.

E. From among the three choices, select the best translation for the English word or phrase given, write the complete sentence, and translate.

1. (You need only to) _____ *le contresigner.*
   (a) *Vous seulement besoin de*
   (b) *Vous avez à*
   (c) *Vous n'avez qu'à*

2. (show me) *Il faudra* _____ *une pièce d'iden-tité.*
   (a) *montrez-moi*
   (b) *me montriez*
   (c) *me montrer*

3. (Give it to me) _____ *en grosses coupures.*
   (a) *Donnez-le-moi*
   (b) *Donnez-le-me*
   (c) *Donnez-moi-le*

4. (I'd like to) _____ *transférer des devises.*
   (a) *Je voudrais*
   (b) *Je voulais*
   (c) *Je me plais à*

5. (to settle) *Vous avez deux questions* _____.
   (a) *de régler*
   (b) *à régler*
   (c) *pour régler*

6. (computerized) *Toutes les transactions sont* _____.
   (a) *ordinateurisées*
   (b) *comptées*
   (c) *informatisées*

7. (as soon as) *Vous aurez votre argent* _____ *lundi.*
   (a) *bientôt*
   (b) *dès*
   (c) *aussi dès que*

8. (at your service) *Nous sommes* _____.
   (a) *à votre disposition*
   (b) *à votre servitude*
   (c) *à votre utilité*

9. (All you have to do is) _____ *nous donner votre adresse permanente.*
   (a) *Il suffit de*
   (b) *Tout ce que vous avez faire*
   (c) *Tout que vous avez à faire, c'est de*

10. (We need) _____ *les mêmes renseignements.*
   (a) *Il nous faut*
   (b) *Nous utilisons*
   (c) *Nous fallons*

# LESSON 17

## À LA POSTE°
## AT THE POST OFFICE

A. DIALOGUE

1. Jane: **Pardon, madame. Je voudrais envoyer ces trois lettres aux États-Unis.**
   Excuse me, ma'am. I would like to send these three letters to the United States.

2. Employée: **Il vous faudra trois timbres à quatre francs quarante.°**
   You'll need three stamps at 4 francs 40.

3. Jane: **J'ai aussi un paquet à envoyer à New York.**
   I also have a package to send to New York.

4. Employée: **Par avion ou par surface?**
   By airmail or by surface mail?

5. Jane: **Par avion, s'il vous plaît.**
   Airmail, please.

6. Employée: **Il faut d'abord que je le pèse. Voyons ... Ça fait quatre-vingt-deux francs trente. Veuillez remplir cette fiche de Douane.**
   I have to weigh it first. Let's see ... That'll be eighty-two francs thirty. Please fill out this custom's form.

7. Jane: **Je voudrais aussi le recommander.**
   I would also like to have it registered.

8. Employée: **Quelle en est la valeur?**
   What's its value?

9. Jane: **Je dirais cinq cent francs.**
   I'd say five hundred francs.

10. Employée: **Très bien. Indiquez cela sur la fiche.**
    Okay. Indicate that on the form.

11. Jane: **D'accord. Et j'ai une lettre à envoyer qui doit arriver demain.**
    All right. And I have a letter to send that has to get there tomorrow.

12. Employée: **Est-ce pour Paris?**
    Is it in Paris?

13. Jane: **Oui, madame.**
    Yes, ma'am.

14. Employée: **Pourquoi ne l'envoyez-vous pas en chronopost?° Ainsi la lettre parviendra au destinataire *en vingt-quatre heures*.**
    Why don't you send it by chronopost? That way it will reach the addressee within twenty-four hours.

15. Jane: **Oui, c'est parfait. Et où dois-je m'adresser pour savoir s'il y a du courrier pour moi?**
    Yes, that's fine. And where do I have to inquire to find out if there's any mail for me?

16. Employée: **Adressez-vous au guichet Poste restante,° madame.**
    Inquire at the General Delivery window, ma'am.

*Au guichet Poste restante.* At the General Delivery window.

17. Jane: **Bonjour, madame. Y a-t-il du courrier pour moi, s'il vous plaît? Je m'appelle Jane Lewis.**

Good day, ma'am. Is there any mail for me, please?
My name is Jane Lewis.

18. Employée: **Voyons ... Oui, madame. Je vois que
vous avez plusieurs cartes postales, un mandat-
poste, et une lettre recommandée ainsi que
quelques imprimés. J'aurai besoin d'une pièce
d'identité.**
Let's see. Yes, ma'am. I see that you have several
postcards, a postal money order, a registered letter as well as some printed matter. I'll
need some identification.

19. Jane: **J'ai mon passeport. Cela suffit?**
I have my passport. Is that enough?

20. Employée: **Oui. Merci beaucoup. Voici votre
courrier.**
Yes, thank you very much. Here is your mail.

21. Jane: **Merci, madame. Au revoir.**
Thank you, sir. Good bye.

## B. NOTES

Title: *La Poste.* Aside from buying stamps, mailing letters,
and such, it is also possible to open an account, to
wire money, to use the Minitel, or to buy life insurance or government bonds at the post office.

2. *quatre francs quarante* (*centimes*): There are one
hundred centimes in a franc.

14. *Chronopost* is express mail in France.

16. *Poste restante:* General Delivery. Many travelers to
larger cities abroad have their mail sent care of large
travel services such as American Express.

## C. GRAMMAR AND USAGE

1. Time expressions: *en* and *dans*
Study these contrasts:

   a. *La lettre lui parviendra en deux heures.*
      The letter will reach him within two hours (before
      the end of two hours).
   b. *Venez prendre votre colis dans deux heures.*
      Come get your package in two hours (after two
      hours have elapsed or at the end of two hours).

2. *Avoir à*—to have to
Study these contrasts:

| Subj. | *avoir* | Object of Inf. | *à* | Infinitive |
|-------|---------|----------------|-----|------------|
| a. *J'* | *ai* | *un paquet* | *à* | *expédier.* |
| b. *Elle* | *a* | *une lettre* | *à* | *écrire.* |

| Subj. | *avoir* | à | Infinitive | Object |
|-------|---------|---|------------|--------|
| c. *J'* | *ai* | *à* | *écrire* | *une lettre.* |
| d. *J'* | *ai* | *à* | *expédier* | *un colis.* |

   a. I have a package to send.
   b. She has a letter to write.

   c. I have to write a letter.
   d. I have to send a package.

Note:
- The difference in position of the object noun (*paquet, lettre*) is simply a question of emphasis. The examples in a. and b. above, would be in response to "*What* do you have to send or write?" That is, "What is to be sent or written?" In these cases the object to be sent or written—a package, a letter—is emphasized. The

statements in c. and d., on the other hand, are in response to "What do you have to do?" in which case *avoir* emphasizes the obligation to do something.

3. Position of pronouns before complementary infinitives

| Main Verb | Prep. | Direct Obj. Pron. | Complementary Infinitive |
|---|---|---|---|
| a. *Je dois* | | *le* | *peser.* |
| b. *Il faut* | | *le* | *faire.* |
| c. *Elle voudrait* | | *la* | *voir.* |
| d. *Je ne peux pas* | | *les* | *expliquer.* |
| e. *Elles veulent* | | *nous* | *accompagner.* |
| f. *Je refuse* | *de* | *l'* | *acheter.* |
| g. *Vous devrez* | | *vous* | *dépêcher.* |
| h. *Nous apprenons* | *à* | *le* | *dire.* |

a. I must weigh it.
b. It's necessary to do it.
c. She would like to see it (fem.).
d. I cannot explain them.
e. They want to go with (accompany) us.
f. I refuse to buy it.
g. You'll have to hurry (yourself).
h. We are learning to say it.


EXERCISES

A. Substitute each of the words in parentheses for the underlined word or expression in the model sentence. Write the complete sentence and say it aloud.

1. *Nous avons une lettre à écrire. (un livre, un billet, une invitation, une note)*

2. *J'ai à faire ce travail.* (*commencer, finir, terminer, voir, chercher*)
3. *Il faut le faire.* (*voir, commencer, comprendre, lire, dire, chercher*)
4. *Elles veulent nous parler.* (*doivent, peuvent, savent, vont*)

B. Expand the following by placing *la voir* at the end of each. Say, write, and translate.

1. *Il veut* _____.
2. *Il voulait* _____.
3. *Il voudra* _____.
4. *Il voudrait* _____.
5. *Il a voulu* _____.
6. *Il avait voulu* _____.
7. *Il aurait voulu* _____.

C. Translate the following sentences into French; then say them aloud.

1. I'll see you again in three weeks.
2. Can you finish the work within an hour?
3. I have something to tell you.
4. Do you have a package to send?
5. We have to write several letters.
6. I can't talk to you now.
7. She's going to do it later.
8. I'd like to see him soon.

D. From among the three choices, select the best translation for the English word or phrase given, write the complete sentence, and translate.

1. (I'd like) _____ *envoyer ces lettres.*
   (a) *Je voulais*
   (b) *Je plais*
   (c) *Je voudrais*

2. (Airmail?) _____?
   (a) *Avion courrier*
   (b) *En avion*
   (c) *Par avion*

3. (within) *Il lui parviendra* _____ *une heure.*
   (a) *en*
   (b) *dans*
   (c) *dedans*

4. (me) *Y a-t-il du courrier pour* _____?
   (a) *me*
   (b) *moi*
   (c) *je*

5. (Weigh them) *Elle doit* _____.
   (a) *les peser*
   (b) *peser les*
   (c) *leur peser*

6. (in/after) *La lettre arrivera* _____ *cinq heures.*
   (a) *en*
   (b) *dans*
   (c) *dedans*

7. (to send) *J'ai aussi un paquet* _____.
   (a) *expédier*
   (b) *pour expédier*
   (c) *à expédier*

8. (have it insured) *Je voudrais aussi* _____.
   (a) *avoir l'assurer*
   (b) *l'avoir assuré*
   (c) *le faire assurer*

9. (five hundred francs) *Je dirais* _____.
   (a) *cinq cent francs*
   (b) *cinq cents francs*
   (c) *cinqs cents francs*

10. (have to send) *Nous* _____ *envoyer ce paquet.*
    (a) *fallons*
    (b) *faut*
    (c) *avons à*

# LESSON 18

## LES VÊTEMENTS
## CLOTHING

### A. DIALOGUE

*Dans un grand magasin°—au rayon Enfants.*
In a department store—in the children's department.

1. Jane: **Bonjour, madame. On voudrait acheter une petite robe pour notre nièce, une fillette de six ans.**
   Hello, ma'am. We would like to buy a little dress for our niece, a little girl who's six years old.

2. Vendeuse: **Oui, madame. Vous voulez quelque chose d'*habillé* ou de *décontracté?***
   Yes, ma'am. Do you want something dressy or casual?

3. Jane: **Plutôt décontracté, n'est-ce pas, Charles?**
   Rather casual, right, Charles?

4. Charles: **Il vaut mieux, oui.**
   That would be better, yes.

5. Vendeuse: **Que pensez-vous de cette robe-ci?**
   What do you think of this dress?

6. Jane: **Qu'est-ce que c'est comme tissu?°**
   What kind of fabric is it?

7. Vendeuse: **C'est du lin.**
   Linen.

8. Jane: **Je pense que le coton ferait mieux l'affaire pour une fille de son âge. Et de toute façon, je**

trouve que la couleur n'est pas très jolie. Quelles couleurs est-ce que Claire aime porter?

I think that cotton would be better for a girl of her age. And anyway, I don't think that color is very pretty. What colors does Claire like to wear?

9. Charles: **Les couleurs vives, elle les adore. Surtout le jaune.**

She loves bright colors. Especially yellow.

10. Vendeuse: **Et celle-ci? Regardez la couleur et le joli motif. C'est du coton.**

How about this one? Look at the color and the pretty pattern. It's cotton.

11. Charles: **Oui, mais ça fait un peu trop habillé, je pense.**

Yes, but it's a little too dressy, I think.

12. Vendeuse: **Alors ... vous cherchiez une robe, mais que pensez vous de cette salopette? Elle est très à la mode.**

Well, you were looking for a dress, but what do you think of this jumper? It's very fashionable.

13. Jane: **C'est adorable! Est-ce que vous l'avez dans d'autres couleurs?**

It's adorable! Do you have it in any other colors?

14. Vendeuse: **En bleu foncé, comme celle-ci, et en bleu clair.**

In dark blue, like this one, and in light blue.

15. Charles: **Parfait! On prendra celle en bleu clair.**

Perfect! We'll take the one in light blue.

16. Jane: **Et avez-vous un chemisier assorti?**

And do you have a matching blouse?

17. Vendeuse: **Il y a ce tee shirt à pois qui irait à merveille.**
There is this polka-dotted tee shirt that would match perfectly.

18. Charles: **Regarde, Jane. Que penses-tu de celui à rayures? Moi, je le *préfère*.**
Look, Jane. What do you think of this striped one? I prefer it.

19. Jane: **Oui! Tu as raison. On le prend. Le tee shirt et la salopette, quel bel ensemble! Claire sera ravie!**
Yes! You're right. We'll take it. The tee shirt and the jumper, what a great outfit. Claire will be delighted.

*Au rayon Hommes.* In the men's department.

20. Charles: **Nous cherchons un vêtement pour notre neveu qui a 19 ans. Il *nous a demandé de lui acheter* une tenue de sport pour son anniversaire.**
We're looking for an outfit for our 19-year-old nephew. He asked us to buy him something athletic for his birthday.

21. Vendeur: **Ce sweat en coton, Monsieur? Ou peut-être ce maillot de bain?°**
This cotton sweatshirt, sir? Or maybe this bathing suit?

22. Charles: **Le maillot est beau, et il aime nager, mais . . .**
The bathing suit is nice, and he likes to swim, but . . .

23. Jane: **Regarde, Charles, ce survêtement serait parfait pour lui. En septembre, il n'ira plus à la**

piscine et il *commencera de nouveau à faire* du jogging.°
Look, Charles. This track suit would be perfect for him. In September he won't be going to the pool anymore and he'll start jogging again.

24. Charles: **Tu as raison. Le survêtement lui sera très utile. Et les baskets là-bas, qu'en penses-tu?**
You're right. The track suit will be useful for him. And those sneakers over there, what do you think of them?

25. Jane: **Il pourrait trouver des chaussures comme ça aux États-Unis, et elles y seraient beaucoup moins chères. Ce n'est pas la peine d'en acheter en France. Mais le survêtement a l'air français, tu ne crois pas?**
He could find shoes like that in the United States, and they would be much less expensive there. It's not worth it to buy any in France. But the track suit looks French, don't you think?

26. Vendeur: **Et il est en solde cette semaine!**
And it's on sale this week!

27. Charles: **Excellent, on le prend.**
Excellent. We'll take it.

28. Vendeur: **Quelle est sa taille?°**
What is his size?

29. Charles: **Il fait du 38.**
Fifteen.

30. Vendeur: **Ouf, il n'en reste qu'un seul. Vous avez de la chance!**
Whew, there's only one left. You're lucky!

31. Jane: **Merci, monsieur.**
Thank you, sir.

32. Charles: **Au revoir.**
Good-bye.

## B. NOTES

Title: *grand magasin:* department store. *Un magasin* is a
store, and *une boutique* is a shop.

6. *Le tissu* and *l'étoffe* both mean "fabric." Some other
fabrics are: *La soie, le nylon, le velours, le velours
côtelé, la laine*—silk, nylon, velvet, corduroy, wool.

21. *un maillot de bain* is often shortened to *un maillot.*

23. *le jogging:* an example of Franglais; the word refers
both to the sport and to the outfit worn for the sport.

28. *la taille:* "size" when referring to all clothes but
gloves and shoes. French sizes are different from
American sizes, so it is advisable to know your
French size when you go to France.

## C. GRAMMAR AND USAGE

1. Prepositions before infinitives (review)

| Verb | *de* | Obj. Pron. | Infinitive |
|------|------|------------|------------|
| a. *Il a décidé* | *de* | *le* | *faire.* |
| b. *Il a fini* | *de* | *les* | *manger.* |
| c. *Il m'a dit* | *de* | | *partir.* |
| d. *Il m'a demandé* | *de* | *l'* | *aider.* |
| e. *Il m'a prié* | *de* | | *ne pas parler.* |
| f. *Essayez* | *de* | | *venir.* |

a. He decided to do it.
b. He finished eating them.

c. He told me to leave.
d. He asked me to help him.
e. He begged me not to speak.
f. Try to come.

| Verb | à | Infinitive | |
|---|---|---|---|
| a. *Elle a commencé* | *à* | *pleurer.* | |
| b. *Elle m'a invité* | *à* | *venir.* | |
| c. *Il m'a aidé* | *à* | *faire* | *le travail.* |
| d. *J'ai appris* | *à* | *conduire.* | |
| e. *Elles ont réussi* | *à* | *finir* | *les devoirs.* |
| f. *Nous tenons* | *à* | *voir* | *Marie.* |

a. She began to cry.
b. She invited me to come.
c. He helped me to do the work.
d. I learned to drive.
e. They succeeded in finishing the homework.
f. We are anxious to see Marie.

| Verb | sans | Infinitive | |
|---|---|---|---|
| a. *Elle est partie* | *sans* | *dire* | *un mot.* |
| b. *Tu parles toujours* | *sans* | *réfléchir.* | |

a. She left without saying a word.
b. You always talk without thinking.

Note:
- The verbs in the two tables above constitute only a brief list of the more common verbs followed by *à* and *de* before an infinitive. You should memorize which verbs are followed by *à* or *de* before an infinitive and which are followed directly by an infinitive, as in *Il faut partir.* See Lesson 1.

- It is important to remember that *sans* plus the infinitive is the equivalent of "without" plus -ing.

2. The present tense of verbs *mener*, "to lead," *préférer*, "to prefer," and verbs like them:

| | |
|---|---|
| *je mène* | *nous menons* |
| *tu mènes* | *vous menez* |
| *il/elle mène* | *ils/elles mènent* |

| | |
|---|---|
| *je préfère* | *nous préférons* |
| *tu préfères* | *vous préférez* |
| *il/elle préfère* | *ils/elles préfèrent* |

Note:
- Compounds of *mener*, "to lead, to take," e.g., *amener*, "to bring," *emmener*, "to take" (someone somewhere), *ramener*, "to bring back" follow the same pattern.
- The common verb *acheter*, "to buy," is also formed like *mener*.
- Other common verbs formed like *préférer: espérer*, "to hope"; *protéger*, "to protect"; *répéter*, "to repeat."
- For other tenses, see Regular Verb Charts.

3. Past participles used as adjectives

| Infinitive | Past Part. as Adj. |
|---|---|
| *habiller* | a. *Elle n'aime pas les robes habillées.* |
| *assortir* | b. *Avez-vous un chemisier assorti?* |
| *serrer* | c. *Ce tee shirt est trop serré.* |
| *cuire* | d. *J'aime la viande bien cuite.* |

a. She doesn't like dresses that are too dressy.
b. Do you have a matching blouse?
c. This tee shirt is too tight.
d. I like meat well done (well cooked).

Note:
- Past participles used as adjectives agree in number and gender with the nouns they modify.

## EXERCISES

A. Substitute each of the words or expressions in parentheses for the underlined word or expression in the model sentence. Write the complete sentence and say it aloud.

1. *Il a décidé de partir. (rentrer, étudier, m'aider, venir, le faire)*
2. *J'ai appris à conduire. (danser, chanter, jouer aux cartes, jouer au tennis, jouer du violon, jouer du piano)*
3. *Ils sont partis sans dire un mot. (entrés, sortis, arrivés, venus, revenus, rentrés)*
4. *Ce veston est trop serré. (tee shirt, manteau, complet, chapeau, pantalon)*

B. Transform these sentences to the negative. Say, write, and translate.

1. *Je préfère ce livre-ci.*
2. *Ils préfèrent les autres chemises.*
3. *Nous répétons la leçon.*
4. *La mère protège ses enfants.*
5. *Elle mène une vie heureuse.*
6. *Il ramène les enfants à l'école.*
7. *Nous achetons les robes les plus chères.*

C. Translate the following sentences into French; then say them aloud.

1. I'll ask her to come.
2. They began to walk quickly.
3. Don't leave without speaking to me.
4. She brings her child back from school at noon.

5. Which fabric do you prefer?
6. This jumper is too casual.
7. This track suit is too big.
8. The steak is well done.


D. From among the three choices, select the best translation
   for the English word or phrase given. Write the complete sentence, and translate.

1. (relaxed) *Elle veut une tenue* _____.
   (a) *fatiguée*
 ‒ (b) *décontractée*
   (c) *serrée*
2. (It would be better) _____.
   (a) *Il vaudrait mieux*
   (b) *Il vaudra mieux*
   (c) *Il vaudrait meilleur*
3. (What kind of fabric) *Qu'est-ce que c'est* _____?
   (a) *tissu*
 ✶(b) *de tissu*
 ‒(c) *comme tissu*
4. (would be better) *Le coton* _____ *que la soie.*
   (a) *ferait mieux*
 ‒ (b) *ferait mieux l'affaire*
   (c) *serait une meilleure affaire*
5. (He's a size) _____ *38.*
   (a) *C'est une taille.*
   (b) *Il fait de la taille*
 ‒ (c) *Il fait du*
6. (polka-dotted jumper) *J'aimerais acheter une* _____.
   (a) *salopette à rayures*
 ‒ (b) *salopette à pois*
   (c) *salopette tachée*
7. (to buy) *Il nous a demandé* _____ *des baskets.*
   (a) *acheter*
   (b) *à acheter*
 ‒ (c) *d'acheter*

8. (prefer) *Je* _____ *celui-ci.*
   (a) *prefere*
   (b) *préféré*
   ↘ (c) *préfère*
9. (on sale) *Cette jupe est* _____.
   (a) *à vendre*
   (b) *en vente*
   ↖ (c) *en solde*
10. (There's only one) _____ *qui reste.*
    ↘ (a) *Il n'y a qu'un seul*
    (b) *Il y a seul qui*
    (c) *Il n'y a que seul*

# LESSON 19

## LE DENTISTE,
## LE MÉDECIN
## ET LE PHARMACIEN
## THE DENTIST,
## THE DOCTOR,
## AND THE PHARMACIST

A. DIALOGUE

*Chez le dentiste.* At the dentist's.

1. Dentiste: **Qu'est-ce qui ne va pas, Madame Lewis?**
   What's wrong, Mrs. Lewis?

2. Jane: **J'ai une dent** *qui me fait terriblement mal depuis deux jours.* **Elle me faisait mal aussi** *il y a trois semaines.*
   I have a tooth that's been hurting me terribly for two days. It also hurt me three weeks ago.

3. Dentiste: *Il se peut que le nerf soit à vif,* puisque vous en souffrez tant.
It's possible that the nerve is exposed, since you're suffering so much from it.

4. Jane: **Croyez-vous que ce soit simplement un nerf exposé? Mes gencives sont tout enflées° ...**
Do you think that it's just an exposed nerve? My gums are all swollen ...

5. Dentiste: **Est-ce qu'elles saignent?**
Are they bleeding?

6. Jane: **Oui, un peu.**
Yes, a little.

7. Dentiste: **Eh bien, je vais prendre une radio. Pencher la tête en arrière et *ouvrez la bouche,* s'il vous plaît ... Voilà!**
Well then, I'm going to X-ray them. Put your head back and open your mouth, please ... There!

8. Jane: **Et ensuite?**
And then?

9. Dentiste: **Les radios seront prêtes dans quelques minutes. En attendant, *je vais examiner la dent.***
The X-rays will be ready in a few minutes. In the meantime, I'm going to examine the tooth.

10. Jane: **Aïe!° Arrêtez! Ne pouvez-vous pas me donner un anesthésique?**
Ouch! Stop! Can't you give me an anesthetic?

11. Dentiste: **Volontiers, madame. Voulez-vous que je vous fasse une piqûre de novocaïne, ou préférez-vous le gaz?**

Gladly, madam. Do you want me to give you an
injection of novocaine, or do you prefer gas?

12. Jane: **De la novocaïne, s'il vous plaît. Je ne peux
pas supporter la douleur. *Il y a deux ans* je me
suis évanouie chez le dentiste.**
Novocaine, please. I can't stand pain. Two years ago
I fainted at the dentist's.

13. Dentiste: **Ah! Je vois maintenant ce dont vous
vous plaignez. C'est une des molaires inférieures,
à gauche. Je ne pense pas que ce soit très grave.**
Oh! I see now what you are complaining about. It's
one of the lower left molars. I don't think it's very
serious.

14. Jane: **Vous ne serez pas obligé d'arracher la dent?**
You won't have to pull the tooth, will you?

15. Dentiste: **Regardons la radiographie. Mmmm ...
La racine paraît saine. Non, il ne faudra pas l'arracher.**
Let's look at the X-ray. Mmmm ... the root seems
healthy. No, it won't be necessary to pull it.

16. Jane: **Ce n'est qu'une dent cariée, alors?**
It's only a decayed tooth, then?

17. Dentiste: **C'est exact, mais c'est une carie assez
profonde. Je vais la plomber.**
Exactly, but it's a rather large cavity. I'm going to
fill it.

*Le médecin.*   The doctor.

18. Charles: **Je ne vais pas bien du tout.° J'ai mal
partout—*à la gorge, à la tête, à l'estomac, aux
yeux* ... J'ai aussi mal *au cœur.*°**

I don't feel well at all. Everything hurts me—my throat, my head, my stomach, my eyes . . . I also feel nauseated.

19. Docteur: *Ouvrez la bouche,* monsieur. **Je vais prendre votre température.°** Ah! Vous avez justement un peu de fièvre, et *vous avez la gorge toute rouge.* **Toussez, maintenant.** *Je veux écouter les poumons.*

   Open your mouth, sir. I'm going to take your temperature. Ah! You do have a little fever, and your throat is all red. Now, cough. I want to listen to your lungs.

20. Charles: **Qu'est-ce qu'il faut faire, docteur?**
   What do I have to do, Doctor?

21. Docteur: **Vous devez garder le lit pendant deux ou trois jours, jusqu'à ce que° vous n'ayez plus de fièvre.**
   You have to stay in bed for two or three days until you have no more fever.

22. Charles: **Est-ce que je peux manger de tout?**
   Can I eat everything?

23. Docteur: **Mais non. Vous devez prendre des repas légers et boire beaucoup de jus de fruits. Vous devrez aussi prendre les cachets° que je vais vous prescrire maintenant.**
   No, indeed. You must take light meals and drink a lot of fruit juice. You'll also have to take the pills that I'm going to prescribe for you now.

24. Charles: **Quels sont vos honoraires, docteur°?**
   What is your fee, Doctor?

25. Docteur: **Cent trente francs, monsieur. Mais ça ne presse pas. Je voudrais vous revoir demain dans l'après-midi.**
One hundred thirty francs, sir. But there's no hurry. I'd like to see you again tomorrow during the afternoon.

*À la pharmacie.*   At the pharmacy.

26. Charles: **Voici l'ordonnance que m'a prescrit le médecin.**
Here's the prescription my doctor filled out for me.

27. Pharmacien: **Je vais vous chercher le médicament tout de suite ... Le malade doit prendre deux cachets trois fois par jour, avant les repas.**
I'll get the medication for you right away ... The patient has to take two pills three times a day, before meals.

28. Charles: **Ah! J'avais presque oublié. Il me faut de l'aspirine et des pastilles contre la toux.**
Oh! I almost forgot. I need some aspirin and some cough drops.

29. Pharmacien: **Les voilà, monsieur.**
Here they are, sir.

30. Charles: **Merci, monsieur.**
Thank you.

B. NOTES

4. *tout enflées:* all swollen. *Tout(e)(s)*, in this adverbial context, is used as an intensifier (the equivalent of entirely, all, very, awfully, quite).

10. *Aïe:* "Ouch" is expressed in different ways in all languages of the world.

18. *pas du tout:* not at all. The phrase *du tout* is very commonly used to express the negative "at all."

Notice that for parts of the body the definite article is often used, rather than the possessive. (See Grammar and Usage, Section 4.)

*mal au cœur* has nothing to do with heart.

19. *température:* temperature is measured in degrees Centigrade; 37°C is normal body temperature.

21. *jusqu'à ce que:* until (followed by a clause).

23. *Un cachet,* or *un comprimé,* is a pill. *Une pillule* or *des pillules* are also used to mean pill, but *la pillule* refers to the birth control pill.

24. *Un médecin* refers to the profession, whereas *docteur* is the title.

## C. GRAMMAR AND USAGE

1. The present tense with *depuis*

| Present of Verb | Complement | *depuis* | Time Expression |
|---|---|---|---|
| a. *J'ai* | *mal aux dents* | depuis | *deux jours.* |
| b. *Elle lit* | | depuis | *trois heures.* |
| c. *Nous sommes* | *en France* | depuis | *six ans.* |
| d. *Ils étudient* | *le français* | depuis | *sept mois.* |

a. I've had a toothache for two days.
b. She's been reading for three hours.
c. We've been in France for six years.
d. They've been studying French for seven months.

Note:
- The time expression with *depuis* always comes at the end of the sentence.

- Another way of expressing the same idea is to use *il y a* + time + *que* + the present tense.

Examples:

a. *Il y a deux jours que j'ai mal aux dents.*
   I've had a toothache for two days.
b. *Il y a deux heures que j'étudie.*
   I've been studying for two hours.

2. *Il y a* + time + *que* + past tense = ago

| Il y a | Time | que | Past Tense |
|--------|------|-----|------------|
| a. *Il y a* | *trois heures* | *que* | *je l'ai vu.* |
| b. *Il y a* | *deux jours* | *que* | *je l'ai vue.* |
| c. *Il y a* | *huit jours* | *que* | *nous l'avons vu.* |
| d. *Il y a* | *quinze jours* | *que* | *vous l'avez reçu.* |
| e. *Il y a* | *trois semaines* | *que* | *tu y es allé(e).* |
| f. *Il y a* | *un an* | *qu'* | *ils y sont allés.* |

a. I saw him three hours ago.
b. I saw her two days ago.
c. We saw him a week ago. (Notice the use of *huit jours* to mean "a week.")
d. You received it two weeks ago. (Notice the use of *quinze jours* to mean "two weeks.")
e. You went there three weeks ago.
f. They went there a year ago.

Compare the word order in these sentences with the sentences above.

| Past Tense | il y a | Time |
|------------|--------|------|
| a. *Je l'ai vu* | *il y a* | *deux ans.* |
| b. *Tu l'as reçu* | *il y a* | *huit jours.* |
| c. *Il y est allé* | *il y a* | *plus d'un an.* |

a. I saw him two years ago.
b. You received it a week ago.
c. He went there more than one year ago.

Note:
- When you wish to express *time ago,* you can use either *Il y a* + time + *que* + past tense or past tense + *il y a* + time.
- All the above sentences denote action *completed in the past.*

3. *Il se peut* + subjunctive (subjunctive of possibility)

| *Il se peut* | *que* | Subject | Subjunctive | Complement |
|---|---|---|---|---|
| a. *Il se peut* | *qu'* | *elle* | *soit* | *malade.* |
| b. *Il se peut* | *que* | *vous* | *ayez* | *raison.* |
| c. *Il se peut* | *qu'* | *il* | *ne puisse pas* | *venir.* |
| d. *Il se peut* | *que* | *nous* | *finissions* | *le travail.* |
| e. *Il se peut* | *qu'* | *ils* | *aient vendu* | *la maison.* |

a. It's possible that she is sick.
b. It's possible that you are right.
c. It's possible that he may not be able to come.
d. It's possible that we may finish the work.
e. It's possible that they have sold the house.

4. Definite article with parts of the body

| | *à* + Def. Art. | Part of Body |
|---|---|---|
| a. *J'ai mal* | *à l'* | *estomac.* |
| b. *Elle a mal* | *au* | *pied.* |
| c. *Elle a mal* | *aux* | *dents.* |
| d. *Il a mal* | *à la* | *gorge.* |

a. I have a stomach ache.
b. Her foot hurts.
c. She has a toothache.
d. He has a sore throat.

|  | Def. Art. | Part of Body |  |
|---|---|---|---|
| a. *Il a* | *les* | *yeux* | *bleus.* |
| b. *Elle a* | *les* | *cheveux* | *noirs.* |
| c. *Elle a* | *les* | *lèvres* | *rouges.* |
| d. *Elle a* | *le* | *nez* | *retroussé.* |
| e. *Elle a* | *l'* | *oreille* | *fine.* |

a. He has blue eyes.
b. She has black hair.
c. She has red lips.
d. She has a turned-up nose.
e. She has sharp ears.

### EXERCISES

A. Substitute each of the words or expressions in parentheses for the underlined word or expression in the model sentence. Write the complete sentence and say it aloud.

1. *Ils étudient le français depuis sept mois. (l'italien, l'espagnol, l'anglais, l'allemand, le japonais)*
2. *J'étudie le français depuis sept mois. (trois ans, huit jours, quinze jours, six semaines, cinq ans)*
3. *Il y a trois ans que j'habite ici. (deux ans, six mois, quinze jours, huit semaines, une quinzaine d'années)*
4. *Il y a une heure que je l'ai vu. (huit jours, un mois, deux mois, un an, longtemps)*
5. *Il se peut qu'elle soit malade. (fâchée, fatiguée, triste, malheureuse, morte)*
6. *Il se peut que nous partions demain. (arrivions, sortions, revenions, rentrions, venions)*

7. *Elle a les cheveux noirs. (blonds, blancs, gris, roux, châtains)*

B. Transform the sentences with *Il y a* to sentences with *depuis*. Say, write, and translate.

   Example: *Il y a un an que je suis ici./Je suis ici depuis un an.*

   1. *Il y a deux jours que j'attends.*
   2. *Il y a un mois qu'elle est malade.*
   3. *Il y a trois semaines que je veux vous parler.*
   4. *Il y a quatre ans qu'il conduit.*
   5. *Il y a six ans que j'habite cette maison.*

C. Translate the following sentences into French. Then say them aloud.

   1. She's been working since four o'clock.
   2. He's been waiting for me since noon.
   3. I've been living here for five years.
   4. It's possible that she doesn't know the answer.
   5. It's possible that he's hungry.
   6. It's possible that they arrived too late.
   7. Do you have a headache?
   8. She has blond hair.
   9. It's possible that he has a sore throat.
   10. They arrived an hour ago.
   11. She studied two hours ago.
   12. We have been waiting for a day.
   13. I spoke to him a week ago.

D. From among the three choices, select the best translation for the English word or phrase given. Write the complete sentence, and translate.

1. (What) _____ ne va pas?
   - (a) *Quoi*
   - (b) *Qu'est-ce que*
   - (c) *Qu'est-ce qui*
2. (It may be) _____ que le nerf soit à vif.
   - (a) *Il se peut*
   - (b) *Il peut*
   - (c) *Il laisse être*
3. (back) *Penchez la tête* _____.
   - (a) *au dos*
   - (b) *derrière*
   - (c) *en arrière*
4. (I'm not well) _____, docteur.
   - (a) *Je ne vais pas bon*
   - (b) *Je ne vais pas bien*
   - (c) *Je ne suis pas bon*
5. (stay in bed) *Vous devez* _____.
   - (a) *garder couché*
   - (b) *se coucher*
   - (c) *garder le lit.*
6. (light meals) *Il doit prendre des* _____.
   - (a) *lumière à manger*
   - (b) *repas légers*
   - (c) *légers dîners*
7. (your fee) *Quels sont* _____?
   - (a) *votre prix*
   - (b) *vos honoraires*
   - (c) *votre honoraire*
8. (everything) *Vous pouvez manger* _____.
   - (a) *de tout*
   - (b) *tous*
   - (c) *du tout*
9. (in the afternoon) *Je voudrais vous revoir* _____.
   - (a) *en après-midi*
   - (b) *à l'après-midi*
   - (c) *dans l'après-midi*

10. (immediately) *Je vais vous chercher le médicament*
_____ .

➤ (a) *tout de suite*
   (b) *tout à fait*
   (c) *tout à l'heure*

# LESSON 20

## LES CULTES
## RELIGIONS

### A. DIALOGUE

*Les offices divins.*   Religious services.

  1. Charles: **Y a-t-il une église protestante près de l'hôtel? Ma femme et moi,** *nous avons l'habitude d'aller à l'église le dimanche.*
Is there a Protestant church near the hotel? My wife and I are in the habit of going to church on Sunday.

  2. Concierge: **À Paris, monsieur, comme dans toutes les grandes villes de France, on célèbre tous les cultes, y compris le culte protestant. Pour aller à l'office, vous n'avez qu'à vous rendre au temple,° quai d'Orsay.° C'est tout près.**
In Paris, sir, as in all the big cities of France, all religions are practiced, including the Protestant religion. To go to the service, all you have to do is go to the temple on the Quai d'Orsay. It's quite near here.

  3. Charles: **Vous avez dit "au temple" et non pas "à l'église . . ."**
You said "to the temple" and not "to the church . . ."

4. Concierge: *C'est exact.* **Les maisons du culte protestant s'appellent "temples."**
   That's right. Protestant houses of worship are called
   "temples."

5. Charles: **À quelle heure commence l'office?**
   At what time does the service begin?

6. Concierge: **Généralement à onze heures. Et tout
   se passera comme chez vous. Le pasteur fera un
   sermon, vous chanterez vos hymnes favoris, on
   fera la quête . . .**
   Generally at eleven o'clock. And everything will be
   as it is in your country. The minister will give a
   sermon, you'll sing your favorite hymns, they'll take
   up a collection . . .

7. Charles: *C'est tout en français,* **bien entendu.**
   It's all in French, of course.

8. Concierge: **À Paris, vous pouvez choisir entre
   l'office en anglais ou en français. Voici une liste
   d'églises, de temples, de mosquées, et de synagogues . . .**
   In Paris, you can choose between the service in English or in French. Here's a list of churches, temples,
   mosques, and synagogues.

9. Charles: *Il serait très intéressant d'assister aussi à
   un service* **de l'église catholique . . . à la cathédrale Notre-Dame,° ou à la Madeleine.°**
   It would be very interesting to attend a Catholic
   service also . . . at Notre Dame Cathedral, or the
   Madeleine.

10. Concierge: *Le dimanche matin on célèbre toujours
    au moins deux messes, et souvent trois.*
    On Sunday morning at least two masses, and often
    three, are celebrated.

11. Charles: **Je note ici que la Grande Synagogue se trouve rue de la Victoire.**

I notice here that the Main Synagogue is located on the rue de la Victoire.

12. Concierge: *Les offices du culte juif°* ont *lieu le vendredi soir et le samedi matin,* **comme vous devez le savoir. Le rabbin et le chantre seraient heureux de vous accueillir si vous vouliez assiter à un office.**

The services of the Jewish religion take place on Friday night and Saturday morning, as you must know. The rabbi and the cantor would be glad to welcome you if you wished to attend a service.

13. Charles: **Y a-t-il aussi des mosquées à Paris?**

Are there also mosques in Paris?

14. Concierge: **Oui, naturellement, pour le culte musulman.°**

Yes, naturally, for the Islamic religion.

15. Jane: **Où étais-tu, Charles? Je te cherchais partout.**

Where were you, Charles? I was looking for you everywhere.

16. Charles: **Je parlais au concierge au sujet des cultes. Il m'a dit où se trouve le temple protestant le plus près.°**

I was talking to the concierge about religions. He told me where the nearest Protestant church is located.

17. Jane: **Nous aurons bientôt l'occasion d'assister à une messe catholique aussi.**

We'll soon have the opportunity to attend a Catholic mass also.

*Un mariage français.* A French wedding.

18. Jane: **Nous venons de recevoir un faire-part. Regarde.**

We've just received an invitation. Look.

19. Charles: **Tiens!** *C'est le neveu* **de Michel qui se marie!**

Well! It's Michel's nephew who is getting married!

(*Lisant*)

**M. et Mme Dupuy**

**M. et Mme Bernard**

**ont la joie de vous annoncer le mariage de leurs enfants Isabelle et Paul qui recevront le sacrement de mariage le 3 juillet à ll heures en l'église Saint-François-Xavier.**

**Les fiancés et leurs parents seraient heureux si vous pouviez participer à la cérémonie religieuse à laquelle ils vous invitent cordialement.**

(Reading)

Mr. and Mrs. Dupuy, Mr. and Mrs. Bernard are happy to announce the marriage of their children Isabelle and Paul who will receive the sacrament of marriage on July 3 at 11 o'clock at the church of Saint Francis Xavier. The betrothed couple and their parents would be happy if you would take part in the religious ceremony to which they cordially invite you.

**Je vais donner un coup de fil à Michel tout de suite. On pourrait peut-être y aller ensemble.**

I'm going to give Michel a ring right now. Perhaps we might be able to go there together.

*Charles parle au teléphone avec Michel.* Charles speaks to Michel on the phone.

20. Charles: **Nous n'avons jamais assisté à un mariage en France, et nous avons pensé que, si cela vous convient, on irait ensemble.**
We've never attended a wedding in France, and we thought that, if it's all right with you, we would go together.

21. Michel: **Je regrette, Charles, mais malheureusement** *ce ne sera pas possible.* **Il faut que je sois témoin au mariage civil° d'Isabelle et Paul qui aura lieu à la mairie du XVIᵉ arrondissement° le même jour à neuf heures et demie du matin. Il faut que j'y aille d'abord.**
I'm sorry, Charles, but unfortunately it will not be possible. I have to be a witness at Isabelle and Paul's civil ceremony which will take place at the town hall of the sixteenth arrondissement the same day at nine-thirty in the morning. I have to go there first.

22. Charles: **Pensez-vous que nous puissions assister aussi à ce mariage civil?**
Do you think we might also be able to attend this civil ceremony?

23. Michel: **Ah, oui, certainement. Ma sœur sera enchantée de vous voir.**
Oh, yes, certainly. My sister will be delighted to see you.

24. Charles: **À** *samedi,* **alors, à neuf heures quinze, à la mairie du XVIᵉ°** ...
Until Saturday, then, at nine-fifteen, at the town hall of the XVIth ...

## B. NOTES

2. *vous rendre au temple: Se rendre à* + place name is equivalent to *aller à* + place name. Example:

*Je me rends à l'école*
*Je vais à l'école.* } I'm going to school.

*quai d'Orsay:* one of the many quays along the Seine. The Ministry of Foreign Affairs is located on this quay.

9. *cathédrale de Notre-Dame:* the Cathedral of Notre Dame of Paris is one of the world's most magnificent works of Gothic architecture. Construction was begun in 1163 and was not completed until 1245. Notre Dame has been the site of many of the greatest events in French history, including the coronation of Napoleon and the great Te Deum celebrating the Liberation of Paris. The cathedral is referred to in conversation as *la cathédrale de Notre-Dame,* or, most often, simply as *Notre-Dame.*
*la Madeleine:* A Greek-style church on the Right Bank of the Seine, not far from the Opera. The Madeleine is the site of many fashionable weddings.

12. Some words associated with Judaism:
*juif* (m.)
*juive* (f.) } Jew/Jewish;
*l'hébreu* (m.), Hebrew; *Israël,* Israel.
France has the largest Jewish population of Western Europe: over 600,000.

14. France also has the largest Muslim population of Western Europe: about five million people.

16. *le plus près:* It is equally correct to say *le plus proche.*

21. *mariage civil:* A civil marriage is required in France. An optional religious marriage ceremony may follow the civil ceremony. The priest, minister, imam, or rabbi must have the civil marriage certificate before performing the religious cermony.

*arrondissement:* Administratively, France is divided into 94 *départements* and la Ville de Paris. Paris is divided into *arrondissements*, each of which is headed by a *maire* whose offices are in the *mairie*. There are 20 *arrondissements* in Paris.

24. *XVI$^e$ arrondissement:* the arrondissement of Passy, a fashionable residential district of Paris. Notice that the number is in Roman numerals. The little $^e$ is an abbreviation for *-ième,* equivalent to English "th," "nd," "rd," as in "16th," "2nd," "3rd."

## C. GRAMMAR AND USAGE

1. *Falloir* + the subjunctive

| Falloir | que | Subjunctive | Complement |
|---|---|---|---|
| a. *Il faut* | *que* | *j'aille* | *à la mairie.* |
| b. *Il faut* | *qu'* | *il garde* | *le lit.* |
| c. *Il fallait* | *qu'* | *il prenne* | *ses cachets.* |
| d. *Il faudra* | *que* | *nous fassions* | *de notre mieux.* |
| e. *Il faudrait* | *qu'* | *ils viennent* | *à trois heures.* |

a. I have to go [It is necessary that I go] to the town hall.
b. He has to stay [It is necessary that he stay] in bed.
c. He had to take [It was necessary that he take] his pills.
d. We will have to do [It will be necessary that we do] our best.
e. They would have to come [It would be necessary that they come] at three o'clock.

Note:
- *Falloir* is used only impersonally, that is, with the subject *il.*

- Refer to Lesson 13 for *falloir* with indirect object pronouns, and to Lesson 4 for review of subjunctive.

2. Time expressions with days of the week

   a. *Il vient dimanche à trois heures.*
     He is coming Sunday at three o'clock.
   b. *Il vient le dimanche (or les dimanches).*
     He comes on Sundays.
   c. *Il n'est pas allé à l'école mercredi.*
     He didn't go to school Wednesday.
   d. *Il ne va pas à l'école le jeudi (or les jeudis).*
     He doesn't go to school on Thursdays.

3. Some uses of *il/elle est* and *c'est*
   Study these contrasts:

| Il/Elle est | Prof., etc. | C'est | Indef. | Modifier | Prof., etc. |
|---|---|---|---|---|---|
| a. *Il est* | *médecin.* | *C'est* | *un* | *bon* | *médecin.* |
| b. *Elle est* | *catholique.* | *C'est* | *une* | | *catholique.* |
| c. *Il est* | *français.* | *C'est* | *un* | | *Français.* |

| a. He is a doctor. | He is a good doctor. |
|---|---|
| b. She is Catholic. | She is a Catholic. |
| c. He is French. | He is a Frenchman. |

Note:

- Use *il/elle est* without an article; use *c'est* with an article.
- A modifier cannot be used with *il/elle est*. Contrast:

| *C'est un bon médecin.* | He's a good doctor. |
|---|---|
| *Il est médecin.* | He's a doctor. |

| Il est + Adjective | de + Inf. | Comp. | C'est + Adjective | à + Inf. |
|---|---|---|---|---|
| a. *Il est facile* | *de voir* | *Paris.* | *C'est facile* | *à voir.* |
| b. *Il est difficile* | *de faire* | *cela.* | *C'est difficile* | *à faire.* |
| c. *Il est important* | *de savoir* | *son nom.* | *C'est important* | *à savoir.* |

| | |
|---|---|
| a. It is easy to see Paris. | It is easy to see. |
| b. It is difficult to do that. | It is difficult to do. |
| c. It is important to know his name. | It is important to know. |

Note:

- When the infinitive takes an object, use *il est* + adjective + *de* + infinitive + complement.
- When there is no object, use *c'est* + adjective + *à* + infinitive.

| Il est | Adjective | que + verb | C'est | Adjective |
|---|---|---|---|---|
| a. *Il est* | *vrai* | *qu'elle est venue.* | *C'est* | *vrai.* |
| b. *Il est* | *probable* | *qu'elle est arrivée.* | *C'est* | *probable.* |
| c. *Il est* | *certain* | *que vous avez tort.* | *C'est* | *certain.* |
| d. *Il est* | *possible* | *qu'elle soit venue.* | *C'est* | *possible.* |

| | |
|---|---|
| a. It is true that she came. | It's (That's) true. |
| b. It is probable that she arrived. | It's probable. |
| c. It is certain that you are wrong. | It is certain. |
| d. It is possible that she came. | It is possible. |

Note:

- Use *Il est* when the adjective is followed by a clause; use *C'est* when the adjective is used alone.

| C'est/Ce sont | Noun/Pronoun | English |
|---|---|---|
| C'est | **Jean.** | It's John. |
| C'est | **une table.** | It's a table. |
| C'est | **une petite fille.** | It's a little girl. |
| C'est | **moi.** | It's I. |
| C'est | **le mien.** | It's mine. |
| C'est | **celui-là** | It's that one. |
| C'est | **tout.** | It's everything. (That's all.) |
| Ce sont | **mes amis.** | They are my friends. |
| Ce sont | **ceux de mon frère.** | They are my brother's. |

## EXERCISES

A. Substitute each of the words or expressions in parentheses for the underlined word or expression in the model sentence. Write the complete sentence and say it aloud.

1. *Il faut que j'aille à la bibliothèque. (au magasin, à l'opéra, à la banque, à la poste, au garage)*
2. *Il faut qu'il apprenne le français. (les mathématiques, l'histoire, les sciences, la biologie, la chimie)*
3. *Il est médecin. (avocat, professeur, banquier, chirurgien, dentiste, pharmacien, tailleur, coiffeur)*
4. *C'est le mien. (le tien, le sien, le vôtre, le nôtre, le leur)*
5. *Ce sont les miennes. (les tiennes, les vôtres, les leurs, les siennes, les nôtres)*
6. *C'est facile à voir. (faire, comprendre, dire, apprendre, lire)*
7. *Il est possible qu'elle soit malade. (regrettable, triste, étonnant, douteux, incroyable)*

B. Translate the following sentences into French. Then say them aloud.

1. I have to go to the bank now.
2. We have to do our work now.
3. She'll have to take the plane.
4. On Sundays, they go to church.
5. She went to church on Sunday.
6. He's a teacher.
7. He's a good teacher.
8. It's not easy.
9. That's not easy to say.
10. It's possible that she can't come.
11. That pen? It's mine.

C. From among the three choices, select the best translation for the English word or phrase given, write the complete sentence, and translate.

1. (near) *Y a-t-il une temple* _____ *l'hôtel?*
   (a) *voisin*
   ‿ (b) *près de*
   (c) *près*
2. (All you have to do is) _____ *vous rendre à la mosquée.*
   (a) *Tout vous avez à faire est*
   (b) *Tout à faire est*
   ‿ (c) *Vous n'avez qu'à*
3. (naturally) *C'est tout en français,* _____ .
   (a) *nature*
   (b) *entendu*
   ‿ (c) *bien entendu*
4. (take place) *Les offices* _____ *le vendredi soir.*
   (a) *prennent place*
   (b) *prennent lieu*
   ‿ (c) *ont lieu*

5. (attend) *Si vous voulez* _____ *un service,*
   *allez-y.*
   (a) *assister à*
   (b) *attendre*
   (c) *aller*

6. (about) *Je parlais* _____ *de temples.*
   (a) *autour*
   (b) *au sujet*
   (c) *vers*

7. (to call) *Je vais* _____ *à Michel.*
   (a) *donner un téléphone*
   (b) *donner un coup*
   (c) *donner un coup de fil*

8. (If that's all right with you) _____ , *on irait*
   *ensemble.*
   (a) *Si c'est juste avec vous*
   (b) *Si cela a raison*
   (c) *Si cela vous convient*

9. (in the morning) *Il se marie à 9 h 30* _____ .
   (a) *du matin*
   (b) *dans le matin*
   (c) *en matin*

10. (could) *Pensez-vous que nous* _____ *assister à*
    *ce mariage civil?*
    (a) *pouvons*
    (b) *pouvions*
    (c) *puissions*

## SUMMARY OF FRENCH GRAMMAR

1. About the Sounds

Very few sounds are exactly alike in both English and French. The pronunciation equivalents given below can therefore be only approximate. Although exceptions exist for almost every pronunciation rule, the guidelines in this section should prove useful to the student.

*The Consonants.* French consonant sounds are generally softer than those of English. A number of them are produced by bringing the tongue in contact with different parts of the mouth cavity than for the equivalent English consonant, or by changing the pressure of the airstream. For example, the English speaker produces the sound of *d, t,* or *n* by placing the tip of the tongue against the gum ridge behind the upper teeth. The French speaker produces these sounds by placing the tip of the tongue against the back of the upper teeth.

In pronouncing a *p* at the beginning of a word such as "pat" or "pen," the English speaker produces a puff of air, whereas the French speaker does not. Try holding your hand in front of your mouth and saying the words "pit," "pack," and "punch." You will feel the puff of air each time you say the *p* at the beginning of each of these words. The French speaker, on the other hand, produces the *p* at the beginning of words *without* the puff of air. The French *p* is close in sound to the English *p* in words like "speak" or "spot."

The pronunciation of the sound *l* also varies in the two languages. American English has two *l* sounds—one that is used at the beginning of a word (the "light" *l*), and another that is used in the middle or at the end of a word (the "dark" *l*). Contrast the *l* sound in the words "like" and "beautiful." The *l* in "like" is a "light" *l*, and this is the *l* sound pronounced in French.

*The Vowels.* Some of the vowel sounds of French resemble the vowels in English. Many vowel sounds, however, are quite different, and some do not exist in English at all.

For example, the sound represented by *é* resembles the English *ay* in the word "day," but the two sounds are not the same. When an English speaker says "day," he is actually pronouncing two sounds: an *a* and a *y*, which glide together to form a diphthong. Try holding your hand on your jaw and saying the words listed below. As you do so, notice how your jaw closes up a bit toward the end of the *ay* sound:

day    say    may    ray    nay    tray    jay

In French, however, the jaw does not move as you say the *é* sound; it remains steady. Pronounce the following French words, while holding the jaw still.

*des    bébé    faché    mes    réalité*

A similar phenomenon occurs with the sound *o*. Say the following words in English:

bow    tow    know    so

Note that the jaw rises at the end of the sound as though to close on the sound *w*. Hold your hand on your jaw and say the above words in slow motion. Now, leaving off the *w* sound at the end by holding the jaw steady, say the following words in French:

*beau    tôt    nos    sot*
(The final consonants are silent.)

Space does not permit us to compare every English sound with its French counterpart, but the charts below will help to clarify the sounds. Repeated imitation of the speakers on the recordings is the best way to learn how to pronounce French correctly.

## 2. The Alphabet

| LETTER | NAME | LETTER | NAME | LETTER | NAME |
|--------|------|--------|------|--------|------|
| a | *a* | f | *effe* | k | *ka* |
| b | *bé* | g | *gé* | l | *elle* |
| c | *cé* | h | *ache* | m | *emme* |
| d | *dé* | i | *i* | n | *enne* |
| e | *é* | j | *ji* | o | *o* |

| p | *pé* | t | *té* | x | *iks* |
|---|------|---|------|---|-------|
| q | *ku* | u | *u* | y | *i grec* |
| r | *erre* | v | *vé* | z | *zède* |
| s | *esse* | w | *double vé* | | |

## 3. The Consonants

The letters *b, d, f, k, l, m, n, p, s, t, v,* and *z* are pronounced approximately as in English when they are not in final position, but with the differences indicated above. Note, however:

*c*  before *a, o, u, l,* and *r* is like the *c* in "cut." Ex., *carte, cœur, cuisine, clarté, croire*

before *e* and *i* is like *s* in "see." Ex., *centre, cinéma*

*ç*  (c with cedilla) is like *s* in "see." Ex., *français, garçon*

*ch*  is like *sh* in "ship." Ex., *chéri, cheval.* But: *chr* is pronounced like English *kr.* Ex., *chrétien*

*g*  before *a, o, u, l, r* is like *g* in "go." Ex., *gare, goût, guerre, glace, grand;*

before *e* and *i* is like the *s* sound in "measure." Ex., *genre, voyageur, Gigi*

*gn*  is like *ni* in "onion" or *ny* in "canyon." Ex., *oignon, soigner*

*h*  is not pronounced. Ex., *heure*

*j*  is like the *s* sound in "measure." Ex., *bonjour, joie*

*l*  is always "light" (as explained above) when it is pronounced as *l.* However, in the following combinations it is pronounced like the *y* in "yes": *-ail, -eil, -eille, -aille, -ille, -ill.* Ex., *chandail, vermeil, oreille, grisaille, vieillard.* But: in *mille, ville* the *l*'s are pronounced as *l.*

*qu*  before *a, e, i, o, u* is like *k.* Ex., *qui, quotidien;* before *oi* is like *kwa.* Ex., *quoi*

*r*  is made farther back in the throat than the English *r;* almost like a gargle. There is also the *trilled r,* which is used by some people in various parts of the country, particularly in the South. The *trilled r* is formed by the tip of the tongue against the gum ridge back of the upper teeth in a rapid succession of taps.

*s*    is generally like the *s* in "see." Ex., *soir, estimer*;
       between vowels it is like the *s* in "rose." Ex., *rose,
       vase*
*w*    (occurring only in foreign words) is generally pro-
       nounced *v*. Ex., *wagon*; the first letter in *whisky*,
       however, is pronounced *w*.

### Final Consonants

As a general rule, final consonants are silent. However, words ending in *c, f, l,* and *r* often do pronounce the final consonant. Ex.:
  *-c: parc, sac, trafic*
  *-f: bref, chef, œuf*
  *-l: moral, Noël, journal*
  *-r: sur, erreur, manoir*
There are several cases in which the final *r* is generally silent:

• The infinite ending of *-er* verbs. Ex., *parler, aller,
  jouer*
• Names of certain tradespeople. Ex., *le boucher, le
  boulanger, le plombier*
• Nouns ending in *-er*. Ex., *verger, soulier, tablier*

There are many common words ending in *c, l,* and *f*
in which the final consonant is silent. Ex., *estomac,
banc, blanc, gentil, pareil, clef* ·

### 4. Simple Vowels

*a*    as in "ah!" or "father." Ex., *pâté, mâle, Jacques*
       as in "marry." Ex., *ami, mal*
*e*    as in "let." Ex., *belle, cher, cette*
       as in "day," without the *y* sound at the end (as ex-
       plained above). This occurs in monosyllables or
       words ending in *-er, -et,* or *-ez,* and is the same
       sound as *é*. Ex., *les, des, laver, filet, allez*
       as in "the" (the "mute" *e* between two single con-
       sonants or in monosyllabic words). Ex., *depuis, le,
       petit, tenir, besoin*
       The unaccented *e* is silent ("mute") at the end of a
       word. Ex., *parle, femme, limonade*

| | |
|---|---|
| é | (*accent aigu*) as in "day," without the *y* sound at the end. Ex., *église, école, fâché, réalité* |
| è | (*accent grave*) as in "let." Ex., *père, mètre, Agnès* |
| ê | (*accent circonflexe*) as in "let." Ex., *tête, être* |
| i | as in "machine." The letter *y*, when it acts as a vowel, is pronounced the same way. Ex., *machine, lycée, qui, bicyclette* |
| o | (closed *o*) as in "go" (without the *w* sound at the end, as explained above). Ex., *tôt, mot, dos*<br>(open *o*) as in the *ou* in "southern." Ex., *robe, alors, bonne, gosse* |
| u | has no equivalent in English. To approximate the sound, say *ee*, keep the tongue in the position of *ee* (with the tip of the tongue against the bottom teeth), and then round the lips. Ex., *lune, nuit, assure* |
| ai | as in "day" (without the *y* sound at the end). Ex., *mais, caisson, lait* |
| ei | as in "let." Ex., *reine, peine* |
| au<br>eau | as in "go" (without the *w* sound at the end). Ex., *auprès, pauvre, eau, eau(x)* |
| eu | has no equivalent in English. To approximate the sound, place the tongue as if for *é*, but round the lips as for *o*. Ex., *deux, feu, peu, ceux* |
| œ | has no equivalent in English. It is more "open" than *eu*. To form the sound, place the tongue as if for the *e* of "let," but round the lips. This sound is usually followed by a consonant, as in *sœur, cœur* |
| oi | pronounced *wa*. Ex., *moi, voilà* |
| ou | as in "too." Ex., *nous, vous, cousin, rouge, amour* |

## 5. The Nasalized Vowels

When the consonants *n* and *m* are preceded by a vowel, the sound is generally nasalized; that is, the airstream escapes partly through the nose. The four categories of nasalized vowels are as follows:

    a. *an, am, en,* and *em* are like the *au* in the British *aunt* pronounced through the nose:

| | |
|---|---|
| *an* | year |
| *ample* | ample |

| | |
|---|---|
| *en* | in |
| *enveloppe* | envelope |
| *temps* | time |

b. *on* and *om* are like the vowel in *north* pronounced through the nose:

| | |
|---|---|
| *bon* | good |
| *tomber* | to fall |

c. *in, im, ein, eim, ain,* and *aim* are like the vowel in *at* pronounced through the nose:

| | |
|---|---|
| *fin* | end |
| *simple* | simple |
| *faim* | hunger |
| *plein* | full |

d. *un* and *um* are like the vowel in *burn* pronounced through the nose:

| | |
|---|---|
| *un* | one |
| *chacun* | each one |
| *humble* | humble |

Vowels are nasalized in the following cases:

a. When the *n* or *m* is the final consonant or one of the final consonants:

| | |
|---|---|
| *fin* | end |
| *pont* | bridge |
| *champ* | field |
| *temps* | time |

b. In the middle of a word, when the *n* or *m* is not followed by a vowel:

### Nasalized

| | | | |
|---|---|---|---|
| *chambre* | room | *impossible* | impossible |

### Not Nasalized

| | | | |
|---|---|---|---|
| *inutile* | useless | *inoccupé* | unoccupied |
| *initial* | initial | *imitation* | imitation |

Note: *mm* and *nn* do not cause the nasalization of the preceding vowel:

| | | | |
|---|---|---|---|
| *flamme* | flame | *innocent* | innocent |
| *donner* | to give | *immense* | immense |

## 6. The Apostrophe

Certain one-syllable words ending in a vowel drop ("elide") the vowel when they come before words beginning with a vowel sound.

This dropping of the vowel or "elision" is marked by an apostrophe. Common cases are:

a. The *a* of *la*:

| | | | |
|---|---|---|---|
| *je l'aime* | I like her (or it) | *l'heure* | the hour |
| *l'amande* | the almond | | |

b. The vowel *e* in one-syllable words (*le, je, se, me, que,* etc.):

| | | | |
|---|---|---|---|
| *l'argent* | the money | *j'habite* | I live |
| *j'ai* | I have | | |

c. The vowel *i* in *si* "if," when it comes before *il* "he" or *ils* "they":

| | |
|---|---|
| *s'il vous plaît* | please ("if it pleases you") |

d. *moi* and *toi* when they come before *en* are written *m'* and *t':*

| | |
|---|---|
| *Donnez-m'en* | Give me some of it (of them). |

e. A few words like *aujourd'hui* (today), etc.

## 7. The Definite Article

| | SINGULAR | PLURAL |
|---|---|---|
| Masculine | *le* | *les* |
| Feminine | *la* | *les* |

Singular

| | |
|---|---|
| *le garçon* | the boy |
| *la fille* | the girl |

Plural

| | |
|---|---|
| *les garçons* | the boys |
| *les filles* | the girls |

a. *Le* and *la* become *l'* before words beginning with a vowel sound.

This contraction takes place before most words beginning with *h* (this *h* is called a "mute" *h*). There are a few words where this contraction does not occur (this *h* is called an "aspirate" *h*):

| | | | |
|---|---|---|---|
| *l'ami* | the friend | *l'heure* | the hour |
| *le héros* | the hero | *la hache* | the ax |

b. Unlike English, the definite article is used in French before a noun used in a general sense, before titles, days of the week, parts of the body, etc.:

| | |
|---|---|
| *l'avion* | the airplane |
| *le dimanche* | Sunday (or Sundays) |
| *le Comte . . .* | Count . . . |
| *J'aime les livres.* | I like books. |
| *Le fer est utile.* | Iron is useful. |
| *L'avarice est un vice.* | Avarice is a vice. |
| *Je vais me laver les mains.* | I'm going to wash my hands. |

c. The definite article is used with names of languages, unless preceded by *en:*

| | |
|---|---|
| *Le français est difficile.* | French is difficult. |
| But— | |
| *Elle raconte l'histoire en français.* | She tells the story in French. |

Note: The article is usually omitted with the name of a language used immediately after the verb *parler:*

| | |
|---|---|
| *Elle parle français.* | She speaks French. |

d. Unlike English, definite articles must be repeated before each noun they modify.

*les portes et les fenêtres*    the doors and windows

## 8. The Indefinite Article

|  | SINGULAR | PLURAL |
|---|---|---|
| Masculine | *un* | *des* |
| Feminine | *une* | *des* |

### Singular

| *un homme* | a man |
|---|---|
| *une femme* | a woman |

### Plural

| *des hommes* | men; some men; a few men |
|---|---|
| *des femmes* | women; some women; a few women |

a. The indefinite article is omitted before an unmodified statement of profession, nationality, rank, etc.:

| *Je suis médecin.* | I am a doctor. |
|---|---|
| *Elle est américaine.* | She is an American. |
| *Il est capitaine.* | He is a captain. |

But, with an adjective:

*C'est un bon médecin.*    He is a good doctor.

b. The indefinite articles are repeated before each noun:

*un homme et une femme*    a man and woman

## 9. The Possessive

The possessive is expressed in the following way: State the thing possessed + *de* (of) + the possessor:

| | |
|---|---|
| *le livre de Marie* | Mary's book ("the book of Mary") |
| *le stylo de l'élève* | the pupil's pen ("the pen of the pupil") |

10. Contractions

   a. The preposition *de* "of" combines with the definite
      articles *le* and *les* as follows:

| | | |
|---|---|---|
| *de + le = du:* | *le livre du professeur* | the teacher's book |
| *de + les = des:* | *les stylos des élèves* | the pupils' pens |

   b. The preposition *à* "to" combines with the articles *le*
      and *les* as follows:

| | | |
|---|---|---|
| *à + le = au:* | *Il parle au garçon.* | He's talking to the boy. |
| *à + les = aux:* | *Il parle aux garçons.* | He's talking to the boys. |

11. Gender

All English nouns take the articles *the* or *a(n)*. Adjectives
modifying English nouns do not change their form. In
French, however, all nouns show gender (masculine or feminine),
and adjectives agree with nouns in gender and number
(singular or plural).

Masculine nouns take the definite article *le* in the singular
and *les* in the plural, and the indefinite article *un*. They are
modified by the masculine form of an adjective.

| | |
|---|---|
| *le costume brun* | the brown suit |
| *les costumes bruns* | the brown suits |

Feminine nouns take the definite article *la* in the singular
and *les* in the plural, and the indefinite article *une*. They are
modified by the feminine form of an adjective.

| | |
|---|---|
| *la robe brune* | the brown dress |
| *les robes brunes* | the brown dresses |

The gender of each noun must be learned with the noun. The following tables describing which noun classes are masculine and which are feminine provide a general rule of thumb. There are a number of exceptions to each statement.

The following classes of nouns are generally masculine:

a. Nouns naming a male person. Ex., *le père* father, *le roi* king

   But: *la sentinelle* sentinel

b. Nouns ending in a consonant. Ex., *le parc* park, *le pont* bridge, *le tarif* rate, tariff

   But: Nouns ending in *-ion* and *-son* are generally feminine. Ex., *l'action* action, *la conversation* conversation, *la raison* reason

c. Nouns ending in any vowel except "mute" *e*. Ex., *le pari* bet, wager, *le vélo* bicycle, *le menu* menu

d. Nouns ending in *-ment, -age, -ege* (note that *-age* and *-ege* end in "mute" *e*). Ex., *le ménage* household, *le manège* riding school, *le document* document, *l'usage* usage

e. Names of days, months, seasons, metals, colors, trees, shrubs. Ex.:

| | | | |
|---|---|---|---|
| *le jeudi* | Thursday | *le bleu* | blue |
| (*le*) *septembre* | September | *le chêne* | oak |
| *le printemps* | spring | *l'olivier* | olive tree |
| *l'or* | gold | *le genêt* | broom (a |
| *le plomb* | lead | | shrub) |

f. The names of parts of speech when used as nouns. Ex., *le nom* noun, *le verbe* verb, *le participe* participle

g. Decimal weights and measures. Ex., *le mètre* meter, *le litre* liter, *le kilogramme* kilogram Note the contrast with a nondecimal measure: *la livre* pound

h. The names of the cardinal points. Ex., *le nord* north, *l'est* east, *le sud* south, *l'ouest* west

The following classes of nouns are generally feminine:

a. Nouns naming a female person. Ex., *la mère* mother, *la reine* queen
But: *le professeur* teacher (m. or f.)

b. Nouns ending in *-te, -son, -ion*. Ex., *la détente* détente, *la raison* reason, *la conversation* conversation
But: *le camion* truck, *l'avion* airplane, *le million* million

c. Names of qualities or states of being ending in: *-nce, esse, -eur, -ude*.

| | |
|---|---|
| *la distance* | distance |
| *la gentillesse* | niceness |
| *la largeur* | width |
| *la douceur* | sweetness |
| *la gratitude* | gratitude |

But: *le bonheur* happiness, *le malheur* unhappiness, pain.

d. Most nouns ending in mute *e*. Ex., *la blague* joke, *la voiture* car
But: See exceptions mentioned in item 4, page 308, under nouns of masculine gender.

e. Names of moral qualities, sciences, and arts. Ex., moral qualities: *la bonté* kindness, *l'avarice* greed
science: *l'algèbre* algebra, *la chimie* chemistry
art: *la peinture* painting, *la musique* music
But: *l'art* (m.), art

f. Most names of fruits. Ex., *la pomme* apple, *la cerise* cherry
But: *le pamplemousse* grapefruit, *le raisin* grapes

g. Nouns ending in -té. Ex., *l'activité* activity, *la générosité* generosity, *la proximité* proximity, *la priorité* priority

## 12. Plural of Nouns

a. Most nouns add -*s* to form the plural:

| | | | |
|---|---|---|---|
| *la ville* | the city | *les villes* | the cities |
| *l'île* | the island | *les îles* | the islands |

b. Nouns ending in -*s*, -*x*, -*z* do not change:

| | | | |
|---|---|---|---|
| *le fils* | the son | *les fils* | the sons |
| *la voix* | the voice | *les voix* | the voices |
| *le nez* | the nose | *les nez* | the noses |

c. Nouns ending in -*au* or -*eu* add -*x*:

| | | | |
|---|---|---|---|
| *le chapeau* | the hat | *les chapeaux* | the hats |
| *l'eau* | water | *les eaux* | waters |
| *le jeu* | the game | *les jeux* | the games |

d. Nouns ending in -*al* and -*ail* for the plural with -*aux*.

| | | | |
|---|---|---|---|
| *l'hôpital* | the hospital | *les hôpitaux* | the hospitals |
| *le travail* | work | *les travaux* | works |

Some irregular plurals:

| | | | |
|---|---|---|---|
| *le ciel* | the sky | *les cieux* | the heavens |
| *l'œil* | the eye | *les yeux* | the eyes |
| *Madame* | Madam, Mrs. | *Mesdames* | Madams |
| *Mademoiselle* | Miss | *Mesdemoiselles* | Misses |
| *Monsieur* | Sir, Mr. | *Messieurs* | Sirs |
| *le bonhomme* | the fellow | *les bonshommes* | the fellows |

## 13. Feminine of Adjectives

a. The feminine of adjectives is normally formed by adding -*e* to the masculine singular, but if the masculine singular already ends in -*e*, the adjective has the same form in the feminine:

Masculine

*un petit garçon*          a little boy
*un jeune homme*           a young man

Feminine

*une petite fille*         a little girl
*une jeune femme*          a young woman

  b. Adjectives ending in *-er* change the *e* to *è* and then
     add *-e:*

*étranger* (m.)     *étrangère* (f.)      foreign

  c. Most adjectives ending in *-eux* change this ending to
     *-euse:*

*heureux* (m.)      *heureuse* (f.)       happy
*sérieux* (m.)      *sérieuse* (f.)       serious

  d. Some adjectives double the final consonant and add
     *-e:*

*bon* (m.)          *bonne* (f.)          good
*ancien* (m.)       *ancienne* (f.)       former, ancient
*gentil* (m.)       *gentille* (f.)       nice
*gros* (m.)         *grosse* (f.)         fat

  e. Adjectives ending in *-eau* change the *-au* to *-lle:*

*beau* (m.)         *belle* (f.)          beautiful
*nouveau* (m.)      *nouvelle* (f.)       new

  f. There are a number of irregular feminines:

*actif* (m.)        *active* (f.)         active
*blanc* (m.)        *blanche* (f.)        white
*doux* (m.)         *douce* (f.)          sweet, gentle, soft
*faux* (m.)         *fausse* (f.)         false
*long* (m.)         *longue* (f.)         long
*vieux* (m.)        *vieille* (f.)        old

14. Plural of Adjectives

    a. The plural of adjectives is regularly formed by adding -*s* to the singular, but if the masculine singular ends in -*s* or -*x,* the masculine plural has the same form:

| SINGULAR | | PLURAL | |
|---|---|---|---|
| *un petit garçon* | a little boy | *deux petits garçons* | two little boys |
| *une petite fille* | a little girl | *deux petites filles* | two little girls |
| *un mauvais garçon* | a bad boy | *deux mauvais garçons* | two bad boys |

    b. Adjectives ending in -*au* add -*x:*

| *un nouveau livre* | a new book | *des nouveaux livres* | new books |
|---|---|---|---|

    c. Adjectives ending in -*al* change to -*aux:*

| *un homme loyal* | a loyal man | *des hommes loyaux* | loyal men |
|---|---|---|---|

15. Agreement of Adjectives

    a. Adjectives agree with the nouns they modify in gender and number; that is, they are masculine if the noun is masculine, plural if the noun is plural, etc.:

| *Marie et sa sœur sont petites.* | Mary and her sister are little. |
|---|---|

    b. An adjective that modifies nouns of different gender is in the masculine plural:

| *Marie et Jean sont petits.* | Mary and John are little. |
|---|---|

16. Position of Adjectives

    a. Adjectives usually follow the noun:

| *un livre français* | a French book |
|---|---|
| *un homme intéressant* | an interesting man |
| *une idée excellente* | an excellent idea |

b. When they describe an inherent quality or when they form a set phrase, etc., they precede the noun:

| | |
|---|---|
| *une jeune fille* | a young girl |
| *le savant auteur* | the learned scholar |
| *une étroite amitié* | a close friendship |
| *une éclatante victoire* | a striking victory |

c. The following common adjectives usually precede the nouns they modify:

| | | | |
|---|---|---|---|
| *autre* | other | *jeune* | young |
| *beau* | beautiful | *joli* | pretty |
| *bon* | good | *long* | long |
| *court* | short | *mauvais* | bad |
| *gentil* | nice, pleasant | *nouveau* | new |
| *grand* | great, large, tall | *petit* | small, little |
| *gros* | big, fat | *vieux* | old |

d. The following common adjectives differ in meaning depending on whether they come before or after the noun.

| | BEFORE THE NOUN | AFTER THE NOUN |
|---|---|---|
| *ancien* | former | ancient |
| *grand* | great | tall |
| *brave* | worthy | brave |
| *cher* | dear | expensive |
| *pauvre* | poor (wretched) | poor (indigent) |
| *propre* | own | clean |
| *même* | same | himself, herself, itself, very |

e. The following adjectives have two forms for the masculine singular:

| MASCULINE SINGULAR | | FEMININE SINGULAR | |
|---|---|---|---|
| Before a Consonant | Before a vowel or "Mute" h | | |
| *beau* | *bel* | *belle* | beautiful |

| *nouveau* | *nouvel* | *nouvelle* | new |
| *vieux* | *vieil* | *vielle* | old |

Examples:

| *un beau livre* | a beautiful book |
| *un bel arbre* | a beautiful tree |
| *une belle femme* | a beautiful woman |

17. Comparison of Adjectives

Most adjectives form the comparative and superlative by placing *plus* and *le plus* (*la plus*) before the adjective:

Positive

| *petit* | small |
| *grand* | large |

Comparative

| *plus petit* | smaller |
| *plus grand* | larger |

Superlative

| *le plus petit* | the smallest |
| *le plus grand* | the largest |

Common exceptions:

Positive

| *bon* | good |
| *mauvais* | bad |

Comparative

| *meilleur* | better |
| *plus mauvais* ⎫<br>*pire* ⎭ | worse |

Superlative

| | |
|---|---|
| *le meilleur* | the best |
| *le plus mauvais* ⎫ *le pire* ⎭ | the worst |

18. Possessive Adjectives

   a. Possessive adjectives agree in gender and number with the thing possessed:

| BEFORE SINGULAR NOUNS: | | BEFORE PLURAL NOUNS: | |
|---|---|---|---|
| MASCULINE | FEMININE | MASCULINE AND FEMININE | |
| *mon* | *ma* | *mes* | my |
| *ton* | *ta* | *tes* | your (*fam.*) |
| *son* | *sa* | *ses* | his, her, its |
| *notre* | *notre* | *nos* | our |
| *votre* | *votre* | *vos* | your |
| *leur* | *leur* | *leurs* | their |

Examples:

| | |
|---|---|
| *mon chien* | my dog |
| *sa mère* | his (or her) mother |
| *ma robe* | my dress |
| *votre livre* | your book |
| *leurs crayons* | their pencils |

   b. Notice that these adjectives agree in gender not with the possessor as in English, but with the noun they modify. *Son, sa,* and *ses* may therefore mean "his," "her," or "its."

| | |
|---|---|
| *Jean parle à sa mère.* | John is talking to his mother. |
| *Marie parle à son père.* | Mary is talking to her father. |

   c. Possessive adjectives are repeated before each noun they modify:

| | |
|---|---|
| *mon père et ma mère* | my father and mother |
| *leurs livres et leurs plumes* | their books and pens |

d. Before a feminine word beginning with a vowel or "mute" *h*, the forms *mon, ton, son* are used instead of *ma, ta, sa:*

| | |
|---|---|
| *son histoire* | his story, his history |
| *son école* | his (or her) school |

e. In speaking of parts of the body, the definite article is usually used instead of the possessive adjective (except where it might be ambiguous):

| | |
|---|---|
| *J'ai mal à la tête.* | I have a headache. |

## 19. Possessive Pronouns

| MASCULINE | | FEMININE | | |
|---|---|---|---|---|
| SINGULAR | PLURAL | SINGULAR | PLURAL | |
| *le mien* | *les miens* | *la mienne* | *les miennes* | mine |
| *le tien* | *les tiens* | *la tienne* | *les tiennes* | yours (*fam.*) |
| *le sien* | *les siens* | *la sienne* | *les siennes* | his, hers, its |
| *le nôtre* | *les nôtres* | *la nôtre* | *les nôtres* | ours |
| *le vôtre* | *les vôtres* | *la vôtre* | *les vôtres* | yours |
| *le leur* | *les leurs* | *la leur* | *les leurs* | theirs |

Examples:

| | |
|---|---|
| *Voici le mien.* | Here's mine. |
| *Quel est la vôtre?* | Which is yours? |
| *Apportez les vôtres;* *j'apporterai les miens.* | Bring yours; I'll bring mine. |

## 20. Demonstrative Adjectives

### Masculine Singular

| | | |
|---|---|---|
| *ce* (before a consonant) | *ce livre* | this (that) book |

| *cet* (before a | *cet arbre* | this (that) tree |
| vowel or | *cet homme* | this (that) man |
| "mute" *h*) | | |

## Feminine Singular

| *cette* | *cette femme* | this (that) woman |

## Plural

| *ces* | *ces hommes* | these (those) men |
| | *ces femmes* | these (those) women |

a. The demonstrative adjectives agree with the nouns they modify in gender and number. They must be repeated before each noun:

| *cet homme et cette femme* | this man and this woman |

b. The demonstrative adjective in French stands for both "this" and "that" (plural "these" and "those"). When it is necessary to distinguish between "this" and "that," *-ci* and *-là* are added to the noun.

| *Donnez-moi ce livre-ci.* | Give me this book. |
| *Voulez-vous cette* | Do you want that dress |
| *robe-là?* | (over there)? |
| *J'aime ce livre-ci, mais* | I like this book, but I |
| *je n'aime pas ce livre-là.* | don't like that book. |

## 21. Demonstrative Pronouns

| Masc. sing. | *celui* | this one, that one, the one |
| Fem. sing. | *celle* | this one, that one, the one |
| Masc. pl. | *ceux* | these, those, the ones |
| Fem. pl. | *celles* | these, those, the ones |

Examples:

| *J'aime celui-ci.* | I like that one. |
| *Donne-moi celle de ton* | Give me your brother's |
| *frère.* | (pen, for example). |

## 22. Personal Pronouns

The forms of the pronouns will depend on whether they are:

- the subject of a verb
- the direct object of a verb
- the indirect object of a verb
- the object of a preposition
- used as a reflexive pronoun

a. As the subject of a verb:

| | | | |
|---|---|---|---|
| *je* | I | *nous* | we |
| *tu* | you (fam.) | *vous* | you |
| *il* | he, it | *ils* | they |
| *elle* | she, it | *elles* | they |
| *on* | one, we | | |

- *Vous* is used when speaking to people you do not know well or to whom you want to be especially polite. *Tu* is used with people whom you know well, such as family or friends, or among young people in their peer group.
- *Il, elle, ils,* and *elles* are used as pronouns referring to things as well as to persons. They have the same number and gender as the nouns to which they refer. *Ils* is used to refer to nouns of different genders:

| | |
|---|---|
| *Où est le livre?* | Where's the book? |
| *Il est sur la table.* | It's on the table. |
| *Où est la lettre?* | Where's the letter? |
| *Elle est sur la table.* | It's on the table. |
| *Où sont les livres et les lettres?* | Where are the books and letters? |
| *Ils sont sur la table.* | They're on the table. |

b. As the direct object of a verb:

| | | | |
|---|---|---|---|
| *me* | me | *nous* | us |
| *te* | you | *vous* | you |
| *le* | him, it | *les* | them |
| *la* | her, it | *en* | some, any |

c. As the indirect object of a verb:

| | | | |
|---|---|---|---|
| *me* | to me | *vous* | to you |
| *te* | to you | *leur* | to them |
| *lui* | to him, to her | *y* | to it, there |
| *nous* | to us | | |

d. As the object of a preposition; disjunctive pronouns:

| | | | |
|---|---|---|---|
| *moi* | I, me | *nous* | we, us |
| *toi* | you (fam.) | *vous* | you |
| *soi* | oneself | *eux* | they, them (masc.) |
| *lui* | he, him | *elles* | they, them (fem.) |
| *elle* | she, her | | |

e. As a reflexive pronoun:

| | |
|---|---|
| *me* | myself |
| *te* | yourself |
| *se* | himself, herself, itself, oneself |
| *nous* | ourselves |
| *vous* | yourself, yourselves |
| *se* | themselves |

f. In affirmative commands:

DIRECT OBJECT          INDICT OBJECT

| | | | |
|---|---|---|---|
| | | *moi/toi*[1] | |
| *le* | | *nous* | |
| *la* } | before | *vous* } | before *y* before *en* |
| *les* | | *lui* | |
| | | *leur* | |

## 23. Position of Pronouns

The direct and indirect pronoun objects generally precede the verb except in affirmative commands and requests.

[1] When *moi* or *toi* are used with *en*, they become *m'* and *t'* and precede *en*.

| | |
|---|---|
| Examples: Donnez-*le-moi*. | But: Donnez-*m'en*. |
| Lève-*toi*. | But: Va-t'en. |

a. Position before a verb:

$$\left.\begin{matrix} me \\ te \\ se \\ nous \\ vous \end{matrix}\right\} \text{ before } \left.\begin{matrix} le \\ la \\ les \end{matrix}\right\} \text{ before } \left.\begin{matrix} lui \\ leur \end{matrix}\right\} \text{ before } y \text{ before } en$$

Examples:

| | |
|---|---|
| *Il me le donne.* | He gives it to me. |
| *Il le lui donne.* | He gives it to him (to her, to it). |
| *Je l'y ai vu.* | I saw him there. |
| *Je leur en parlerai.* | I'll speak to them about it. |

b. Position after a verb:

$$\left.\begin{matrix} le \\ la \\ les \end{matrix}\right\} \text{ before } \left.\begin{matrix} me\ (moi) \\ te\ (toi) \\ lui \\ nous \\ vous \\ leur \end{matrix}\right\} \text{ before } y \text{ before } en$$

Examples:

| | |
|---|---|
| *Donnez-le-lui.* | Give it to him. |
| *Donnez-leur-en.* | Give them some. |
| *Allez-vous-en.* | Go away. Get out of here. |

c. In affirmative commands, both the direct and indirect object pronoun follow the verb, the direct preceding the indirect:

| | |
|---|---|
| *Donnez-moi le livre.* | Give me the book. |
| *Donnez-le-moi.* | Give it to me. |
| *Montrez-moi les pommes.* | Show me the apples. |
| *Montrez-m'en.* | Show me some. |
| *Écrivez-lui une lettre.* | Write him a letter. |
| *Écrivez-la-lui.* | Write it to him. |

d. The pronoun objects precede *voici* and *voilà:*

| | |
|---|---|
| *Où est le livre?* | Where's the book? |
| *Le voici.* | Here it is. |

## 24. Relative Pronouns

a. As the subject of a verb:

| | |
|---|---|
| *qui* | who, which, that |
| *ce qui* | what, that which |

b. As the object of a verb:

| | |
|---|---|
| *que* | whom, which, that |
| *ce que* | what, that which |

c. As the object of a preposition:

| | |
|---|---|
| *qui* (for a person) | whom |
| *lequel* (for a thing) | which |

Note that *dont* means "whose, of whom, of which":

| | |
|---|---|
| *Le problème dont je connais la solution* . . . | The problem whose solution I know . . . |
| *Le professeur dont je vous ai parlé* . . . | The teacher about whom I talked to you . . . |

## 25. Indefinite Pronouns

| | |
|---|---|
| *quelque chose* | something |
| *quelqu'un* | someone |
| *chacun* | each (one) |
| *on* | one, people, they, etc. |
| *ne . . . rien* | nothing |
| *ne . . . personne* | no one |

## 26. Noun Used as Indirect Object

A noun used as an indirect object is always preceded by the preposition *à:*

| | |
|---|---|
| *Je donne un livre à la jeune fille.* | I'm giving the girl a book. |

## 27. Repetition of Prepositions

The prepositions *à* and *de* must be repeated before each of their objects:

| | |
|---|---|
| *Je parle au député et à son secrétaire.* | I'm speaking to the deputy and his secretary. |
| *Voici les cahiers de Jean et ceux de Marie.* | Here are John's and Mary's notebooks. |

## 28. The Partitive

a. When a noun is used in such a way as to express or imply quantity, it is preceded by *de* with the article. This construction very often translates as the English "some" or "a few."

| | |
|---|---|
| *J'ai de l'argent.* | I have some money. |
| *Il a des amis.* | He has a few friends. |

In many cases, however, the article is used where we don't use "some" or "a few" in English:

| | |
|---|---|
| *A-t-il des amis ici?* | Does he have friends here? |

b. The article is omitted:

• When an expression of quantity is used:

| | |
|---|---|
| *J'ai beaucoup d'argent.* | I have a lot of money. |
| *Combien de livres avez-vous?* | How many books do you have? |

Exceptions: *bien* much, many; and *la plupart* most, the majority:

| | |
|---|---|
| *bien des hommes* | many men |
| *la plupart des hommes* | most men |

• When the noun is preceded by an adjective:

| | |
|---|---|
| *J'ai acheté de belles cravates.* | I bought some nice ties. |

- When the sentence is negative:

| | |
|---|---|
| *Il n'a pas d'amis.* | He has no friends. |
| *Mon ami n'a pas d'argent.* | My friend hasn't any money. |

## 29. Negation

A sentence is made negative by placing *ne* before the verb and *pas* after it:

| | |
|---|---|
| *Je sais.* | I know. |
| *Je ne sais pas.* | I don't know. |
| *Je ne l'ai pas vu.* | I haven't seen it. |

Other negative expressions:

| | |
|---|---|
| *ne . . . guère* | hardly |
| *ne . . . point* | not (at all) (literary) |
| *ne . . . rien* | nothing |
| *ne . . . nul, nulle* | no one, no |
| *ne . . . jamais* | never |
| *ne . . . personne* | nobody |
| *ne . . . plus* | no longer |
| *ne . . . ni . . . ni* | neither . . . nor |
| *ne . . . que* | only |
| *ne . . . aucun, aucune* | no one |

## 30. Word Order in Questions

a. Questions with pronoun subjects:
   There are two ways of asking a question with a pronoun subject:

- Place the pronoun after the verb:

| | |
|---|---|
| *Parlez-vous français?* | Do you speak French? |

- Place *est-ce que* ("is it that") before the sentence:

| | |
|---|---|
| *Est-ce que je parle trop vite?* | Am I talking too fast? |
| *Est-ce que vous parlez français?* | Do you speak French? |

b. Questions with noun subjects:
When a question begins with a noun, the pronoun is repeated after the verb:

| | |
|---|---|
| *Votre frère parle-t-il français?* | Does your brother speak French? |
| *Votre sœur a-t-elle quitté la maison?* | Has your sister left the house? |

c. Questions introduced by interrogative words:
In questions that begin with an interrogative word (*quand, comment, où, pourquoi*), the order is usually: interrogative word—noun subject—verb—personal pronoun:

| | |
|---|---|
| *Pourquoi votre ami a-t-il quitté Paris?* | Why did your friend leave Paris? |

31. Adverbs

a. Most adverbs are formed from the adjectives by adding *-ment* to the feminine form:

| | | | |
|---|---|---|---|
| *froid* | cold | *froidement* | coldly |
| *certain* | certain | *certainement* | certainly |
| *naturel* | natural | *naturelle-ment* | naturally |
| *facile* | easy | *facilement* | easily |

b. There are many irregular adverbs that must be learned separately:

| | | | |
|---|---|---|---|
| *vite* | quickly | *mal* | badly |

c. Adverbs are compared like adjectives

| POSITIVE | COMPARATIVE | SUPERLATIVE |
|---|---|---|
| *loin*　far | *plus loin*　farther | *le plus loin*　the farthest |

d. Some common adverbs of place:

| | |
|---|---|
| *ici* | here |
| *là* | there |

| *à côté* | at the side |
| *de côté* | aside |
| *devant* | before, in front of |
| *derrière* | behind |
| *dessus* | on top |
| *dessous* | underneath |
| *dedans* | inside |
| *dehors* | outside |
| *partout* | everywhere |
| *nulle part* | nowhere |
| *loin* | far |
| *près* | near |
| *où* | where |
| *y* | there |
| *ailleurs* | elsewhere |
| *là-haut* | up there |
| *là-bas* | over there |

e. Some common adverbs of time:

| *aujourd'hui* | today |
| *demain* | tomorrow |
| *hier* | yesterday |
| *avant-hier* | the day before yesterday |
| *après-demain* | the day after tomorrow |
| *maintenant* | now |
| *alors* | then |
| *avant* | before |
| *autrefois* | once, formerly |
| *jadis* | once, formerly |
| *tôt* | early |
| *bientôt* | soon |
| *tard* | late |
| *souvent* | often |
| *ne . . . jamais* | never |
| *toujours* | always, ever |
| *longtemps* | long, for a long time |
| *tantôt* | soon, presently |
| *tantôt . . . tantôt* | now . . . now, sometimes . . . sometimes |
| *encore* | still, yet |
| *ne . . . plus* | no longer, no more |

f. Adverbs of manner:

| | |
|---|---|
| *bien* | well |
| *mal* | ill, badly |
| *ainsi* | thus, so |
| *de même* | similarly |
| *autrement* | otherwise |
| *ensemble* | together |
| *fort* | much, very |
| *volontiers* | willingly |
| *surtout* | above all, especially |
| *exprès* | on purpose, expressly |

g. Adverbs of quantity or degree:

| | |
|---|---|
| *beaucoup* | much, many |
| *assez* | enough |
| *ne . . . guère* | not much, scarcely |
| *peu* | little |
| *plus* | more |
| *ne . . . plus* | no more |
| *moins* | less |
| *encore* | more |
| *bien* | much, many |
| *très* | very |
| *trop* | too, too much, too many |
| *tellement* | so much, so many |

## 32. The Infinitive

The most common endings of the infinitive are:

### I. The First Conjugation

*-er*          *parler* (to speak)

### II. The Second Conjugation

*-ir*          *finir* (to finish)

### III. The Third Conjugation

*-re*          *vendre* (to sell)

## 33. The Past Participle

### Forms

|     | INFINITIVE | PAST PARTICIPLE |
| --- | ---------- | --------------- |
| I   | *parler*   | *parlé*         |
| II  | *finir*    | *fini*          |
| III | *perdre*   | *perdu*         |

### Agreement

a. When a verb is conjugated with *avoir,* the past participle agrees in gender and number with the preceding direct object:

| | |
| --- | --- |
| *La pièce que j'ai vue hier était mauvaise.* | The play I saw yesterday was bad. |
| *Avez-vous vu le livre qu'il a acheté?* | Have you seen the book he bought? |
| *Avez-vous donné la plume à Charles?* | Did you give the pen to Charles? |
| *Non, je l'ai donnée à Claire.* | No, I gave it to Claire. |

b. In the case of reflexive verbs the past participle agrees with the reflexive direct object:

| | |
| --- | --- |
| *Ils se sont levés.* | They got up. |
| *Elle s'est lavée.* | She washed herself. |

c. In the case of intransitive verbs conjugated with *être,* the past participle agrees with the subject:

| | |
| --- | --- |
| *Marie est arrivée hier.* | Mary arrived yesterday. |
| *Jean et Pierre se sont levés.* | John and Peter got up. |
| *Ils sont arrivés.* | They arrived. |
| *Nous sommes rentrés très tard.* | We came back very late. |

## 34. The Indicative

### Simple Tenses

a. The present tense is formed by the verb stem plus the endings *-e, -es, -e, -ons, -ez, -ent.* It has several English translations:

| *je parle* | I speak, I am speaking, I do speak |
| *ils mangent* | They eat, they are eating, they do eat |
| *je me lève* | I get up, I'm getting up |

b. The imperfect tense is formed by dropping the *-ant* of the present participle and adding *-ais, -ais, -ait, -ions, -iez, -aient*. It expresses a continued or habitual action in the past. It also indicates an action that was happening when something else happened:

| *Je me levais à sept heures.* | I used to get up at seven o'clock. |
| *Il dormait quand Jean est entré.* | He was sleeping when John entered. |
| *Il parlait souvent de cela.* | He often spoke about that. |

c. The future tense is formed by adding to the infinitive or future stem the endings, *-ai, -as, -a, -ons, -ez, -ont*. It indicates a future action:

| *Je me lèverai tôt.* | I'll get up early. |
| *Il arrivera demain.* | He'll arrive tomorrow. |
| *Je le vendrai demain.* | I'll sell it tomorrow. |

d. The past definite tense (used only in formal written French) is formed by adding to the root the endings *-ai, -as, -a, -âmes, -âtes, -èrent* for *-er* verbs; the endings *-is, -is, -it, -îmes, -îtes, -irent* for *-ir* verbs; and for all other verbs either these last or *-us, -us, -ut, -ûmes, -ûtes, -urent*. It expresses an action begun and ended in the past, and it is not generally used in the first person.

| *Le roi fut tué.* | The king was killed. |
| *Les soldats entrèrent dans la ville.* | The soldiers entered the city. |

## Compound Tenses

a. The past indefinite tense or ''conversational past'' is formed by adding the past participle to the present indicative of *avoir* or, in a few cases, *être*. It is used to indicate a past action that has been completed.

| | |
|---|---|
| *Je me suis levé tôt.* | I got up early. |
| *Il ne m'a rien dit.* | He didn't tell me anything. |
| *J'ai fini mon travail.* | I finished my work. I have finished my work. |
| *L'avez-vous vu?* | Have you seen him? Did you see him? |
| *Ils sont arrivés.* | They arrived. |

b. The pluperfect or past perfect tense is formed by adding the past participle to the imperfect of *avoir* or, in a few cases, *être*. It translates the English past perfect:

| | |
|---|---|
| *Il l'avait fait.* | He had done it. |
| *Lorsque je suis revenu, il était parti.* | When I came back, he had gone. |

c. The past anterior tense is formed by adding the past participle to the past definite of *avoir* or, in a few cases, *être*. It is used for an event that happened just before another event. It is rarely found except after *quand* and *lorsque* (when), *après que* (after), *dès que* (as soon as). It is used only in literary style.

| | |
|---|---|
| *Après qu'il eut dîné, il sortit.* | As soon as he had eaten, he went out. |
| *Quand il eut fini, il se leva.* | When he had finished, he got up. |

d. The future perfect tense is formed by adding the past participle to the future of *avoir* or, in a few cases, *être*. It translates the English future perfect:

| | |
|---|---|
| *Il aura bientôt fini.* | He will soon have finished. |

Sometimes it indicates probability:

| | |
|---|---|
| *Il le lui aura sans doute dit.* | No doubt he must have told him. |
| *Il aura été malade.* | He probably was sick. |
| *Je me serai trompé.* | I must have been mistaken. |

e. The most common intransitive verbs that are conjugated with the verb *être* in the compound tenses are the following:

*aller, arriver, descendre, devenir, entrer, monter, mourir, naître, partir, rentrer, rester, retourner, revenir, sortir, tomber, venir.*

Examples:

| | |
|---|---|
| *Je suis venu.* | I have come. |
| *Il est arrivé.* | He has arrived. |
| *Nous sommes partis.* | We have left. |

f. Reflexive verbs are conjugated with the auxiliary *être* in the past indefinite:

| | |
|---|---|
| *Je me suis lavé les mains.* | I have washed my hands. |
| *Je me suis levé à sept heures ce matin.* | I got up at seven o'clock this morning. |
| *Elle s'est levée.* | She got up. |

35. The Conditional

a. The conditional is formed by adding to the infinitive the endings *-ais, -ais, -ait, -ions, -iez, -aient.* It translates the English "would" or "should":

| | |
|---|---|
| *Je le prendrais si j'étais à votre place.* | I would take it if I were you. |
| *Je ne ferais jamais une chose pareille.* | I would never do such a thing. |

b. The conditional perfect is formed by adding the past participle to the conditional of *avoir* or, in a few cases, *être*. It translates the English "if I had" or "if I would have," etc.:

| | |
|---|---|
| *Si j'avais su, je n'y se-rais jamais allé.* | If I had (would have) known, I should never have gone there. |
| *Si j'avais eu assez d'ar-gent, je l'aurais acheté.* | If I had (would have had) the money, I would have bought it. |

### 36. The Imperative

a. The imperative of most verbs is generally formed from the present indicative tense. (In the verbs of the first conjugation, however, the second person singular loses the final *s*):

| | | | |
|---|---|---|---|
| *donner* (to give) | *donne!* | *donnez!* | *donnons!* |
| *finir* (to finish) | *finis!* | *finissez!* | *finissons!* |
| *vendre* (to sell) | *vends!* | *vendez!* | *vendons!* |

b. Imperatives of *être* and *avoir*:

| | | | |
|---|---|---|---|
| *être* (to be) | *sois!* | *soyez!* | *soyons!* |
| *avoir* (to have) | *aie!* | *ayez!* | *ayons!* |

### 37. Verbs Followed by the Infinitive

a. Some verbs are followed by the infinitive without a preceding preposition:

| | |
|---|---|
| *Je vais parler à Jean.* | I am going to talk to John. |
| *J'aime parler français.* | I like to speak French. |
| *Je ne sais pas danser.* | I don't know how to dance. |

b. Some verbs are followed by *à* plus the infinitive:

| | |
|---|---|
| *J'apprends à parler français.* | I am learning to speak French. |
| *Je l'aiderai à le faire.* | I'll help him do it. |

c. Some verbs are followed by *de* plus the infinitive:

| | |
|---|---|
| *Il leur a demandé de fermer la porte.* | He asked them to shut the door. |

## 38. The Subjunctive

The indicative makes a simple statement; the subjunctive indicates a certain attitude toward the statement—uncertainty, desire, emotion, etc. The subjunctive is used in subordinate clauses when the statement is unreal, doubtful, indefinite, subject to some condition, or is affected by will or emotion.

### Forms

a. For the Present Subjunctive, drop the -ent of the third person plural present indicative and add -e, -es, -e, -ions, -iez, -ient. See the forms of the regular subjunctive in the Regular Verb Charts.

The irregular verbs *avoir* and être conjugate as follows:

| AVOIR | ÊTRE |
|---|---|
| *que j'aie* | *que je sois* |
| *que tu aies* | *que tu sois* |
| *qu'il ait* | *qu'il soit* |
| *que nous ayons* | *que nous soyons* |
| *que vous ayez* | *que vous soyez* |
| *qu'ils aient* | *qu'ils soient* |

b. For the Imperfect Subjunctive, drop the ending of the first person singular of the past definite and add -sse, -sses, -t, -ssions, -ssiez, -ssent, putting a circumflex over the last vowel of the third person singular:

| (THAT) I GAVE, MIGHT GIVE | (THAT) I FINISHED, MIGHT FINISH |
|---|---|
| *que je donnasse* | *que je finisse* |
| *que tu donnasses* | *que tu finisses* |
| *qu'il donnât* | *qu'il finît* |
| *que nous donnassions* | *que nous finissions* |
| *que vous donnassiez* | *que vous finissiez* |
| *qu'ils donnassent* | *qu'ils finissent* |

(THAT) I SOLD, MIGHT SELL

> *que je vendisse*
> *que tu vendisses*
> *qu'il vendît*
> *que nous vendissions*
> *que vous vendissiez*
> *qu'ils vendissent*

c. For the Perfect Subjunctive, add the past participle to the present subjunctive of *avoir* (or, in a few cases, *être*):

*avoir: que j'aie donné, que tu aies donné, etc.*
*être: que je sois allé, que tu sois allé, etc.*

d. For the Pluperfect Subjunctive,[1] add the past participle to the imperfect subjunctive of *avoir* (or, in a few cases, *être*):

*avoir: j'eusse donné, etc.*
*être: je fusse allé, etc.*

## Uses

a. After verbs of command, request, permission, etc.:

| | |
|---|---|
| *Je tiens à ce que vous y alliez.* | I insist on your going there. |

b. After expressions of approval and disapproval, necessity, etc.:

| | |
|---|---|
| *Il n'est que juste que vous le lui disiez.* | It's only fair that you tell him that. |
| *Il faut que vous fassiez cela.* | You have to do that. |

---

[1] The imperfect and the pluperfect subjunctive are not used today in conversational French.

c. After verbs of emotion (desire, regret, fear, joy, etc.):

| | |
|---|---|
| *Je voudrais bien que vous veniez avec nous.* | I'd like you to come with us. |
| *Je regrette que vous ne puissiez pas venir.* | I'm sorry you can't come. |

d. After expressions of doubt, uncertainty, denial:

| | |
|---|---|
| *Je doute que j'y aille.* | I doubt that I'll go there. |
| *Il est possible qu'il ne puisse pas venir.* | It's possible that he may not be able to come. |

e. In relative clauses with an indefinite antecedent:

| | |
|---|---|
| *Il me faut quelqu'un qui fasse cela.* | I need someone to do that. |

f. In adverbial clauses after certain conjunctions denoting purpose, time, concessions, etc.:

| | |
|---|---|
| *Je viendrai à moins qu'il ne pleuve.* | I'll come unless it rains. |
| *Asseyez-vous en attendant que ce soit prêt.* | Sit down until it's ready. |

g. In utterances expressing a wish or command:

| | |
|---|---|
| *Qu'ils s'en aillent!* | Let them go away! |
| *Dieu vous bénisse!* | God bless you! |
| *Vive la France!* | Long live France! |

# VERB CHARTS

## I. FORMS OF THE REGULAR VERBS

### A. Classes I, II, III

| Infinitive | Pres. & Past Participles | Present Indicative | Present Subjunctive* | Conversational Past | Past Subjunctive | Imperfect Indicative |
|---|---|---|---|---|---|---|
| -er ending parler | parlant parlé | parl + e<br>es<br>e<br>ons<br>ez<br>ent | parl + e<br>es<br>e<br>ions<br>iez<br>ent | j'ai + parlé<br>tu as<br>il a<br>nous avons<br>vous avez<br>ils ont | que j'aie + parlé<br>que tu aies<br>qu'il ait<br>que nous ayons<br>que vous ayez<br>qu'ils aient | parl + ais<br>ais<br>ait<br>ions<br>iez<br>aient |
| -ir ending finir | finissant fini | fin + is<br>is<br>it<br>issons<br>issez<br>issent | finiss + e<br>es<br>e<br>ions<br>iez<br>ent | j'ai + fini<br>tu as<br>il a<br>nous avons<br>vous avez<br>ils ont | que j'aie + fini<br>que tu aies<br>qu'il ait<br>que nous ayons<br>que vous ayez<br>qu'ils aient | finiss + ais<br>ais<br>ait<br>ions<br>iez<br>aient |

\* Like the past subjunctive, the present subjunctive verb is always preceded by *que* or *qu'* + the appropriate pronoun, as in *Il faut que je parte* and *Je veux qu'il quitte la maison.*

276

| Infinitive | Pres. & Past Participles | Present Indicative | Present Subjunctive* | Conversational Past | Past Subjunctive | Imperfect Indicative |
|---|---|---|---|---|---|---|
| -re ending vendre | vendant vendu | vend + s s — ons ez ent | vend + e es e ions iez ent | j'ai + vendu tu as il a nous avons vous avez ils ont | que j'aie + vendu que tu aies qu'il ait que nous ayons que vous ayez qu'ils aient | vend + ais ais ait ions iez aient |

| Past Perfect | Future | Future Perfect | Conditional | Conditional Perfect | Imperative |
|---|---|---|---|---|---|
| j'avais + parlé | parler + ai | j'aurai + parlé | parler + ais | j'aurais + parlé | parle |
| tu avais | as | tu auras | ais | tu aurais | |
| il avait | a | il aura | ait | il aurait | |
| nous avions | ons | nous aurons | ions | nous aurions | parlons |
| vous aviez | ez | vous aurez | iez | vous auriez | parlez |
| ils avaient | ont | ils auront | aient | ils auraient | |
| j'avais + fini | finir + ai | j'aurai + fini | finir + ais | j'aurais + fini | finis |
| tu avais | as | tu auras | ais | tu aurais | |
| il avait | a | il aura | ait | il aurait | |
| nous avions | ons | nous aurons | ions | nous aurions | finissons |
| vous aviez | ez | vous aurez | iez | vous auriez | finissez |
| ils avaient | ont | ils auront | aient | ils auraient | |
| j'avais + vendu | vendr + ai | j'aurai + vendu | vendr + ais | j'aurais + vendu | vends |
| tu avais | as | tu auras | ais | tu aurais | |
| il avait | a | il aura | ait | il aurait | |
| nous avions | ons | nous aurons | ions | nous aurions | vendons |
| vous aviez | ez | vous aurez | iez | vous auriez | vendez |
| ils avaient | ont | ils auront | aient | ils auraient | |

B. Verbs Ending in –cer and –ger

| Infinitive | Pres. & Past Participles | Present Indicative | Present Subjunctive† | Conversational Past | Past Subjunctive | Imperfect Indicative |
|---|---|---|---|---|---|---|
| placer[1] | plaçant[3] | place | place | j'ai + placé | que j'aie + placé | plaçais[3] |
| | placé | places | places | tu as | que tu aies | plaçais |
| | | place | place | il a | qu'il ait | plaçait |
| | | plaçons | placions | nous avons | que nous ayons | placions |
| | | placez | placiez | vous avez | que vous ayez | placiez |
| | | placent | placent | ils ont | qu'ils aient | plaçaient |
| manger[2] | mangeant[3] | mange | mange | j'ai + mangé | que j'aie + mangé | mangeais |
| | mangé | manges | manges | tu as | que tu aies | mangeais |
| | | mange | mange | il a | qu'il ait | mangeait |
| | | mangeons | mangions | nous avons | que nous ayons | mangions |
| | | mangez | mangiez | vous avez | que vous ayez | mangiez |
| | | mangent | mangent | ils ont | qu'ils aient | mangeaient |

[1] Similarly conjugated: commencer, lancer, etc.
[2] Similarly conjugated: plonger, ranger, arranger, etc.
[3] All spelling changes in verb forms will be italicized in this section.

279

| Past Perfect | | Future | | Future Perfect | | Conditional | | Conditional Perfect | | Imperative |
|---|---|---|---|---|---|---|---|---|---|---|
| j'avais | + placé | placer | + ai | j'aurai | + placé | placer | + ais | j'aurais | + placé | place |
| tu avais | | | as | tu auras | | | ais | tu aurais | | |
| il avait | | | a | il aura | | | ait | il aurait | | *plaçons* |
| nous avions | | | ons | nous aurons | | | ions | nous aurions | | placez |
| vous aviez | | | ez | vous aurez | | | iez | vous auriez | | |
| ils avaient | | | ont | ils auront | | | aient | ils auraient | | |
| j'avais | + mangé | manger | + ai | j'aurai | + mangé | manger | + ais | j'aurais | + mangé | mange |
| tu avais | | | as | tu auras | | | ais | tu aurais | | *mangeons* |
| il avait | | | a | il aura | | | ait | il aurait | | mangez |
| nous avions | | | ons | nous aurons | | | ions | nous aurions | | |
| vous aviez | | | ez | vous aurez | | | iez | vous auriez | | |
| ils avaient | | | ont | ils auront | | | aient | ils auraient | | |

C. Verbs Ending in *-er* with Changes in the Stem

| Infinitive | Pres. & Past Participles | Present Indicative | Present Subjunctive† | Conversational Past | Past Subjunctive | Imperfect Indicative |
|---|---|---|---|---|---|---|
| **acheter**[1] | achetant<br>acheté | achète<br>achètes<br>achète<br>achetons<br>achetez<br>achètent | achète<br>achètes<br>achète<br>achetions<br>achetiez<br>achètent | j'ai  + acheté<br>tu as<br>il a<br>nous avons<br>vous avez<br>ils ont | que j'aie  + acheté<br>que tu aies<br>qu'il ait<br>que nous ayons<br>que vous ayez<br>qu'ils aient | achet  + ais<br>ais<br>ait<br>ions<br>iez<br>aient |
| **appeler**[2] | appelant<br>appelé | appelle<br>appelles<br>appelle<br>appelons<br>appelez<br>appellent | appelle<br>appelles<br>appelle<br>appelions<br>appeliez<br>appellent | j'ai  + appelé<br>tu as<br>il a<br>nous avons<br>vous avez<br>ils ont | que j'aie  + appelé<br>que tu aies<br>qu'il ait<br>que nous ayons<br>que vous ayez<br>qu'ils aient | appel  + ais<br>ais<br>ait<br>ions<br>iez<br>aient |

281

| Infinitive | Pres. & Past Participles | Present Indicative | Present Subjunctive† | Conversational Past | Past Subjunctive | Imperfect Indicative |
|---|---|---|---|---|---|---|
| payer³ | payant <br> payé | paie/paye <br> paies/payes <br> paie/paye <br> payons <br> payez <br> paient/payent | paie/paye <br> paies/payes <br> paie/paye <br> payons <br> payez <br> paient/payent | j'ai + payé <br> tu as <br> il a <br> nous avons <br> vous avez <br> ils ont | que j'aie + payé <br> que tu aies <br> qu'il ait <br> que nous ayons <br> que vous ayez <br> qu'ils aient | pay + ais <br> ais <br> ait <br> ions <br> iez <br> aient |
| préférer⁴ | préférant <br> préféré | préfère <br> préfères <br> préfère <br> préférons <br> préférez <br> préfèrent | préfère <br> préfères <br> préfère <br> préférions <br> préfériez <br> préfèrent | j'ai + préféré <br> tu as <br> il a <br> nous avons <br> vous avez <br> ils ont | que j'aie + préféré <br> que tu aies <br> qu'il ait <br> que nous ayons <br> que vous ayez <br> qu'ils aient | préfér + ais <br> ais <br> ait <br> ions <br> iez <br> aient |

| Past Perfect | Future | Future Perfect | Conditional | Conditional Perfect | Imperative |
|---|---|---|---|---|---|
| j'avais + acheté | *acheter* + ai | j'aurai + acheté | *acheter* + ais | j'aurais + acheté | |
| tu avais | as | tu auras | ais | tu aurais | *achète* |
| il avait | a | il aura | ait | il aurait | |
| nous avions | ons | nous aurons | ions | nous aurions | achetons |
| vous aviez | ez | vous aurez | iez | vous auriez | achetez |
| ils avaient | ont | ils auront | aient | ils auraient | |
| j'avais + appelé | *appeller* + ai | j'aurai + appelé | *appeller* + ais | j'aurais + appelé | |
| tu avais | as | tu auras | ais | tu aurais | *appelle* |
| il avait | a | il aura | ait | il aurait | |
| nous avions | ons | nous aurons | ions | nous aurions | appelons |
| vous aviez | ez | vous aurez | iez | vous auriez | appelez |
| ils avaient | ont | ils auront | aient | ils auraient | |

| Past Perfect | | Future | | Future Perfect | | Conditional | | Conditional Perfect | | |
|---|---|---|---|---|---|---|---|---|---|---|
| j'avais | + payé | *paier* | + ai | j'aurai | + payé | *paier* | + ais | j'aurais | + payé | |
| tu avais | | or | as | tu auras | | or | ais | tu aurais | | *paie/paye* |
| il avait | | payer | + a | il aura | | payer | + ait | il aurait | | |
| nous avions | | | ons | nous aurons | | | ions | nous aurions | | payons |
| vous aviez | | | ez | vous aurez | | | iez | vous auriez | | payez |
| ils avaient | | | ont | ils auront | | | aient | ils auraient | | |
| j'avais | + préféré | préférer | + ai | j'aurai | + préféré | préférer | + ais | j'aurais | + préféré | |
| tu avais | | | as | tu auras | | | ais | tu aurais | | *préfère* |
| il avait | | | a | il aura | | | ait | il aurait | | |
| nous avions | | | ons | nous aurons | | | ions | nous aurions | | préférons |
| vous aviez | | | ez | vous aurez | | | iez | vous auriez | | préférez |
| ils avaient | | | ont | ils auront | | | aient | ils auraient | | |

# D. Verbs Ending in –OIR

| Infinitive | Pres. & Past Participles | Present Indicative | Present Subjunctive | Conversational Past | | Past Subjunctive | | Imperfect Indicative | |
|---|---|---|---|---|---|---|---|---|---|
| **recevoir**[1] | recevant | reçois | reçoive | j'ai | + reçu | que j'aie | + reçu | recev | + ais |
| | reçu | reçois | reçoives | tu as | | que tu aies | | | ais |
| | | reçoit | reçoive | il a | | qu'il ait | | | ait |
| | | recevons | recevions | nous avons | | que nous ayons | | | ions |
| | | recevez | receviez | vous avez | | que vous ayez | | | iez |
| | | reçoivent | reçoivent | ils ont | | qu'ils aient | | | aient |

| Future | | Future Perfect | | Conditional | | Conditional Perfect | | Imperative |
|---|---|---|---|---|---|---|---|---|
| recevr | + ai | j'aurai | + reçu | recevr | + ais | j'aurais | + reçu | |
| | as | tu auras | | | ais | tu aurais | | reçois |
| | a | il aura | | | ait | il aurait | | |
| | ons | nous aurons | | | ions | nous aurions | | recevons |
| | ez | vous aurez | | | iez | vous auriez | | recevez |
| | ont | ils auront | | | aient | ils auraient | | |

| Past Perfect | | |
|---|---|---|
| j'avais | + reçu | |
| tu avais | | |
| il avait | | |
| nous avions | | |
| vous aviez | | |
| ils avaient | | |

[1] Verbs like recevoir: devoir (dois, doive, dû).

## E. Verbs Ending in –NDRE

| Infinitive | Pres. & Past Participles | Present Indicative | Present Subjunctive | Conversational Past | Past Subjunctive | Imperfect Indicative |
|---|---|---|---|---|---|---|
| craindre[1] | craignant | crains | craigne | j'ai + craint | que j'aie + craint | craign + ais |
| | craint | crains | craignes | tu as | que tu aies | ais |
| | | craint | craigne | il a | qu'il ait | ait |
| | | craignons | craignions | nous avons | que nous ayons | ions |
| | | craignez | craigniez | vous avez | que vous ayez | iez |
| | | craignent | craignent | ils ont | qu'ils aient | aient |
| éteindre[2] | éteignant | éteins | éteigne | j'ai + éteint | que j'aie + éteint | éteign + ais |
| | éteint | éteins | éteignes | tu as | que tu aies | ais |
| | | éteint | éteigne | il a | qu'il ait | ait |
| | | éteignons | éteignions | nous avons | que nous ayons | ions |
| | | éteignez | éteigniez | vous avez | que vous ayez | iez |
| | | éteignent | éteignent | ils ont | qu'ils aient | aient |

[1] Verbs like *craindre*: *plaindre*, to pity. The reflexive form, *se plaindre*, means "to complain" and in the compound tenses is conjugated with *être*.
[2] Verbs like *éteindre*: *peindre*, to paint; *teindre*, to dye.

| Past Perfect | Future | Future Perfect | Conditional | Conditional Perfect | Imperative |
|---|---|---|---|---|---|
| j'avais   + *craint* | craindr + ai | j'aurai   + *craint* | craindr + ais | j'aurais   + *craint* |  |
| tu avais |  as | tu auras |  ais | tu aurais | *crains* |
| il avait |  a | il aura |  ait | il aurait |  |
| nous avions |  ons | nous aurons |  ions | nous aurions | *craignons* |
| vous aviez |  ez | vous aurez |  iez | vous auriez | *craignez* |
| ils avaient |  ont | ils auront |  aient | ils auraient |  |
| j'avais   + *éteint* | éteindr + ai | j'aurai   + *éteint* | éteindr + ais | j'aurais   + *éteint* |  |
| tu avais |  as | tu auras |  ais | tu aurais | *éteins* |
| il avait |  a | il aura |  ait | il aurait |  |
| nous avions |  ons | nous aurons |  ions | nous aurions | *éteignons* |
| vous aviez |  ez | vous aurez |  iez | vous auriez | *éteignez* |
| ils avaient |  ont | ils auront |  aient | ils auraient |  |

F. Compound Tenses of Verbs Conjugated with *ÊTRE*

| Conversational Past | Past Subjunctive | Past Perfect | Future Perfect | Conditional Perfect |
|---|---|---|---|---|
| je suis allé(e) | que je sois allé(e) | j'étais allé(e) | je serai allé(e) | je serais allé(e) |
| tu es allé(e) | que tu sois allé(e) | tu étais allé(e) | tu seras allé(e) | tu serais allé(e) |
| il est allé | qu'il soit allé | il était allé | il sera allé | il serait allé |
| elle est allée | qu'elle soit allée | elle était allée | elle sera allée | elle serait allée |
| nous sommes allé(e)s | que nous soyons allé(e)s | nous étions allé(e)s | nous serons allé(e)s | nous serions allé(e)s |
| vous êtes allé(e)(s) | que vous soyez allé(e)(s) | vous étiez allé(e)(s) | vous serez allé(e)(s) | vous seriez allé(e)(s) |
| ils sont allés | qu'ils soient allés | ils étaient allés | ils seront allés | ils seraient allés |
| elles sont allées | qu'elles soient allées | elles étaient allées | elles seront allées | elles seraient allées |

## G. Compound Tenses of Reflexive Verbs (All Reflexive Verbs Are Conjugated with *ÊTRE*)

| Conversational Past | Past Subjunctive | Past Perfect | Future Perfect | Conditional Perfect |
|---|---|---|---|---|
| je me suis levé(e) | que je me sois levé(e) | je m'étais levé(e) | je me serai levé(e) | je me serais levé(e) |
| tu t'es levé(e) | que tu te sois levé(e) | tu t'étais levé(e) | tu te seras levé(e) | tu te serais levé(e) |
| il s'est levé | qu'il se soit levé | il s'était levé | il se sera levé | il se serait levé |
| elle s'est levée | qu'elle se soit levée | elle s'était levée | elle se sera levée | elle se serait levée |
| nous nous sommes levé(e)s | que nous nous soyons levé(e)s | nous nous étions levé(e)s | nous nous serons levé(e)s | nous nous serions levé(e)s |
| vous vous êtes levé(e)(s) | que vous vous soyez levé(e)(s) | vous vous étiez levé(e)(s) | vous vous serez levé(e)(s) | vous vous seriez levé(e)(s) |
| ils se sont levés | qu'ils se soient levés | ils s'étaient levés | ils se seront levés | ils se seraient levés |
| elles se sont levées | qu'elles se soient levées | elles s'étaient levées | elles se seront levées | elles se seraient levées |

# H. Infrequently Used and "Literary" Tenses (Classes I, II, III)

| Past Definite[1] | | | Past Anterior[2] | | | Imperfect Subjunctive[3] | | |
|---|---|---|---|---|---|---|---|---|
| parlai | finis | perdis | eus parlé | eus fini | eus perdu | parlasse | finisse | perdisse |
| parlas | finis | perdis | eus parlé | eus fini | eus perdu | parlasses | finisses | perdisses |
| parla | finit | perdit | eut parlé | eut fini | eut perdu | parlât | finît | perdît |
| parlâmes | finîmes | perdîmes | eûmes parlé | eûmes fini | eûmes perdu | parlassions | finissions | perdissions |
| parlâtes | finîtes | perdîtes | eûtes parlé | eûtes fini | eûtes perdu | parlassiez | finissiez | perdissiez |
| parlèrent | finirent | perdirent | eurent parlé | eurent fini | eurent perdu | parlassent | finissent | perdissent |

[1] Used in formal narrative only. In informal conversation and writing, use the conversational past (*j'ai parlé*, etc.) All other regular verbs use either the *–er*, *–ir*, or *–re* endings, depending upon the conjugation to which they belong. The past definite forms of irregular verbs must be memorized.

[2] Used in literary style only, after *quand*, *lorsque*, *après que*, *dès que* for an event that happened just before another event. Example: *Après qu'il eut dîné, il sortit.* As soon as he had eaten, he went out.

[3] "That I spoke," "that I might speak," etc. This tense is infrequently found in ordinary conversation, but is used fairly often in literary works.

## Past Perfect Subjunctive[4]

| | | |
|---|---|---|
| que j'eusse parlé | que j'eusse fini | que j'eusse perdu |
| que tu eusses parlé | que tu eusses fini | que tu eusses perdu |
| qu'il eût parlé | qu'il eût fini | qu'il eût perdu |
| que nous eussions parlé | que nous eussions fini | que nous eussions perdu |
| que vous eussiez parlé | que vous eussiez fini | que vous eussiez perdu |
| qu'ils eussent parlé | qu'ils eussent fini | qu'ils eussent perdu |

[4] "That I had spoken," "that I might have spoken," etc. A predominantly literary tense.

## II. FREQUENTLY USED IRREGULAR VERBS

The correct auxiliary verb is indicated in parentheses below each verb.
For compound tenses, use the appropriate form of the auxiliary verb + past participle.

| Infinitive | Pres. & Past Participles | Present Indicative | Present Subjunctive | Imperfect Indicative | Future | Conditional | Imperative |
|---|---|---|---|---|---|---|---|
| **aquérir** to acquire (*avoir*) | acquériant acquis | acquiers acquiers acquiert acquérons acquérez acquièrent | acquière acquières acquière acquérions acquériez acquièrent | acquér + ais ais ait ions iez aient | acquerr + ai as a ons ez ont | acquerr + ais ais ait ions iez aient | acquiers acquérons acquérez |
| **aller** to go (*être*) | allant allé(e)(s) | vais vas va allons allez vont | aille ailles aille allions alliez aillent | all + ais ais ait ions iez aient | ir + ai as a ons ez ont | ir + ais ais ait ions iez aient | va allons allez |

| Infinitive | Pres. & Past Participles | Present Indicative | Present Subjunctive | Imperfect Indicative | Future | Conditional | Imperative |
|---|---|---|---|---|---|---|---|
| (s')asseoir¹ to sit (down) (*être*) | asseyant assis(e)(s) | assieds assieds assied asseyons asseyez asseyent | asseye asseyes asseye asseyions asseyiez asseyent | assey + ais ais ait ions iez aient | asseyer *or* assiér *or* assoir + ai as ons ez ont | asseyer *or* assiér *or* assoir + ais ais ait ions iez aient | assieds-toi asseyons-nous asseyez-vous |
| avoir to have (*avoir*) | ayant eu | ai as a avons avez ont | aie aies ait ayons ayez aient | av + ais ais ait ions iez aient | aur + ai as a ons ez ont | aur + ais ais ait ions iez aient | aie ayons ayez |
| battre to beat (*avoir*) | battant battu | bats bats bat battons battez battent | batte battes batte battions battiez battent | batt + ais ais ait ions iez aient | battr + ai as a ons ez ont | battr + ais ais ait ions iez aient | bats battons battez |

¹ There is a variant form of the conjugation of *s'asseoir* based on the present participle *assoyant* and first person singular *assois*, but this is rather archaic and is rarely used. There are also two variant forms for the future stem: *assiér*- and *assoir*-. *Assiér*- is frequently used.

| Infinitive | Pres. & Past Participles | Present Indicative | Present Subjunctive | Imperfect Indicative | Future | Conditional | Imperative |
|---|---|---|---|---|---|---|---|
| **boire** to drink (*avoir*) | buvant bu | bois bois boit buvons buvez boivent | boive boives boive buvions buviez boivent | buv + ais ais ait ions iez aient | boir + ai as a ons ez ont | boir + ais ais ait ions iez aient | bois buvons buvez |
| **conclure** to conclude (*avoir*) | concluant conclu | conclus conclus conclut concluons concluez concluent | conclue conclues conclue concluions concluiez concluent | conclu + ais ais ait ions iez aient | conclur + ai as a ons ez ont | conclur + ais ais ait ions iez aient | conclus concluons concluez |

| Infinitive | Pres. & Past Participles | Present Indicative | Present Subjunctive | Imperfect Indicative | Future | Conditional | Imperative |
|---|---|---|---|---|---|---|---|
| **conduire**<br>to drive<br>to lead<br>(*avoir*) | conduisant<br>conduit | conduis<br>conduis<br>conduit<br>conduisons<br>conduisez<br>conduisent | conduise<br>conduises<br>conduise<br>conduisions<br>conduisiez<br>conduisent | conduis + ais<br>ais<br>ait<br>ions<br>iez<br>aient | conduir + ai<br>as<br>a<br>ons<br>ez<br>ont | conduir + ais<br>ais<br>ait<br>ions<br>iez<br>aient | conduis<br>conduisons<br>conduisez |
| **connaître**<br>to know<br>(*avoir*) | connaissant<br>connu | connais<br>connais<br>connaît<br>connaissons<br>connaissez<br>connaissent | connaisse<br>connaisses<br>connaisse<br>connaissions<br>connaissiez<br>connaissent | connaiss + ais<br>ais<br>ait<br>ions<br>iez<br>aient | connaîtr + ai<br>as<br>a<br>ons<br>ez<br>ont | connaîtr + ais<br>ais<br>ait<br>ions<br>iez<br>aient | connais<br>connaissons<br>connaissez |
| **courir**<br>to run<br>(*avoir*) | courant<br>couru | cours<br>cours<br>court<br>courons<br>courez<br>courent | coure<br>coures<br>coure<br>courions<br>couriez<br>courent | cour + ais<br>ais<br>ait<br>ions<br>iez<br>aient | courr + ai<br>as<br>a<br>ons<br>ez<br>ont | courr + ais<br>ais<br>ait<br>ions<br>iez<br>aient | cours<br>courons<br>courez |

| Infinitive | Pres. & Past Participles | Present Indicative | Present Subjunctive | Imperfect Indicative | Future | Conditional | Imperative |
|---|---|---|---|---|---|---|---|
| **croire** to believe (*avoir*) | croyant cru | crois crois croit croyons croyez croient | croie croies croie croyions croyiez croient | croy + ais ais ait ions iez aient | croir + ai as a ons ez ont | croir + ais ais ait ions iez aient | crois croyons croyez |
| **cueillir** to gather to pick (*avoir*) | cueillant cueilli | cueille cueilles cueille cueillons cueillez cueillent | cueille cueilles cueille cueillions cueilliez cueillent | cueill + ais ais ait ions iez aient | cueiller + ai as a ons ez ont | cueiller + ais ais ait ions iez aient | cueille cueillons cueillez |
| **devoir** to owe to ought (*avoir*) | devant dû | dois dois doit devons devez doivent | doive doives doive devions deviez doivent | dev + ais ais ait ions iez aient | devr + ai as a ons ez ont | devr + ais ais ait ions iez aient | *not used* |

| | | Present | Present subj. | Imperfect | Future | Conditional | Imperative |
|---|---|---|---|---|---|---|---|
| **dire**<br>to say<br>to tell<br>(*avoir*) | disant<br>dit | dis<br>dis<br>dit<br>disons<br>dites<br>disent | dise<br>dises<br>dise<br>disions<br>disiez<br>disent | dis + ais<br>ais<br>ait<br>ions<br>iez<br>aient | dir + ai<br>as<br>a<br>ons<br>ez<br>ont | dir + ais<br>ais<br>ait<br>ions<br>iez<br>aient | dis<br>disons<br>dites |
| **dormir**<br>to sleep<br>(*avoir*) | dormant<br>dormi | dors<br>dors<br>dort<br>dormons<br>dormez<br>dorment | dorme<br>dormes<br>dorme<br>dormions<br>dormiez<br>dorment | dorm + ais<br>ais<br>ait<br>ions<br>iez<br>aient | dormir + ai<br>as<br>a<br>ons<br>ez<br>ont | dormir + ais<br>ais<br>ait<br>ions<br>iez<br>aient | dors<br>dormons<br>dormez |
| **écrire**<br>to write<br>(*avoir*) | écrivant<br>écrit | écris<br>écris<br>écrit<br>écrivons<br>écrivez<br>écrivent | écrive<br>écrives<br>écrive<br>écrivions<br>écriviez<br>écrivent | écriv + ais<br>ais<br>ait<br>ions<br>iez<br>aient | écrir + ai<br>as<br>a<br>ons<br>ez<br>ont | écrir + ais<br>ais<br>ait<br>ions<br>iez<br>aient | écris<br>écrivons<br>écrivez |

| Infinitive | Pres. & Past Participles | Present Indicative | Present Subjunctive | Imperfect Indicative | Future | Conditional | Imperative |
|---|---|---|---|---|---|---|---|
| **envoyer** to send (*avoir*) | envoyant envoyé | envoie envoies envoie envoyons envoyez envoient | envoie envoies envoie envoyions envoyiez envoient | envoy + ais ais ait ions iez aient | enverr + ai as a ons ez ont | enverr + ais ais ait ions iez aient | envoie envoyons envoyez |
| **être** to be (*avoir*) | étant été | suis es est sommes êtes sont | sois sois soit soyons soyez soient | ét + ais ais ait ions iez aient | ser + ai as a ons ez ont | ser + ais ais ait ions iez aient | sois soyons soyez |
| **faillir**[1] to fail (*avoir*) | faillant failli | *not used* | *not used* | *not used* | faillir + ai as a ons ez ont | faillir + ais ais ait ions iez aient | *not used* |

[1] Used in expressions such as *Il a failli tomber.* He nearly fell (lit.: He failed to fall).

| Infinitive | Participles | Present | Present Subjunctive | Imperfect | Future | Conditional | Imperative |
|---|---|---|---|---|---|---|---|
| **faire**<br>to do<br>to make<br>(*avoir*) | faisant<br>fait | fais<br>fais<br>fait<br>faisons<br>faites<br>font | fasse<br>fasses<br>fasse<br>fassions<br>fassiez<br>fassent | fais + ais<br>ais<br>ait<br>ions<br>iez<br>aient | fer + ai<br>as<br>a<br>ons<br>ez<br>ont | fer + ais<br>ais<br>ait<br>ions<br>iez<br>aient | fais<br>faisons<br>faites |
| **falloir**<br>to be<br>necessary,<br>must<br>(used only<br>with *il*)<br>(*avoir*) | *no pres. part.*<br>fallu | il faut | il faille | il fallait | il faudra | il faudrait | *not used* |
| **fuir**<br>to flee<br>(*avoir*) | fuyant<br>fui | fuis<br>fuis<br>fuit<br>fuyons<br>fuyez<br>fuient | fuie<br>fuies<br>fuie<br>fuyions<br>fuyiez<br>fuient | fuy + ais<br>ais<br>ait<br>ions<br>iez<br>aient | fuir + ai<br>as<br>a<br>ons<br>ez<br>ont | fuir + ais<br>ais<br>ait<br>ions<br>iez<br>aient | fuis<br>fuyons<br>fuyez |

| Infinitive | Pres. & Past Participles | Present Indicative | Present Subjunctive | Imperfect Indicative | Future | Conditional | Imperative |
|---|---|---|---|---|---|---|---|
| **haïr** to hate (*avoir*) | haïssant haï | hais hais hait haïssons haïssez haïssent | haïsse haïsses haïsse haïssions haïssiez haïssent | haïss + ais ais ait ions iez aient | haïr + ai as a ons ez ont | haïr + ais ais ait ions iez aient | hais haïssons haïssez |
| **lire** to read (*avoir*) | lisant lu | lis lis lit lisons lisez lisent | lise lises lise lisions lisiez lisent | lis + ais ais ait ions iez aient | lir + ai as a ons ez ont | lir + ais ais ait ions iez aient | lis lisons lisez |
| **mettre** to put to place (*avoir*) | mettant mis | mets mets met mettons mettez mettent | mette mettes mette mettions mettiez mettent | mett + ais ais ait ions iez aient | mettr + ai as a ons ez ont | mettr + ais ais ait ions iez aient | mets mettons mettez |
| **mourir** to die (*être*) | mourant mort(e)(s) | meurs meurs meurt mourons mourez meurent | meure meures meure mourions mouriez meurent | mour + ais ais ait ions iez aient | mourr + ai as a ons ez ont | mourr + ais ais ait ions iez aient | meurs mourons mourez |

| Infinitive | Participles | Present | Pres. Subj. | Imperfect | Future | Conditional | Imperative |
|---|---|---|---|---|---|---|---|
| **mouvoir**[1] to move (*avoir*) | mouvant mû | meus meus meut mouvons mouvez meuvent | meuve meuves meuve mouvions mouviez meuvent | mouv + ais ais ait ions iez aient | mouvr + ai as a ons ez ont | mouvr + ais ais ait ions iez aient | meus mouvons mouvez |
| **naître** to be born (*être*) | naissant né(e)(s) | nais nais naît naissons naissez naissent | naisse naisses naisse naissions naissiez naissent | naiss + ais ais ait ions iez aient | naîtr + ai as a ons ez ont | naîtr + ais ais ait ions iez aient | nais naissons naissez |
| **ouvrir** to open (*avoir*) | ouvrant ouvert | ouvre ouvres ouvre ouvrons ouvrez ouvrent | ouvre ouvres ouvre ouvrions ouvriez ouvrent | ouvr + ais ais ait ions iez aient | ouvrir + ai as a ons ez ont | ouvrir + ais ais ait ions iez aient | ouvre ouvrons ouvrez |
| **partir** to leave to depart (*être*) | partant parti(e)(s) | pars pars part partons partez partent | parte partes parte partions partiez partent | part + ais ais ait ions iez aient | partir + ai as a ons ez ont | partir + ais ais ait ions iez aient | pars partons partez |

[1] *Mouvoir* is seldom used except in compounds like *émouvoir*, to move (emotionally).

301

| Infinitive | Pres. & Past Participles | Present Indicative | Present Subjunctive | Imperfect Indicative | Future | Conditional | Imperative |
|---|---|---|---|---|---|---|---|
| **plaire** to please (to be pleasing to) (*avoir*) | plaisant plu | plais plais plaît plaisons plaisez plaisent | plaise plaises plaise plaisions plaisiez plaisent | plais + ais, ais, ait, ions, iez, aient | plair + ai, as, a, ons, ez, ont | plair + ais, ais, ait, ions, iez, aient | plais plaisons plaisez |
| **pleuvoir** to rain (used only with *il*) (*avoir*) | pleuvant plu | il pleut | il pleuve | il pleuvait | il pleuvra | il pleuvrait | *not used* |
| **pouvoir** to be able, can (*avoir*) | pouvant pu | peux (puis)[1] peux peut pouvons pouvez peuvent | puisse puisses puisse puissions puissiez puissent | pouv + ais, ais, ait, ions, iez, aient | pourr + ai, as, a, ons, ez, ont | pourr + ais, ais, ait, ions, iez, aient | *not used* |

[1] The interrogative of *pouvoir* in the first person singular is always *Puis-je?*

| | | | | Imperfect | Future | Conditional | Imperative |
|---|---|---|---|---|---|---|---|
| **prendre** to take (*avoir*) | prenant pris | prends prends prend prenons prenez prennent | prenne prennes prenne prenions preniez prennent | pren + ais ais ait ions iez aient | prendr + ai as a ons ez ont | prendr + ais ais ait ions iez aient | prends prenons prenez |
| **résoudre** to resolve (*avoir*) | résolvant résolu | résous résous résout résolvons résolvez résolvent | résolve résolves résolve résolvions résolviez résolvent | résolv + ais ais ait ions iez aient | résoudr + ai as a ons ez ont | résoudr + ais ais ait ions iez aient | résous résolvons résolvez |
| **rire** to laugh (*avoir*) | riant ri | ris ris rit rions riez rient | rie ries rie riions riiez rient | ri + ais ais ait ions iez aient | rir + ai as a ons ez ont | rir + ais ais ait ions iez aient | ris rions riez |

| Infinitive | Pres. & Past Participles | Present Indicative | Present Subjunctive | Imperfect Indicative | Future | Conditional | Imperative |
|---|---|---|---|---|---|---|---|
| **savoir** to know (*avoir*) | sachant su | sais sais sait savons savez savent | sache saches sache sachions sachiez sachent | sav + ais ais ait ions iez aient | saur + ai as a ons ez ont | saur + ais ais ait ions iez aient | sache sachons sachez |
| **suffire** to be enough, to suffice (*avoir*) | suffisant suffi | suffis suffis suffit suffisons suffisez suffisent | suffise suffises suffise suffisions suffisiez suffisent | suffis + ais ais ait ions iez aient | suffir + ai as a ons ez ont | suffir + ais ais ait ions iez aient | suffis suffisons suffisez |
| **suivre** to follow (*avoir*) | suivant suivi | suis suis suit suivons suivez suivent | suive suives suive suivions suiviez suivent | suiv + ais ais ait ions iez aient | suivr + ai as a ons ez ont | suivr + ais ais ait ions iez aient | suis suivons suivez |

| Infinitive / meaning | Participles | Present | Present subjunctive | Imperfect | Future | Conditional | Imperative |
|---|---|---|---|---|---|---|---|
| **(se) taire**<br>to be quiet,<br>to say<br>nothing<br>(*être*) | taisant<br>tu(e)(s) | tais<br>tais<br>tait<br>taisons<br>taisez<br>taisent | taise<br>taises<br>taise<br>taisions<br>taisiez<br>taisent | tais + ais<br>ais<br>ait<br>ions<br>iez<br>aient | tair + ai<br>as<br>a<br>ons<br>ez<br>ont | tair + ais<br>ais<br>ait<br>ions<br>iez<br>aient | tais-toi<br>taisons-nous<br>taisez-vous |
| **tenir**<br>to hold,<br>to keep<br>(*avoir*) | tenant<br>tenu | tiens<br>tiens<br>tient<br>tenons<br>tenez<br>tiennent | tienne<br>tiennes<br>tienne<br>tenions<br>teniez<br>tiennent | ten + ais<br>ais<br>ait<br>ions<br>iez<br>aient | tiendr + ai<br>as<br>a<br>ons<br>ez<br>ont | tiendr + ais<br>ais<br>ait<br>ions<br>iez<br>aient | tiens<br>tenons<br>tenez |
| **vaincre**<br>to conquer<br>(*avoir*) | vainquant<br>vaincu | vaincs<br>vaincs<br>vainc<br>vainquons<br>vainquez<br>vainquent | vainque<br>vainques<br>vainque<br>vainquions<br>vainquiez<br>vainquent | vainqu + ais<br>ais<br>ait<br>ions<br>iez<br>aient | vaincr + ai<br>as<br>a<br>ons<br>ez<br>ont | vaincr + ais<br>ais<br>ait<br>ions<br>iez<br>aient | vaincs<br>vainquons<br>vainquez |
| **venir**<br>to come<br>(*être*) | venant<br>venu(e)(s) | viens<br>viens<br>vient<br>venons<br>venez<br>viennent | vienne<br>viennes<br>vienne<br>venions<br>veniez<br>viennent | ven + ais<br>ais<br>ait<br>ions<br>iez<br>aient | viendr + ai<br>as<br>a<br>ons<br>ez<br>ont | viendr + ais<br>ais<br>ait<br>ions<br>iez<br>aient | viens<br>venons<br>venez |

| Infinitive | Pres. & Past Participles | Present Indicative | Present Subjunctive | Imperfect Indicative | Future | Conditional | Imperative |
|---|---|---|---|---|---|---|---|
| **vivre** to live (*avoir*) | vivant vécu | vis vis vit vivons vivez vivent | vive vives vive vivions viviez vivent | viv + ais ais ait ions iez aient | vivr + ai as a ons ez ont | vivr + ais ais ait ions iez aient | vis vivons vivez |
| **voir** to see (*avoir*) | voyant vu | vois vois voit voyons voyez voient | voie voies voie voyions voyiez voient | voy + ais ais ait ions iez aient | verr + ai as a ons ez ont | verr + ais ais ait ions iez aient | vois voyons voyez |
| **vouloir** to want (*avoir*) | voulant voulu | veux veux veut voulons voulez veulent | veuille veuilles veuille voulions vouliez veuillent | voul + ais ais ait ions iez aient | voudr + ai as a ons ez ont | voudr + ais ais ait ions iez aient | veuillez[1] |

[1] *Veuillez* is commonly used in polite requests.

306

## ANSWER KEY

## LESSON 1

B. 1. *Je viens de l'acheter.*
   *Tu viens de l'acheter.*
   *Il vient de l'acheter.*
   *Elle vient de l'acheter.*

   *Nous venons de l'acheter.*
   *Vous venez de l'acheter.*
   *Ils viennent de l'acheter.*
   *Elles viennent de l'acheter.*

2. *Je tiens à le voir.*
   *Tu tiens à le voir.*
   *Il tient à le voir.*
   *Elle tient à le voir.*

   *Nous tenons à le voir.*
   *Vous tenez à le voir.*
   *Ils tiennent à le voir.*
   *Elles tiennent à le voir.*

3. *J'ai envie de lui parler.*
   *Tu as envie de lui parler.*
   *Il a envie de lui parler.*
   *Elle a envie de lui parler.*

   *Nous avons envie de lui parler.*
   *Vous avez envie de lui parler.*
   *Ils ont envie de lui parler.*
   *Elles ont envie de lui parler.*

C. 1.

| *Me voici.* | Here I am. |
|---|---|
| *Te voici.* | Here you are. |
| *Le voici.* | Here he is. |
| *La voici.* | Here she is. |
| *Nous voici.* | Here we are. |
| *Vous voici.* | Here you are. |
| *Les voici.* | Here they are. (m. & f.) |

2.

| *Me voilà.* | There I am. |
|---|---|
| *Te voilà.* | There you are. |
| *Le voilà.* | There he is. |
| *La voilà.* | There she is. |
| *Nous voilà.* | There we are. |
| *Vous voilà.* | There you are. |
| *Les voilà.* | There they are. |

D.　1. *Je vais retrouver Charles.*
　　2. *Il ne va pas voir Jane.*
　　3. *Est-ce qu'on trouvera une table libre à cette heure-là?*
　　4. *Je veux téléphoner à mon ami.*
　　5. *Voulez-vous parler français?*
　　6. *Elle veut fixer un rendez-vous.*
　　7. *Il faut s'asseoir à l'intérieur.*
　　8. *Il faut payer l'addition.*
　　9. *Elle peut faire un petit tour* (or *une petite promenade*).
　10. *Nous pouvons fêter votre arrivée.*
　11. *Je sais lire un journal français.*
　12. *Savez-vous écrire une lettre en français?*
　13. *Je commence à défaire les bagages.*

14. *Commencez-vous à comprendre?*
15. *Elle tient à le voir.*
16. *Je refuse de rester ici.*
17. *Il a demandé à Robert de rester.*
18. *Je suis content d'être à Paris.*
19. *C'est le moment de rencontrer Michel.*
20. *J'ai le droit d'accompagner Michel.*
21. *Avons-nous le droit d'entrer?*

E. 1. *Je viens d'arriver.*
    I have just arrived.

  2. *Tout de suite, messieurs.*
    Right away, gentlemen.

  3. *Tiens, voici déjà le serveur qui nous apporte les boissons.*
    Look, here is the waiter bringing us our drinks already.

  4. *Et on ne demande jamais aux clients de partir?*
    And they never ask the customers to leave?

  5. *À la terrasse, bien entendu.*
    On the terrace, naturally (of course).

  6. *Il fait chaud.*
    It's hot.

  7. *J'ai envie de marcher.*
    I feel like walking.

  8. *Je vais régler l'addition et laisser un pourboire.*
    I am going to settle the bill and leave a tip.

## LESSON 2

B.   *C'est une Anglaise./C'est un Anglais.*
    *C'est une Chinoise./C'est un Chinois.*
    *C'est une Américaine./C'est un Américain.*
    *C'est une Marocaine./C'est un Marocain.*
    *C'est une Espagnole./C'est un Espagnol.*

C. 1. *En choisissant ce compact, il s'est trompé.*
    He made a mistake in choosing that CD.

2. *En choisissant ce compact, elle a bien fait.*
   She did well by choosing that CD.

3. *En choisissant ce compact, elle ne s'est pas trompée.*
   In choosing that CD, she made no mistake.

4. *En choisissant ce compact, elle avait raison.*
   She did right to choose that CD.

5. *En choisissant ce compact, nous avons payé trop cher.*
   Because of choosing that CD, we paid too much money.

D. 1. *Pourriez-vous nous dire . . . ?*
   2. *Pourriez-vous nous montrer une revue sur l'informatique?*
   3. *Pourriez-vous nous indiquer un magasin?*
   4. *Auriez-vous une bonne revue littéraire?*
   5. *Si je ne me trompe pas, voici un quotidien canadien.*
   6. *Voici quelque chose d'intéressant au kiosque.*
   7. *Voici quelque chose d'ennuyeux.*
   8. *Il y a quelque chose d'important dans cet hebdomadaire.*
   9. *Il nous faut des cassettes et des compacts.*
   10. *Puis-je voir Jane?*
   11. *Puis-je parler à Charles?*
   12. *Choisissons entre ce numéro-ci et ce numéro-là.*
   13. *Regardez ce monument-ci. Ne regardez pas cet article-là.*
   14. *Je n'aime pas ces journaux-ci. Je préfère ces journaux-là.*
   15. *Je n'aime pas ce plan-ci. Je préfère ce plan-là.*
   16. *Montrez-moi cette chaîne-là.*
   17. *Prenez ces cassettes-là.*
   18. *Achetez ces guides-ci.*
   19. *Voici ce que vous cherchez.*
   20. *Voici ce que je veux dire.*
   21. *Ce que je veux? Une carte routière!*
   22. *Ce qu'il cherche? Un Walkman!*
   23. *Ce qu'elle lit? Notre Michelin!*

24. *Ils vendent tout ce que vous cherchez.*
25. *Je comprends tout ce qu'elle dit.*
26. *Il sait ce qui est important.*
27. *Nous lisons ce qui est nécessaire.*
28. *Voyez-vous ce qui se passe?*
29. *En lisant, on apprend à lire.*
30. *En écrivant, on apprend à écrire.*

E. 1. *Je ne connais pas les journaux.*
   I don't know the newspapers.
   2. *Pourriez-vous nous aider?*
   Could you help us?
   3. *Ces journaux paraissent une fois par semaine.*
   These newspapers appear (or come out) once a week.
   4. *Tant d'images!*
   So many pictures!
   5. *Je commence par Le Monde.*
   I'll begin with *Le Monde.*
   6. *Nous avons des revues de tous les genres.*
   We have all kinds of magazines.
   7. *C'est ça, madame.*
   That's right, ma'am.
   8. *Avez-vous un plan de la ville?*
   Do you have a map of the city?

LESSON 3

B. 1. *Quel livre intéressant!*
   What an interesting book!
   2. *Quel bon garçon!*
   What a good boy!
   3. *Quelle robe exquise!*
   What a lovely dress!
   4. *Quelles jolies images!*
   What pretty pictures!
   5. *Quels beaux arbres!*
   What beautiful trees!

C . 1. *Quand je le verrai, je le saluerai.*
When I see him, I'll say hello.

2. *Quand il viendra, dites-lui de manger.*
When he comes, tell him to eat.

3. *Quand il sortira, fermez la porte.*
When he goes out, close the door.

4. *Quand vous quitterez la salle, on commencera la discussion.*
When you leave the room, we will begin the discussion.

5. *Quand il achètera la voiture, il fera un voyage.*
When he buys the car, he will take a trip.

D. 1. *Je voudrais chercher un numéro.*

2. *Voudriez-vous parler à Charles?*

3. *Quel système intéressant!*

4. *Je ne vois rien.*

5. *Il ne trouve rien.*

6. *Vous ne voulez rien?*

7. *Elle n'a rien vu.*

8. *Nous n'avons rien trouvé.*

9. *Ils n'ont rien voulu.*

10. *Qu'est-ce que vous avez trouvé? Rien.*

11. *Qu'est-ce que vous voulez? Rien.*

12. *Il lui faut l'annuaire.*

13. *Veuillez parler plus fort (or Parlez plus fort, s'il vous plaît).*

E. 1. *Achetez une télécarte.*

2. *Cherchez le numéro dans l'annuaire.*

3. *Décrochez le récepteur.*

4. *Introduire la télécarte.*

5. *Attendez le signal.*

6. *Demandez le numéro au service de renseignements.*

7. *Composez votre numéro.*

8. *Parlez avec votre correspondant.*

9. *Raccrochez si vous avez fait un faux numéro.*

10. *Recommencez de nouveau.*

F. *Mme: Allo! C'est ici 42-81-58-17?*
   *M.: Oui, madame.*
   *Mme: Je voudrais parler avec (or à) Monsieur Dupont, s'il vous plaît.*
   *M.: C'est de la part de qui?*
   *Mme: C'est Madame Lenclos.*
   *M.: Ne quittez pas, s'il vous plaît. Je le regrette, madame, mais sa ligne est occupée. Voulez-vous attendre?*
   *Mme: Non, merci. Je préfère laisser un message. Veuillez lui dire que je le rappellerai demain.*
   *M.: Je vais lui transmettre le message.*
   *Mme: Merci beaucoup. Au revoir, Monsieur.*
   *M.: Au revoir, madame.*

G. 1. *C'est pour quelle ville?*
      What city is it for?
   2. *Cela ne fait rien, monsieur.*
      It doesn't matter, sir.
   3. *La cabine est à droite.*
      The booth is on the right.
   4. *Dès que j'aurai la communication,*
      As soon as I have the connection,
   5. *Veuillez entrer.*
      Please go in.
   6. *Je vous dérange encore une fois.*
      I am disturbing you once again.
   7. *C'est dans Paris même.*
      It's in Paris itself.
   8. *Il vous faudra une télécarte.*
      You'll need a telephone credit card.
   9. *J'y suis, jusqu'ici.*
      I understand, so far.
   10. *Je saurai me débrouiller.*
       I'll know how to manage.

## LESSON 4

B. 1. *Finis/Finissez/Finissons*
   2. *Sois/Soyez/Soyons*

3. *Apprends/Apprenez/Apprenons*
4. *Mange/Mangez/Mangeons*
5. *Choisis/Choisissez/Choisissons*
6. *Mets/Mettez/Mettons*


C. 1. *Quelle est votre adresse?*
2. *Nous devons prendre un bus.*
3. *Elle doit prendre le métro.*
4. *Cela doit être l'arrêt de bus.*
5. *J'ai dû prendre un taxi.*
6. *Ils ont dû prendre un carnet.*
7. *Elle devra faire la queue.*
8. *Ils devront payer.*
9. *Il devrait payer, mais il ne veut pas payer.*
10. *Il aurait dû partir.*
11. *Elles auraient dû venir.*
12. *Allons regarder la Tour Eiffel.*
13. *Allons passer l'après-midi avec Marie.*
14. *Comment fait-on pour aller à la Place des Vosges?*
15. *Comment fait-on pour trouver un taxi?*
16. *Il n'y a qu'une station avant Concorde.*
17. *Il n'y a que deux correspondances à faire.*
18. *Il a dit qu'elle prendrait un taxi.*
19. *Il a dit qu'ils auraient l'argent.*
20. *Ils sont plus riches que les autres.*
21. *Les taxis sont plus chers que le bus.*
22. *On parle anglais ici.*
23. *On peut voir la Tour Eiffel d'ici.*
24. *On voyage loin pour voir la Tour Eiffel.*
25. *Elle veut que vous alliez.*
26. *Je suis content qu'elle soit heureuse.*
27. *Nous doutons qu'il puisse faire cela.*
28. *J'irai à moins qu'il ne pleuve.*


D. 1. *Pour rentrer, prenons un taxi.*
   To get back, let's take a taxi.

2. *Allons prendre nos billets.*
Let's go get our tickets (lit.: Let's go to take our tickets).

3. *L'escalier se trouve au bout du couloir.*
The staircase is at the end of the corridor.

4. *Il y a encore de la place.*
There is still room.

5. *Il y a du monde!*
There's a crowd!

6. *On doit descendre ici.*
We have to get off here.

7. *Oui, ça vaudrait mieux.*
Yes, that would be better.

8. *Celui-là doit être occupé.*
That one must be taken (lit.: occupied).

9. *C'est quelle adresse, s'il vous plaît?*
What address is it, please?

10. *Y-a-t-il une correspondance avant Molitor?*
Is there a train change before Molitor?

## LESSON 5

B. 1. *Je me couche à neuf heures.*
I go to bed at nine.

*Tu te couches à neuf heures.*
You go to bed at nine.
*Il se couche à neuf heures.*
He goes to bed at nine.
*Elle se couche à neuf heures.*
She goes to bed at nine.
*Nous nous couchons à neuf heures.*
We go to bed at nine.
*Vous vous couchez à neuf heures.*
You go to bed at nine.
*Il se couchent à neuf heures.*
They (masc.) go to bed at nine.

*Elles se couchent à neuf heures.*
They (fem.) go to bed at nine.


2.   *Je me suis trompé(e).*
I made a mistake (or I was mistaken).

*Tu t'es trompé(e).*
You made a mistake.
*Il s'est trompé.*
He made a mistake.
*Elle s'est trompée.*
She made a mistake.
*Nous nous sommes trompé(e)s.*
We made a mistake.
*Vous vous êtes trompé(e)(s).*
You made a mistake.
*Ils se sont trompés.*
They (masc.) made a mistake.
*Elle se sont trompées.*
They (fem.) made a mistake.


C.  1. *Nous nous sommes lavé(e)s.*
       We washed.
    2. *Nous nous sommes levé(e)s.*
       We got up.
    3. *Nous nous sommes trompé(e)s.*
       We were mistaken (We made a mistake).
    4. *Nous nous sommes dépêché(e)s.*
       We hurried.
    5. *Nous nous sommes arrêté(e)s.*
       We stopped.


D.  1. *Demandez le chemin au concierge (à la concierge).*
    2. *Ne demandez pas le chemin à ce monsieur.*
    3. *Je ne saurais pas aller à pied.*
    4. *De quel côté voulez-vous aller? Du côté de Paris.*
    5. *Elles se sont regardées.*

6. *Si on allait voir la Sainte-Chapelle?*
7. *Si on allait faire une promenade?*
8. *Nous nous sommes égarés.*
9. *Nous sommes allés au Quartier Latin.*
10. *Tournez à droite.*
11. *Je dois tourner à gauche.*
12. *Vous auriez dû continuer tout droit.*
13. *Elle doit rebrousser chemin.*
14. *La Sorbonne est à deux pas d'ici? Oui, elle est tout près d'ici.*


E. 1. *Si on faisait une promenade à pied?*
   How about taking a walk?
   2. *C'est facile.*
   It's easy.
   3. *Regardez ce plan de Paris.*
   Look at this map of Paris.
   4. *Il faut continuer tout droit.*
   You have to go (to continue) straight ahead.
   5. *Vous allez dans le mauvais sens.*
   You are walking in the wrong direction.
   6. *Nous avons tourné à gauche.*
   We turned left.
   7. *Ah oui, une fois que nous avons trouvé le bon chemin.*
   Oh, yes, once we found the right path.
   8. *C'est nous qui nous sommes trompés.*
   It is we who made the mistake.
   9. *Quel dommage!*
   What a pity!
   10. *N'oublie pas que nous avons vu Notre-Dame.*
   Don't forget that we saw Notre Dame.


LESSON 6


B. 1. *Donnez-moi celui-ci.*
   2. *Je préfère ceux-là.*

3. *Regardez celles-ci.*
4. *Prenez ceux-ci.*

C. 1. *Celui dont je vous ai parlé a été vendu.*
   The one I spoke to you about (lit.: about which I spoke to you) has been sold.
   2. *Celui dont je vous ai parlé coûte trop cher.*
   The one that I spoke to you about costs too much.
   3. *Celui dont je vous ai parlé ne me plaît pas.*
   I don't like the one (the person) I spoke to you about.
   4. *Celui dont je vous ai parlé est excellent.*
   The one I spoke to you about is excellent.
   5. *Celui dont je vous ai parlé est le frère de Michel.*
   The person (the one) about whom I spoke to you is Michel's brother.
   6. *Celui dont je vous ai parlé est venu me voir.*
   The one (the person) whom I spoke to you about came to see me.

D. 1. *Il le lui donne.*
   He is giving it to him.
   2. *Il nous les montre.*
   He is showing them to us.
   3. *Ne me le donnez pas.*
   Don't give it to me.
   4. *Il m'en montre.*
   He shows some to me.
   5. *Je l'y mets.*
   I am putting it there.

E. 1. *Ne la leur montrez pas.*
   Don't show it to them.
   2. *Ne les lui vendez pas.*
   Don't sell them to him.
   3. *Ne m'en donnez pas.*
   Don't give any to me.
   4. *Ne nous la racontez pas.*
   Don't tell it to us.

5. *Ne me le prête pas.*
   Don't lend it to me.

F.  1. *Je préfère celui-là en soie.*
    2. *J'aime celle-ci en rayone.*
    3. *Il aime ceux-là en laine.*
    4. *Elle aime celles-là en cuir.*
    5. *Nous préférons celles-ci en coton.*
    6. *Elle préfère ceux-ci en nylon.*
    7. *Quelle est votre pointure?*
    8. *Quelle est votre taille?*
    9. *Je voudrais celui-ci en rose.*
   10. *Je voudrais celle-là en bleu marine.*
   11. *Je voudrais ceux-ci en blanc.*
   12. *Je voudrais ceux-là en rouge.*
   13. *Je voudrais celles-ci en jaune.*
   14. *Il voudrait celles-là en gris.*
   15. *La robe à manches longues.*
   16. *Celui-ci vous va à merveille.*
   17. *Celle-là te va parfaitement.*
   18. *Voici quelque chose de beau.*
   19. *Il n'y a rien d'autre ici.*
   20. *Il va vous les envoyer (expédier).*
   21. *Il va les lui envelopper.*
   22. *Donnez-les-moi.*
   23. *Ne le leur racontez pas.*
   24. *Pourriez-vous me dire où se trouve le bus?*
   25. *Sauriez-vous le nom de ce monsieur-là?*
   26. *Je voudrais le voir.*
   27. *Auriez-vous la bonté de m'indiquer l'heure?*

G.  1. *Je voudrais des gants pour tous les jours.*
       I would like some gloves for every day.
    2. *Ceux-là sont assez jolis.*
       Those are quite pretty.
    3. *Les pointures pour les gants sont les mêmes.*
       Glove sizes are the same.

4. *Je cherche une robe de soie.*
   I am looking for a silk dress.
5. *C'est une occasion.*
   It's a bargain.
6. *Je la trouve large aux épaules.*
   I find it wide in the shoulders.
7. *Qu'est-ce que vous désirez, madame?*
   What do you wish, madam?
8. *Je cherche des mouchoirs.*
   I am looking for some handkerchiefs.
9. *Ils se vendent à cent francs la douzaine.*
   They sell for 100 francs a dozen.
10. *Voici votre monnaie.*
    Here is your change.

## LESSON 7

A. 1. *Elle parle au garçon qu'elle a rencontré à la banque.*
      She is speaking to the boy she met at the bank.
   2. *Elle parle de l'arbre qui est en fleurs.*
      She is speaking about the tree that is in bloom.
   3. *Elle parle aux enfants qui se rendent à l'épicerie.*
      She is speaking to the children who are going to the grocery store.
   4. *Elle parle constamment du petit truc qu'elle a vu au magasin.*
      She speaks constantly of the little gadget she saw in the store.
   5. *Elle parle souvent de la petite fille du professeur.*
      She speaks often about the little daughter of the professor.

C. 1. *Je me fais laver les cheveux.*
   2. *Je me fais teindre les cheveux.*
   3. *Je me fais raser.*
   4. *Je me fais faire un brushing.*
   5. *Je me fais faire les ongles.*

D. 1. *Je me suis fait raser.*
      I had myself shaved (or I got myself shaved).
   2. *Elle s'est fait faire les ongles.*
      She has had her nails done.
   3. *Il s'est fait couper les cheveux.*
      He had his hair cut.


E. 1. *Qu'est-ce que nous pouvons faire pour vous, madame?*
   2. *En quoi puis-je vous être utile, monsieur?*
   3. *Monsieur (Madame) désire?*
   4. *Elle veut se faire faire un shampooing.*
   5. *Il veut se faire couper les cheveux.*
   6. *Elle veut se faire faire les ongles.*
   7. *Elle veut se faire éclaircir les cheveux.*
   8. *Ne les coupez pas trop courts sur la nuque.*
   9. *Quel luxe que d'être chez le coiffeur!*
  10. *Quel luxe que d'aller à Paris!*
  11. *Je voudrais une coupe de cheveux.*
  12. *Elle voudrait un shampooing.*
  13. *Faites-le comme d'habitude.*
  14. *Faites-le comme toujours.*
  15. *Faites-le comme vous voulez.*
  16. *Elle en aura pour longtemps.*
  17. *Est-ce que j'en aurai pour longtemps?*
  18. *La terrasse du café est toujours ouverte au public.*
  19. *Voulez-vous aller avec lui à la bibliothèque pour parler aux étudiants?*
  20. *Le critique du* Monde *m'a parlé des films d'aujourd'-hui.*
  21. *Viens avec moi à l'école d'agriculture.*
  22. *Chez nous tu trouveras beaucoup de livres.*


F. 1. *Ils poussent plus vite que jamais.*
      They are growing faster than ever.
   2. *Je vous les coupe comme d'habitude.*
      I'll cut it (hair—les cheveux) as usual.

3. *Vous en aurez pour longtemps.*
   You will have a long wait.
4. *Ma femme est à côté.*
   My wife is next door.
5. *Quel luxe de se faire raser de temps en temps.*
   What a luxury to have oneself shaved from time to
   time.
6. *On vous reverra la semaine prochaine.*
   We'll see you (again) next week.
7. *Voilà quelque chose en plus pour vous.*
   Here is something extra for you.
8. *Te voilà, chérie!*
   There you are, dear!
9. *Il y a quelque chose de différent.*
   There is something different.
10. *Pas de manucure cette fois-ci?*
    No manicure this time?

## LESSON 8

A. 1. *Elle n'a que deux sœurs.*
      She has only two sisters.
   2. *Ils n'ont que quatre pièces.*
      They only have four plays.
      Note: *la pièce* also means "the room."
   3. *Elle ne veut que ton bonheur.*
      She wants only your happiness.
   4. *Nous n'avons qu'un peu d'argent.*
      We only have a little money.

B. 1. *Vous avez de bonnes idées.*
      You have (some) good ideas.
      Note: In this sentence, the word "some" could be
      either stated or merely implied.
   2. *J'ai lu de bons livres.*
      I've read some good books.
   3. *Nous avons vu de bons films.*
      We've seen some good films.

4. *J'ai mangé de bonnes frites.*
   I ate some good French fries.
5. *Elle a écrit de bonnes lettres.*
   She's written some good letters.

C. 1. *Ne lui pardonne pas.*
   2. *Ne les regardons pas.*
   3. *Ne nous écoutez pas.*
   4. *Ne l'excusez pas.*
   5. *Ne te lève pas.*

E. 1. *Elle est descendue.*
   She went down.
   2. *Ils sont venus.*
   They have come.
   3. *Elles sont parties.*
   They have left.
   4. *Nous sommes resté(e)s.*
   We stayed.
   5. *Vous êtes entré(e)(s).*
   You came in.

F. 1. *Nous ne voulons que des places au centre.*
   2. *Il y a des places au café.*
   3. *Nous avons de bonnes pièces à Paris.*
   4. *Nous avons d'autres places.*
   5. *Ne me montrez pas le programme.*
   6. *Présentez-nous à Michel.*
   7. *Donnez-nous l'argent. Ne lui donnez pas l'argent.*
   8. *Aujourd'hui il part à neuf heures.*
      *Hier il est parti à neuf heures aussi.*
   9. *Elle est restée au bureau jusqu'à huit heures.*
   10. *Elle se plaît à voir les comédiens.*
   11. *J'aurai le temps de le faire.*
   12. *Auront-ils l'occasion de le faire?*
   13. *Ce qui m'intéresse c'est le décor.*
   14. *Ce qui l intéresse c'est l'action.*

15. *Donnez-moi du sucre.*
16. *Il a de l'argent.*
17. *Nous voudrions des pommes.*
18. *Allez au marché, parce que nous n'avons pas de lait.*
19. *Il a acheté de très bonnes chaussures.*

G.  1. *Quatre places, pas trop sur le côté.*
    Four seats, not too far to the side.
  2. *J'ai encore de bonnes places.*
    I still have some good seats.
  3. *Quel plaisir de vous revoir!*
    What a pleasure to see you again!
  4. *La couleur vous va à merveille.*
    The color becomes you wonderfully.
  5. *Permettez-moi, Charles.*
    Permit me, Charles.
  6. *Par ici, s'il vous plaît.*
    This way, please.
  7. *À vrai dire, il me plaît.*
    To tell the truth, I like him.
  8. *C'est la deuxième chaîne.*
    It's the second channel.
  9. *Dépêchons-nous, alors!*
    Let's hurry, then!

## LESSON 9

B.  1. *Il y a quatre peintures au mur.*
  2. *Il y a vingt personnes dans la salle.*
  3. *Il y a des garçons devant l'école.*
  4. *Il y a de la bonne viande chez le boucher.*
  5. *Il y du sucre dans le placard.*

C.  1. *N'y va pas.*
    Don't go there.
  2. *N'y allez pas.*
    Don't go there.

3. *Il n'y va pas.*
He isn't going there.

4. *Il n'y est pas allé.*
He didn't go there.

5. *Nous n'y sommes pas allés.*
We haven't gone there.

6. *Elles n'y sont pas allées.*
They didn't go there.

D. 1. *L'homme dont je t'avais parlé est arrivé.*
The man about whom I spoke to you has come.

2. *La femme dont j'avais fait la connaissance hier s'appelle Mme Dupont.*
The name of the woman (whom) I met yesterday is Mme Dupont.

3. *Les hommes dont j'avais entendu parler sont partis pour Paris.*
The men (whom) I've heard about have left for Paris.

4. *Les femmes dont vous connaissez les fils ont aussi des filles.*
The women whose sons you know also have daughters.

5. *Le livre dont vous avez besoin n'est pas à la bibliothèque.*
The book (that) you need is not at the library.

E. 1. *Elle vous fera visiter le Louvre.*
2. *Nous lui ferons voir les peintures.*
3. *Je leur ferai regarder les statues.*
4. *Voilà l'Opéra! Il y a aussi un bel Opéra à Milan.*
5. *Voilà la Place de la Concorde. Il y a aussi une belle place à Rome.*
6. *Voilà le Louvre! Il y a aussi un beau musée à New-York.*
7. *Voici les objets d'art dont il vous a parlé.*
8. *Voici les sculptures dont ils lui ont parlé.*
9. *Voici les peintures dont elle leur a parlé.*

10. *Voici les chefs-d'œuvre dont nous vous avons parlé.*

11. *Voilà les peintres dont nous entendons toujours parler.*

12. *Voilà les Impressionnistes dont j'entends toujours parler.*

13. *Ma femme s'y connaît en musique.*

14. *Je m'y connais en livres.*

F. 1. *Je voudrais aller au Louvre.*

   2. *Allons-y tout de suite (or Allons-y immédiatement).*

   3. *Où se trouvent les peintures (or Où sont les peintures)?*

   4. *Je voudrais voir aussi les statues (or Je voudrais voir également les statues).*

   5. *Regardez! Voilà les chefs-d'œuvre (or Regardez! Voilà les œuvres maîtresses).*

G. 1. *Vingt francs chacun, s'il vous plaît.*
    Twenty francs each, please.

   2. *Nous aurions dû venir dimanche.*
    We should have come Sunday.

   3. *Mon mari s'y connaît en peinture.*
    My husband knows about painting.

   4. *On peut admirer les chefs-d'œuvre.*
    One can admire the masterpieces.

   5. *Suivez-moi, s'il vous plaît.*
    Follow me, please.

   6. *Qu'elle [la peinture] est bien exposée!*
    How well displayed it [the painting] is!

   7. *Je ne les vois nulle part.*
    I see them nowhere (or I don't see them anywhere).

   8. *Allons-y tout de suite.*
    Let's go there right away.

   9. *Je préfère le cubisme.*
    I prefer cubism.

  10. *Ne les cherchons pas maintenant.*
    Let's not look for them now.

LESSON 10

B. 1. *La maison que tu as vendue est belle.*
   2. *La maison qu'il a vendue est belle.*
   3. *La maison qu'elle a vendue est belle.*
   4. *La maison que nous avons vendue est belle.*
   5. *La maison que vous avez vendue est belle.*
   6. *La maison qu'ils ont vendue est belle.*
   7. *La maison qu'elles ont vendue est belle.*

C. 1. *Le marchand qui vend la cafetière est sympathique.*
   2. *La dame qui achète les meubles est ma femme.*
   3. *Le marchand que vous voyez est sympathique.*
   4. *La dame que nous aimons est ici.*
   5. *Les vêtements que je porte sont vieux.*
   6. *Les bagues que vous avez sont belles.*
   7. *C'est l'allée la plus longue du marché.*
   8. *C'est la toile la plus riche de la galerie.*
   9. *C'est le peintre le plus reconnu de Paris.*
   10. *C'est le meilleur dessin de la collection.*
   11. *C'est le plus vieux tableau de la collection.*
   12. *Il y aura des meubles au marché.*
   13. *Il y aura des peintures dans la galerie.*
   14. *Il faudra marchander.*
   15. *Il faudra porter de vieux vêtements.*
   16. *Elle a l'air élégant.*
   17. *Est-ce que j'ai l'air riche?*
   18. *Ils n'ont pas l'air sympathique.*
   19. *Je me demande s'il a un canapé.*
   20. *On se demande s'ils ont des peintures.*
   21. *Nous nous demandons si vous avez des objets d'art.*
   22. *Je voudrais le voir de près.*
   23. *Je voudrais le voir de loin.*
   24. *Elle voudrait le voir d'ici.*
   25. *Vous le trouverez au bout de l'allée.*
   26. *Vous le trouverez en face de la galerie.*
   27. *Est-ce que je le trouverai au coin de la rue?*

28. *Montrez-moi un fauteuil bleu ciel.*
29. *Voilà un canapé vert foncé.*
30. *Je voudrais une tapisserie rouge clair.*
31. *Préférez-vous la tapisserie de droite?*
32. *Je préfère la toile du milieu.*
33. *Elle préfère la toile de gauche.*

D. 1. *Nous avons si souvent entendu parler du Marché aux Puces.*
     We have heard so often of the Flea Market.
   2. *Si on y allait tous les trois?*
     How about all three of us going there?
   3. *Il y aura quelque chose que nous pourrions acheter.*
     There will be something that we could buy.
   4. *Il faut marchander.*
     One must bargain.
   5. *Regardez en face.*
     Look across the way.
   6. *Ne soyez pas trop impulsif.*
     Don't be too impulsive.
   7. *Celui qui a exposé à Beaubourg . . .*
     The one who has exhibited at Beaubourg . . .
   8. *Il nous en reste encore quelques-unes [les toiles].*
     We still have a few [canvases] left.
   9. *Elle [la toile] doit être très chère.*
     It [the canvas] must be very expensive.

LESSON 11

B. 1. *Qu'est-ce que se passe?*
   2. *Qu'est-ce qui ne marche pas?*
   3. *Qu'est-ce qui vous ennuie?*
   4. *Qu'est-ce qui est arrivé?*
   5. *Qu'est-ce qui l'inquiète?*

C. 1. *J'en ai acheté.*
     I bought some.

2. *J'en voudrais.*
   I'd like some.
3. *Nous en avons assez.*
   We have enough (of it, of them).
4. *Il m'en a donné quatre.*
   He gave me four (of them).
5. *Prêtez-m'en.*
   Lend me some.


D.   1. *Des photos? Il en a pris plusieurs.*
2. *J'en voudrais quatre.*
3. *Ne me donnez pas de pellicules; j'en ai assez.*
4. *Avez-vous assez de pellicules pour l'appareil?*
5. *Oui, mais il n'y a pas assez de lumière.*
6. *Qu'est-ce qui est sur la table?*
7. *Qu'est-ce qui va arriver?*
8. *Qu'est-ce qui vous ennuie?*
9. *Pour apprendre, il faut comprendre.*
10. *Je n'ai pas assez d'argent pour acheter ce camé-scope.*
11. *Faut-il prendre un avion pour y aller?*


E.   1. *Tu as assez pellicules-diapo?*
     Do you have enough slide film?
2. *Peut-être même des agrandissements aussi.*
   Maybe even some enlargements too.
3. *Il nous en faudra au moins deux.*
   We'll need at least two.
4. *Je voudrais me souvenir des couleurs.*
   I'd like to remember the colors.
5. *Les voici.*
   Here they are.
6. *Je l'ai acheté aux États-Unis.*
   I bought it in the United States.
7. *Veuillez aussi jeter un coup d'œil à cet appareil?*
   Would you please also glance (or take a look) at this camera?

8. *Y a-t-il autre chose?*
   Is there anything else?
9. *Je vois jusqu'à l'Arc de Triomphe.*
   I see up to the Arch of Triumph.
10. *Je ferais mieux de changer l'ouverture.*
    I'd better change the shutter.

## LESSON 12

B. 1. *Croit-il que tu sois stupide?*
      *Croit-il qu'il soit stupide?*
      *Croit-il qu'elle soit stupide?*
      *Croit-il que nous soyons stupides?*
      *Croit-il que vous soyez stupide(s)?*
      *Croit-il qu'ils soient stupides?*
      *Croit-il qu'elles soient stupides?*
   2. *Il ne pense pas que tu aies de l'argent.*
      *Il ne pense pas qu'il ait de l'argent.*
      *Il ne pense pas qu'elle ait de l'argent.*
      *Il ne pense pas que nous ayons de l'argent.*
      *Il ne pense pas que vous ayez de l'argent.*
      *Il ne pense pas qu'ils aient de l'argent.*
      *Il ne pense pas qu'elles aient de l'argent.*

C. 1. *Ils sont allés en Italie l'année dernière.*
   2. *Il y a une belle cathédrale à Chartres.*
   3. *En France, on parle français.*
   4. *Nous avons reçu une lettre du Québec.*
   5. *Elle est revenue de Paris hier.*
   6. *Ce vin vient du Portugal.*
   7. *Ils voyagent toujours en voiture.*
   8. *Je suis rentré à pied.*
   9. *Je ne pense pas qu'ils soient très chers.*
   10. *Croyez-vous qu'il soit venu hier?*

D. 1. *Je voudrais voyager en dehors de Paris.*
      I would like to travel outside of Paris.

2. *Vous pouvez aller n'importe où.*
You can go anywhere. (Lit.: You can go no matter where.)

3. *Vous pouvez y aller en train.*
You can go there by railroad.

4. *J'ai besoin d'une carte routière.*
I need a road map.

5. *Vous gagnerez ainsi beaucoup de temps.*
You will save a lot of time that way.

6. *Qu'est-ce que vous avez décidé?*
What have you decided? (Lit.: What is it that you have decided?)

7. *On peut voir les Grandes Eaux seulement le dimanche.*
You can see the fountains only on Sundays.

8. *Voudriez-vous bien nous retenir des chambres d'hôtel?*
Would you please reserve hotel rooms for us?

9. *Si vous y tenez, vous pourriez le faire.*
If you insist you can do it.

## LESSON 13

B. 1. *Il mange trois fois par jour.*
He eats three times a day.

2. *Ils se voient deux fois par jour.*
They see each other twice a day.

3. *Elles sortent une fois par jour.*
They go out once a day.

4. *Il me téléphone plusieurs fois par jour.*
He telephones me several times a day.

5. *Nous les changeons une fois par jour.*
We change them once a day.

C. 1. *Il nous faut trois livres.*
2. *Il lui faut un ami.*

3. *Il leur faut de l'argent.*
4. *Il vous faut des conseils.*
5. *Il lui faut du sommeil.*

D.  1. *Quelle est sa question?*
    2. *Quel est votre problème?*
    3. *Quelles étaient ses raisons?*
    4. *Quelle robe préférez-vous?*
    5. *Quelle voiture a-t-il achetée?*
    6. *Quel voyage feront-ils?*
    7. *Je la vois une fois par an.*
    8. *Les enfants vont à l'école cinq jours par semaine.*
    9. *Combien de fois par jour mangez-vous?*
   10. *Il me faut une voiture pour mon travail.*
   11. *Il lui fallait de l'argent.*
   12. *Vous faut-il une nouvelle voiture?*
   13. *Elle pensait travailler hier soir.*
   14. *Que pensez-vous faire samedi?*
   15. *Je pense aller au cinéma.*

E.  1. *C'est pour vous deux.*
       It's for the two of you.
    2. *Nous pensions aller en Espagne.*
       We were thinking about going to Spain.
    3. *Cela dépend du tarif.*
       That depends on the rate.
    4. *Une Peugeot 504 fera votre affaire.*
       A Peugeot 504 will meet your needs.
    5. *Qu'est-ce qui est inclus dans le tarif?*
       What's included in the rate?
    6. *Quant à l'essence, c'est trop cher.*
       As for gasoline, it's too expensive.
    7. *Nous payerons quand nous rendrons la voiture.*
       We will pay when we (will) return the car.
    8. *Mais si on la laisse ailleurs?*
       But if we leave it somewhere else?
    9. *Nous sommes en panne d'essence.*
       We're out of gas.

10. *Faite le plein du super, s'il vous plaît.*
    Fill it up with super, please.

## LESSON 14

A. 1. *Elle y restera.*
      She will stay there.
   2. *J'y passerai mes vacances.*
      I will spend my vacation there.
   3. *Il lui parle.*
      He is speaking to him.
   4. *J'y ai trouvé mes chaussettes.*
      I found my shoes there.
   5. *Il y est entré.*
      He went in there.
   6. *Elle lui lit le roman.*
      She is reading the novel to him (her).
   7. *Il leur a posé une question.*
      He asked them a question.
   8. *Il y a passé trois semaines.*
      He spent three weeks there.

B. 1. *Je n'y suis pas.*
   2. *Je n'y reste pas.*
   3. *Il n'y obéit pas.*
   4. *Elle n'y répond pas.*
   5. *Nous n'y pensons pas.*
   6. *N'y allez pas.*
   7. *N'y va pas.*
   8. *N'y allons pas.*
   9. *N'y répondons pas.*
   10. *N'y entrez pas.*

C. 1. *Elle va partir ce soir.*
      She is going to leave this evening.
   2. *Ils vont sortir plus tard.*
      They are going out later.

3. *Elles vont arriver à sept heures.*
   They will arrive at seven.
4. *Nous allons faire une promenade.*
   We are going to take a walk.
5. *Elle va voir sa sœur demain.*
   She is seeing her sister tomorrow.

D. 1. *J'y vais dans trois semaines.*
   2. *Nous y sommes restés pendant un mois.*
   3. *Son voyage? Elle y pense tous les jours.*
   4. *Nous allons partir demain.*
   5. *Va-t-elle venir plus tard?*
   6. *Je vais remplacer le pneu crevé.*
   7. *C'est une longue histoire.*
   8. *Quelle belle voiture!*
   9. *Il n'est pas très heureux aujourd'hui.*

E. 1. *Je ne sais pas, au juste.*
   I don't know, exactly.
   2. *Il y a un drôle de bruit.*
   There is a funny noise.
   3. *Je croyais en avoir encore quelques litres.*
   I thought I still had a few litres.
   4. *Nous allons faire un voyage à travers les Alpes.*
   We are going to take a trip across the Alps.
   5. *Il y a une roue de secours dans le coffre.*
   There's a spare tire in the trunk.
   6. *Je vais vérifier les bougies s'il le faut.*
   I'll check the spark plugs if necessary.
   7. *Elle [la voiture] est neuve.*
   It [the car] is new.
   8. *Pas du tout, monsieur.*
   Not at all, sir.
   9. *J'aurai besoin de la voiture.*
   I'll need the car.
   10. *Nous faisons de notre mieux.*
   We do our best.

## LESSON 15

B. 1. *J'ai entendu dire qu'elle était arrivée.*
     I heard that she has arrived.
  2. *J'ai entendu dire que vous étiez malade.*
     I've heard that you were sick.
  3. *J'ai entendu dire qu'ils étaient très pauvres.*
     I've heard (people say) that they are very poor.
  4. *J'ai entendu dire que tu étais parti hier.*
     I heard that you had left yesterday.
  5. *J'ai entendu dire qu'il ne voulait pas venir.*
     I heard (tell) that he doesn't want to come.
  6. *Il ne veut pas que vous dormiez en classe.*
     He doesn't want you to sleep in class.
  7. *Il ne veut pas qu'elle sache la vérité.*
     He doesn't want her to know the truth.
  8. *Il ne veut pas que nous parlions trop fort.*
     He doesn't want us to speak too loudly.
  9. *Il ne veut pas que je fasse ce voyage.*
     He doesn't want me to take this trip.
  10. *Il ne veut pas qu'ils aillent à Paris.*
     He doesn't want them to go to Paris.
  11. *Il ne veut pas que je finisse ce travail.*
     He doesn't want me to finish this work.
  12. *Il ne veut pas qu'elles apprennent cette nouvelle.*
     He doesn't want them to learn this news.

C. 1. *Avez-vous entendu parler de ce livre?*
  2. *J'ai entendu dire qu'elle partira demain.*
  3. *Je vois venir le marchand.*
  4. *Il ne veut pas que je sois triste.*
  5. *Voulez-vous que je vienne à trois heures?*
  6. *Je veux que vous partiez tout de suite!*
  7. *Les livres que j'ai lus étaient excellents.*
  8. *Je les ai lus l'année dernière.*
  9. *Elle est arrivée en retard.*
  10. *Nous nous sommes rencontrés, mais nous ne nous sommes pas écrits.*

11. *Mangeons ensemble.*
12. *Je commençais à lire quand il est entré.*
13. *Nous commençons à nous fatiguer.*
14. *Elle mangeait lentement.*

D. 1. *Regarde cette queue!*
Look at that line!
   2. *C'est le tunnel entre la France et l'Angleterre.*
It's the tunnel between France and England.
   3. *C'est l'escalier qui mène au terminal.*
It's the stairway that leads to the terminal.
   4. *J'ai entendu dire qu'ils sont efficaces.*
I've heard that they are efficient.
   5. *Nous voici déjà installés.*
Here we are already settled.
   6. *Nous en aurons pour longtemps.*
We'll be waiting for a long time.
   7. *Que lumineux!*
How bright it is!
   8. *Nous avons mis trois heures pour y aller.*
It took us three hours to get there.
   9. *Te souviens-tu de notre dernier voyage?*
Do you remember our last trip?
   10. *On les a fouillées.*
They searched them.

## LESSON 16

B. 1. *Reposez-vous avant de commencer.*
Rest before you begin.
   2. *Il faut réfléchir avant de commencer.*
It's necessary to reflect before beginning.
   3. *Vous devez manger avant de commencer.*
You must eat before you begin.
   4. *Avant de commencer, je viendrai vous voir.*
Before I begin, I'll come to see you.
   5. *Avant de commencer, elle a téléphoné à son amie.*
Before beginning, she telephoned her friend.

6. *Pensez bien avant de commencer ce travail.*
   Think well before you begin this work.
7. *Réfléchissez bien avant de commencer ce que vous allez faire.*
   Reflect carefully before beginning what you are going to do.
   Note: *Avant de commencer* means literally, ''before beginning,'' but it is often freely translated, as in some of the preceding sentences.

C. 1. *Il parle constamment.*
   2. *Il parle prudemment.*
   3. *Il parle poliment.*
   4. *Il parle intelligemment.*
   5. *Il parle suffisamment.*

D. 1. *Elle a dit au revoir avant de partir.*
   2. *Avant de dire ''non,'' faites un effort.*
   3. *Je me lave les mains avant de manger.*
   4. *Après les avoir lus, j'ai rendu les livres à Marie.*
   5. *Après être rentrée, elle s'est couchée.*
   6. *Après avoir montré mon passeport, j'ai ouvert un compte en banque.*
   7. *Si elle lui donne assez d'information, il pourra remplir le formulaire.*
   8. *Je vous écrirais plus souvent si j'en avais le temps.*
   9. *S'il avait neigé, je serais resté chez moi.*
   10. *Heureusement, nous avons assez d'argent.*
   11. *Elle est évidemment très intelligente.*
   12. *Vous avez absolument raison.*
   13. *J'aurais dû lui parler.*
   14. *Ils seraient partis.*

E. 1. *Vous n'avez qu'à le contresigner.*
   You need only to countersign it.
   2. *Il faudra me montrer une pièce d'identité.*
   You will have to show me some identification.

3. *Donnez-le-moi [l'argent] en grosses coupures.*
   Give it [the money] to me in large bills.
4. *Je voudrais transférer des devises.*
   I'd like to transfer some funds.
5. *Vous avez deux questions à régler.*
   You have two matters to settle.
6. *Toutes les transactions sont informatisées.*
   All transactions are computerized.
7. *Vous aurez votre argent dès lundi.*
   You'll have your money as soon as Monday.
8. *Nous sommes à votre disposition.*
   We're at your service.
9. *Il suffit de nous donner votre adresse permanente.*
   All you have to do is give us your permanent address.
10. *Il nous faut les mêmes renseignements.*
    We need the same information.

## LESSON 17

B. 1. *Il veut la voir.*
      He wants to see her.
   2. *Il voulait la voir.*
      He wanted to see her.
   3. *Il voudra la voir.*
      He will want to see her.
   4. *Il voudrait la voir.*
      He would like to see her.
   5. *Il a voulu la voir.*
      He wanted to see her.
   6. *Il avait voulu la voir.*
      He had wanted to see her.
   7. *Il aurait voulu la voir.*
      He would have wanted to see her.
      Note: *La* as a direct object means either "her" or "it" (when referring to a feminine noun). Thus, these sentences could also be translated, "He wants to see it," "He wanted to see it," etc.

C. 1. *Je vous reverrai dans trois semaines.*
2. *Pouvez-vous finir le travail en une heure?*
3. *J'ai quelque chose à vous dire.*
4. *Avez-vous un paquet à envoyer?*
5. *Nous avons à écrire plusieurs lettres.*
6. *Je ne peux pas vous parler maintenant.*
7. *Elle va le faire plus tard.*
8. *Je voudrais le voir bientôt.*

D. 1. *Je voudrais envoyer ces lettres.*
   I would like to send these letters.
2. *Par avion?*
   By airmail?
3. *Il lui parviendra en une heure.*
   It will reach him within an hour.
4. *Y a-t-il du courrier pour moi?*
   Is there some mail for me?
5. *Elle doit les peser.*
   She has to weigh them.
6. *La lettre arrivera dans cinq heures.*
   The letter will arrive in five hours.
7. *J'ai aussi un paquet à expédier.*
   I also have a package to send.
8. *Je voudrais aussi le faire assurer.*
   I'd also like to have it insured.
9. *Je dirais cinq cents francs.*
   I'd say five hundred francs.
10. *Nous avons à envoyer ce paquet.*
   We have to send this package.

## LESSON 18

B. 1. *Je ne préfère pas ce livre-ci.*
   I don't prefer this book.
2. *Ils ne préfèrent pas les autres chemises.*
   They don't prefer the other shirts.
3. *Nous ne répétons pas la leçon.*
   We aren't repeating the lesson.

4. *La mère ne protège pas ses enfants.*
The mother doesn't protect her children.

5. *Elle ne mène pas une vie heureuse.*
She doesn't lead a happy life.

6. *Il ne ramène pas les enfants de l'école.*
He isn't taking the children from school.

7. *Nous n'achetons pas les robes les plus chères.*
We aren't buying the most expensive dresses.

C. 1. *Je lui demanderai de venir.*

2. *Ils ont commencé à marcher rapidement.*

3. *Ne partez pas sans me parler.*

4. *Elle ramène son enfant de l'école à midi.*

5. *Quel tissu préférez-vous?*

6. *Cette salopette est trop décontractée.*

7. *Ce survêtement est trop grand.*

8. *Le bifteck est bien cuit.*

D. 1. *Elle veut une tenue décontractée.*
She wants a casual outfit.

2. *Il vaudrait mieux.*
It would be better.

3. *Qu'est-ce que c'est comme tissu?*
What kind of fabric is it?

4. *Le coton ferait mieux l'affaire que la soie.*
Cotton would be better than silk.

5. *Il fait du 38.*
He's a size 38.

6. *J'aimerais acheter une salopette à pois.*
I would like to buy a polka-dotted jumper.

7. *Il nous a demandé d'acheter des baskets.*
He asked us to buy some sneakers.

8. *Je préfère celui-ci.*
I like this one.

9. *Cette jupe est en solde.*
This skirt is on sale.

10. *Il n'y a qu'un seul qui reste.*
There's only one left.

LESSON 19

B.  1. *J'attends depuis deux jours.*
       I've been waiting for two days.
    2. *Elle est malade depuis un mois.*
       She's been sick for a month.
    3. *Je veux vous parler depuis trois semaines.*
       I've been wanting to speak to you for three weeks.
    4. *Il conduit depuis quatre ans.*
       He's been driving for four years.
    5. *J'habite cette maison depuis six ans.*
       I've been living in that hotel for six years.

C.  1. *Elle travaille depuis quatre heures.*
    2. *Il m'attend depuis midi.*
    3. *J'habite ici depuis cinq ans.*
    4. *Il se peut qu'elle ne sache pas la réponse.*
    5. *Il se peut qu'il ait faim.*
    6. *Il se peut qu'ils soient arrivés trop tard.*
    7. *Avez-vous mal à la tête?*
    8. *Elle a les cheveux blonds.*
    9. *Il se peut qu'il ait mal à la gorge.*
   10. *Ils sont arrivés il y a une heure (or Il y a une heure qu'ils sont arrivés).*
   11. *Elle a étudié il y a deux heures (or Il y a deux heures qu'elle a étudié).*
   12. *Nous attendons depuis un jour.*
   13. *Je lui ai parlé il y a une semaine (or Il y a une semaine que je lui ai parlé).*

D.  1. *Qu'est-ce qui ne va pas?*
       What's wrong? (What's the trouble?)
    2. *Il se peut que le nerf soit à vif.*
       It's possible that the nerve is exposed.
    3. *Penchez la tête en arrière.*
       Put your head back.
    4. *Je ne vais pas bien, docteur.*
       I'm not well, Doctor.

5. *Vous devez garder le lit.*
   You must stay in bed.
6. *Il doit prendre des repas légers.*
   He must take light meals.
7. *Quels sont vos honoraires?*
   What is your fee?
8. *Vous pouvez manger de tout.*
   You can eat everything.
9. *Je voudrais vous revoir dans l'après-midi.*
   I'd like to see you again in the afternoon.
10. *Je vais vous chercher le médicament tout de suite.*
    I'll go get your medicine right away.

LESSON 20

B.  1. *Il faut que j'aille à la banque maintenant.*
    2. *Il faut que nous fassions notre travail maintenant.*
    3. *Il faudra qu'elle prenne l'avion.*
    4. *Le dimanche ils vont à l'église.*
    5. *Elle est allée à l'église dimanche.*
    6. *Il est professeur.*
    7. *C'est un bon professeur.*
    8. *Ce n'est pas facile.*
    9. *Ce n'est pas facile à dire.*
   10. *Il est possible qu'elle ne puisse pas venir.*
   11. *Ce stylo? C'est à moi (or C'est le mien).*

C.  1. *Y a-t-il une temple près de l'hôtel?*
       Is there a temple near the hotel?
    2. *Vous n'avez qu'à vous rendre à la mosquée.*
       All you have to do is go to the mosque.
    3. *C'est tout en français, bien entendu.*
       It's all in French, naturally.
    4. *Les offices ont lieu le vendredi soir.*
       Services take place (are held) on Friday.
    5. *Si vous voulez assister à un service, allez-y.*
       If you wish to attend a service, go there.

6. *Je parlais au sujet de temples.*
   I spoke about temples.
7. *Je vais donner un coup de fil à Michel.*
   I'm going to call Michael.
8. *Si cela vous convient, on irait ensemble.*
   If that's all right with you, we'll go together.
9. *Il se marie à 9h. 30 du matin.*
   He is getting married at 9:30 in the morning.
10. *Pensez-vous que nous puissions assister à ce mariage civil?*
    Do you think we might attend this civil marriage?